Fifty Black Women

Who Changed America

Fifty Black Women Who Changed America

AMY ALEXANDER

KENSINGTON PUBLISHING CORP.
www.kensingtonbooks.com

For my mother, Hazel N. Fermon,
a glorious example of all that black women
have contributed to America

DAFINA BOOKS are published by

Kensington Publishing Corp.
850 Third Avenue
New York, NY 10022

First Citadel Press Printing: January 2001
First Kensington Trade Paperback Printing: January 2003

10 9 8 7 6 5 4 3 2 1

Printed in the United States of America

CONTENTS

ACKNOWLEDGMENTS

I am indebted to Phoebe Flowers for her research assistance. My husband, Joseph P. Williams Jr. provided love and support throughout. Thank you. Special thanks also to Irene Monroe, whose intrepid nature and extensive library of black American literature proved invaluable.

INTRODUCTION

When talk show host Oprah Winfrey speaks the praises of black women writers like Toni Morrison and Maya Angelou, she is doing much more than merely promoting another book. Indeed, for more than three hundred years, black American women have helped the United States develop into a world leader. As Johnnetta Cole, one of several prominent black woman educators of the twentieth century observed, "It is black women who are able to see out of their blackness, out of their womanness, often out of their poverty and sometimes out of their privilege. So I believe it is going to be black women who will find the answers to many of the problems we face today."

It is appropriate to celebrate their contribution to this nation's development and to examine the lives and work of women who have been sadly overlooked by many American historians. From the first black American woman poet (Phillis Wheatley), to the titan of modern entertainment (Oprah Winfrey), this book sheds light on the many ways in which black women have come to define America at the cusp of a new millenium. And for those of us who follow in the footsteps of these women, their lives provide a shining beacon of hope, determination, and compassion.

The women chronicled in this book represent a wide range of academic and social interests, from health and beauty to business and education to arts and entertainment. Interestingly, the majority of the fifty women selected for this book made their mark in the world of arts and letters. But, like all of the women chronicled in this pages, they overcame incredible odds to pursue their artistic visions while remaining true to themselves. Consequently, one cannot overestimate the impact of African-American women on the nation's cultural landscape.

Imagine the world without the bluesy tones of Billie Holiday or the snappy versatility of Ella Fitzgerald. For that matter, our nation's international standing as a cultural innovator would be greatly diminished if Alberta Hunter's lonely days in Chicago had not produced the classic "Downhearted Blues" or if Gwendolyn Brooks's keen observation of racial discrimination in the North had not given birth to the work of poetry *Annie Allen*. Millions of Americans might never have gained access to the fluid emotionalism of Afro-Caribbean dance had Katherine Dunham not made it her business to investigate the indigenous traditions in those far-off locations.

Since the seventeenth century, oral tradition has played a vital role in the development of African Americans' identity (and in the definition of the United States' cultural identity). From Phillis Wheatley to Gwendolyn Brooks and Nikki Giovanni, black women writers have preserved the ancient tradition of storytelling. Today, popular fiction and nonfiction writing represents the postmodern versions of the old oral histories which provided such seminal documents as the slave narratives. It is in this realm that black American women have perhaps made the most significant impact on life in the United States. Indeed, Alice Walker, one of the most celebrated writers of the late twentieth century, sees her achievements as part of a long continuum of black women storytellers in America: "For where my duty as a black poet, writer, and teacher would take me, people would have little need of Keats, Byron or even Robert Frost, but much need of . . . Gwendolyn Brooks and Margaret Walker."

Viewed in that continuum, black American women have influenced some of the greatest social and cultural movements in the United States, from the abolitionist movement to the suffrage movement to the Jazz Age to the civil rights movement of the sixties. And while the annals of hard sciences and military history bear few names of black American women, other fields, such as literature, social sciences, education, and the arts, have been unmistakably shaped by women like Mary McLeod Bethune, Josephine Baker, Zora Neale Hurston, and Lena Horne.

Even a cursory glimpse at the history of popular entertainment in America reveals a long tradition of black women adding their voices and talents to the canon. The formidable folksinger Odetta, for example, plumbed the archives of Southern gospels and spirituals to give her repertoire a vital historic link. Classical singers Marian Anderson and

Leontyne Price both discovered their glorious singing voices while young choirgirls in their family's churches. Dancers and femme fatales like Josephine Baker and Eartha Kitt fled the constrictions of segregated America and found welcoming fans in Europe before returning home to appreciative audiences.

In the political arena black American women have indeed been an important defining force. Barbara Jordan, Shirley Chisholm, and Angela Davis have predecessors worthy of closer scrutiny. In the eighteenth century women like Sojourner Truth and Harriet Tubman helped shape the fight to end slavery. In Tubman's case, this struggle involved organizing and maintaining the legendary Underground Railroad, the furtive network of safehouses and conspirators that spread from the Deep South into the "free" states and Canada.

In the proud, straight-backed figure of Sojourner Truth, we can trace not only the abolition movement but the beginnings of the women's rights movement in America. Truth's famous address to an Ohio convention of woman suffragists in the eighteen fifties marks one of the most startling examples of how black American women have represented the vanguard of social change in our history. "Ain't I a woman?" Sojourner Truth asked the gathering of woman political and social activists at that convention, words that ring in the ears of Americans of all races some 150 years later.

During the twentieth century, women like Barbara Jordan and Shirley Chisholm began to build upon the political foundations set down by women like Sojourner Truth. While the feminist movement produced such cultural stars as Gloria Steinem and Betty Friedan, Jordan and Chisholm went about the nuts-and-bolts work of convincing thousands of politically silent black American women to begin showing their power. These two became the first black women since Reconstruction to hold top elected positions of power in American politics.

At the grassroots level, activists like Fannie Lou Hamer and Ella Baker paved the way for voting rights legislation and increased funding for the homeless in America. As the stalwart educator Mary McLeod Bethune noted, progress for women is inextricably linked with progress for blacks in America. "It seems almost paradoxical but nevertheless true," Bethune said in 1933, "that the history of women and the history of Negroes are, in the essential features of the struggle for status, quite parallel."

In Mary Church Terrell and Dorothy Height, we see the alluring combination of steely intelligence, well-born grace, and deep compassion. As educators and founders of some of the most prominent civic clubs in America, Terrell and Height provided the foundation for millions of modern, young black women who pledge their dedication to sororities and social causes in cities and towns across the nation.

In the second half of the twentieth century, as the economic status of black women in America lagged behind that of white men and women, many African-American women continued the work begun by Tubman and Wheatley. In America and abroad, the accomplishments of these women have been recognized as not only vivid examples of black achievement, but also remarkably top-notch work of experts in their chosen fields, including the social sciences, education, and the arts. Among these women are Nobel laureates, Pulitzer Prize winners, National Book Award winners, and recipients of the Presidential Medal of Honor.

In the seventies Maya Angelou, Toni Morrison, and Alice Walker began writing books, essays, and poems that described the black woman's experience in America. For Morrison, a former teacher and book editor, the opportunity to write also afforded her the opportunity to tell the world some of the stories that black American women had been sharing with each other for centuries—stories of loss and retribution, of love fulfilled and love unrequited. The universal acceptance of Morrison as a supremely talented writer is unmistakable proof that the black woman's experience holds valuable lessons for all humankind.

To be sure, these fifty women emerged from varied economic and educational backgrounds, from the hardscrabble agricultural fields of the South, to the secure middle-class communities of Washington, D.C., and New York and Chicago. From Tina Turner and Aretha Franklin, to Betty Shabazz and June Jordan, their steadfast commitment to uplifting other black Americans (whether through art or activism) is a treasured hallmark of U.S. history.

Moreover, their stories—and their ultimate success at changing the face of America—have a common thread: Each of the fifty women managed to overcome the double whammy of being born a woman and black in America. The struggle for civil rights occupied many of these black women for much of the century.

So here now is a closer look at fifty African-American women who changed America. They are only a tiny percentage of the thousands of black American women throughout our history who have dedicated their lives to improving the United States. Yet because of their spirit, their unbreakable resolve, and their passionate devotion to humanity, they are emblematic of all the black women who have helped make America a powerful leader on the global stage.

As we celebrate the triumphs and relive the hardships of these fifty women, we would be wise to keep in mind the essential humanity of their stories. We celebrate their uniqueness, yes. But we also remember that the truth of their lives is the key to much of American history.

Fifty Black Women
Who Changed America

1

Phillis Wheatley

c. 1753–1784

From African Slave to American Literary Pioneer

ALTHOUGH HER LIFE was tragically short, Phillis Wheatley left an indelible mark on American culture. Her contribution to our literary history is unquestioned. As a child of seven, she was kidnapped in Senegal, in west Africa, and shipped across the Atlantic Ocean to slavery in the New World. From that inauspicious beginning, Phillis emerged less than twenty years later as a poet of incredible grace and insight. By the time of her death, in her early thirties, she would hold the distinction of being the first published African-American poet.

Read today, her works astound by their poignant expression of religious faith and her belief in the goodness of mankind. Writing in heroic couplets, Wheatley transformed her newfound Christian religious beliefs into soaring poems of redemption and salvation. More than two hundred years after her death, she remains an inspiration to millions of American writers—and especially to the long line of black women who have sought to live up to her literary legacy.

In 1773 a wealthy supporter agreed to print a collection of Phillis's poems. Though she was barely twenty years old, the former slave girl had exhibited a sharp intelligence and a deep understanding of the Bible. All the same, she had to overcome firmly entrenched white perceptions of blacks as "savages" and suffered the stinging rebuke of many whites who refused to believe that Phillis could possibly have written such polished, heartfelt verse.

Indeed, Phillis was subjected to a humiliating grilling by white Bostonians who set up a council to determine whether she had been merely mimicking the speech and writing lessons of her white masters. Phillis passed their oral examination with flying colors and subsequently created a sensation when her first collection of poems, *Poems on Various Subjects, Religious and Moral,* was printed in Britain. The collection contained a testament to the authenticity of Phillis's work, prepared and signed by the Boston group who had interviewed the young poet:

> We whose Names are underwritten, do assure the World that the poems specified in the following Page, were (as we verily believe) written by Phillis, a young Negro Girl, who was but a few Years since, brought an uncultivated Barbarian from Africa, and has ever since been, and now is, under the Disadvantage of serving as a Slave in a Family in this Town. She has been examined by some of the best judges and is thought qualified to write them.

For several years after the publication of her poems, Phillis was a literary celebrity. She visited groups in London and around New England, where she gave readings of her work, and on one appearance at Harvard University, she stunned the assembled students by reading for them a lengthy poem she'd written especially for the occasion. And by 1780, Phillis had become one of the best-known writers in colonial

America. Fluent in English, Greek, and Latin, Phillis would astound the burgeoning artistic community with her clear, concise readings of her poems as well as of the works of classic poets like Milton and Pope. Nevertheless, her fortunes continued to depend on the circumstances of her white owners. And while Phillis had been lucky to belong to an American family that was kind to her, she held little control over her own fate.

When she died penniless and virtually alone barely a decade after her first literary success, few Americans gave Phillis Wheatley credit for enlightening the world with her beautiful poetry. Several volumes of her unpublished poems are thought to have survived her, but no one has been able to find the lost work. All the same, Phillis's published work is a vital part of this nation's literary canon. Her legacy can now be found in textbooks and literary compilations everywhere. And for black women writers who have followed her—including AUDRE LORDE, NIKKI GIOVANNI, and JUNE JORDAN—Wheatley provides a spiritual touchstone.

Believed to have been born in Senegal in the seventeen fifties, the girl who would become Phillis Wheatley endured the long, torturous "middle passage" between Africa and the New World aboard a slave ship. Few reliable records exist which might shed light on exactly when and where Phillis landed on colonial shores although one estimate dates it at 1761; and no one seems to know what became of her parents. The first written record of Phillis shows that she was bought by a wealthy Boston family in that year.

For John and Susannah Wheatley, the little African girl they encountered at auction seemed to draw them to her with some inexplicable energy. The couple purchased her and brought her into their prosperous household. There the girl was named Phillis and given the family name of Wheatley. Over the next few years, young Phillis worked for the couple doing household chores. John Wheatley was a successful merchant in the booming young town. For her part, Susannah Wheatley grew attached to young Phillis. Indeed, her husband had purchased Phillis for Susannah. She taught the frail girl to sew and knit and was delighted to see her blossom. The Wheatleys encouraged her to learn the strange new language, and soon Phillis spoke English in halting phrases. Encouraged by her quick intelligence, the Wheatleys decided on an extraordinary step. At the time, few whites believed that Africans were even human beings: many whites believed that blacks were soulless creatures more akin to animals. Yet as the Wheatleys grew accustomed to Phillis's unique development, they realized that she was indeed human and imbued with a special spirit.

So, despite the conventions of the day, the Wheatleys endeavored to teach Phillis to read and write. At first the young slave girl struggled with the alphabet. Once she grasped the rudiments of the English language, she began to read well. Further, she seemed to be intrigued by the imagery and dramatic parables found in the Bible. By the time she reached adolescence, she was not only reading expertly but also beginning to write.

Throughout these years, the Wheatleys drew Phillis into their religious faith. For three decades, a British evangelical minister, George Whitefield, had led a religious awakening in the colonies. During his visits to Massachusetts, he attracted hundreds of worshippers to revivals and religious sermons. For the Wheatleys he was an important religious leader, and Phillis came to revere him as well. When Whitefield died in 1770, Phillis began composing an ode to him. Once it was completed, the shy girl showed it to John and Susannah, and they were amazed. "An Elegaic Poem on the Death of the Celebrated Divine . . . George Whitefield" delighted the Wheatleys. At the age of fourteen, she had written a thoughtful tribute to the evangelist, and the Wheatleys saw that their charge had a special gift. After the couple arranged to have the poem published in a local newspaper, some townsfolk whispered that they had actually written the poem and were merely having a joke on everyone. Yet other townsfolk were flabbergasted by the implications: a slave had actually learned to read and write. Thereafter the townsfolk looked skeptically at the Wheatleys. But the couple was protective of Phillis and resolved to continue her education despite the controversy swirling around them.

Over the next few years, Phillis continued to improve her literary skills. She studied Greek and Latin and eventually discovered the works of poets long dead. Under Susannah's watchful eye, Phillis began writing almost daily, her quill pen setting down ideas and images that grew from her religious studies. By the early 1770s Phillis had completed a collection of poems focusing on religion and the afterlife. In her early poems, Phillis seems to have adopted some of the more questionable beliefs of her masters (including the widely held belief that blacks had been given dark skin by God as proof of their moral inferiority); she nonetheless showed great technical skill and a deep understanding of the English language.

John Wheatley's pride in Phillis was boundless. When he endeavored to have her collected poems published, the controversy was rekindled with a vengeance. In his book examining the black literary tradition in America, *Loose Canons,* Harvard black studies scholar Henry Louis Gates Jr. imagined the meeting between Phillis and the prominent Bostonians who gathered to test the young girl in 1772:

> One bright morning in the spring, . . . a young African girl walked demurely into the courthouse at Boston to undergo an oral examination, the results of which would determine the direction of her life and work. Perhaps she was shocked upon entering the appointed room. For there, gathered in a semicircle, sat eighteen of Boston's most notable citizens. Among them was John Erving, a prominent Boston merchant; the Reverend Charles Chauncey, paster of the Tenth Congregational Church . . . and John Hancock, who would later gain fame for his signature on the Declaration of Independence.

Also present at the inquiry were the governor of the colony and his lieutenant governor. As Gates describes it, it's likely that the assembled men were skeptical about Phillis's English skills and her ability to write and understand complicated ideas. Unfortunately, no record of the meeting exists, and Gates proposes that the tribunal showered Wheatley with difficult questions:

> We can only speculate on the nature of the questions posed to the fledgling poet. Perhaps they asked her to explain for all to hear exactly who were the Greek and Latin gods and poets alluded to so frequently in her work. Or perhaps they asked her to conjugate a verb in Latin, or even to translate randomly selected passages from the Latin, which she and her master, John Wheatley, claimed that she had "made some progress" in. Or, perhaps they asked her to recite from memory key passages from the texts of Milton and Pope, the two poets by whom the African claimed to be most directly influenced.

Whatever the exact questions, historians are certain that Phillis passed the grueling examination. After she had left the courthouse and returned to the Wheatley home, the impromptu panel issued a two-paragraph "attestation" to the veracity of her skills. It was a remarkable moment, a public confirmation of John and Susannah's oft-stated claim that the young slave girl had indeed produced mature poetry.

For the rest of the seventeen seventies Phillis's fame grew. Her first collection of poetry, on faith and Christianity, *Poems on Various Subjects, Religious and Moral,* created a smash when it appeared in London. Some Britishers viewed Americans' use of Africans as slaves as a moral abomination, and many Londoners saw Phillis's book as proof that blacks were indeed humans with souls and spirits of their own. When Phillis arrived in London accompanied by John, Susannah, and their son Nathaniel, an eager audience of Britishers awaited her. For the next month, she toured England and the provinces, giving readings of her poetry and speaking about her life in Boston.

Back in New England, Phillis stunned a group of students at Harvard by reading a poem she'd written especially for her visit. As always, religion and faith lay at the center of Phillis's poetry, and the students at the small, exclusive university were awestruck as she read to them:

> *What matchless mercy in the Son of God!*
> *When the whole human race by sin had fall'n,*
> *He deigned to die that they might rise again,*
> *And share with in the sublimest skies,*
> *Life without death, and glory without end.*

Rarely did Phillis write about being captured and sold into slavery, and no records show how she felt about being human property. Still, in one short poem, Phillis alluded to having been brought from a "pagan land," and, at the poem's end, urges Christians to remember that "Negroes black as Cain / May be refin'd and join th'angelic train." Apparently, Phillis's religious grounding helped her to accept her enslavement. It also helped that the Wheatleys considered her a part of their family rather than merely a human chattel. For example, Phillis was a sickly young woman, whose frail constitution did not withstand the brutally cold New England winters well. The Wheatleys gave Phillis warm clothing and tried to keep her well. She developed an asthmatic condition, though, and suffered greatly through several difficult illnesses.

As Phillis continued living and working in Boston, her poetry and sonnets brought a constant stream of admirers and curiosity seekers to the Wheatleys' doorstep. Phillis was gracious and kind to the visitors and sometimes agreed to a short reading. It was an exciting time for the family, and Phillis wrote and published several other poems, including an ode to General George Washington. Sadly, however, Phillis's secure life would change dramatically.

After her triumphant trip to London, Phillis was devastated by the deaths of Susannah Wheatley (in 1774) and John (in 1778). Phillis struggled to find work as a seamstress. She would have preferred to make a living by writing, but few outlets existed for a talented young African-American poet, and Phillis had to make do with menial jobs.

In 1778 Phillis married a handsome young black man named John Peters, and the couple set up their own household in the predominantly black section of Boston. John was a craftsman, but few whites were willing to hire him for more than an odd job. They had three children and worked hard to keep their family together. The pressure of trying to keep his family clothed and fed proved a burden to John, and he told his young wife that he needed to travel to find work. John Peters placed Phillis and the children in a blacks-only boardinghouse in Boston and headed out into the colonies seeking work. Despondent, Phillis fell into a malaise from which she never recovered. Living conditions in the boardinghouse were so miserable that all of her children contracted fatal illnesses and died before John Peters returned to Boston.

Throughout this hardship, Phillis continued writing poetry, her artistic vision and religious faith undimmed by her wretched circumstances. In 1779 she placed an ad in two local newspapers saying she was seeking subscriptions for her newest volumes of poetry. As the Revolutionary War raged all around New England, Phillis was heartbroken to learn that there was no interest in her work. However, some of her latest works, including poems celebrating the end of the war against British redcoats, were published in local journals.

The harsh winters and impoverished living conditions finally took their toll on Phillis. In her early thirties—an age when most young women today are truly beginning their lives—Phillis died. Her passing went largely unnoticed, as the fighting between British armies and Revolutionaries had created confusion and upheaval. It was a sad end for a woman who had shown so much promise.

Lost along with her radiant light are the final works Phillis produced. As historians describe it, John Peters finally returned to Boston, only to find his wife and children dead. When some neighbors told him they believed Phillis had left behind some unpublished poetry, the grieving husband hurried to the boardinghouse where Phillis had last lived.

There a woman told him that Phillis had left behind some sheaves of paper covered with writing. John Peters claimed his wife's last works and vanished into rural New England, never to be seen again.

Phillis Wheatley continues today to embody the artistic contribution of black American women. This nation has been enlightened, improved, and shaped by the poetry and insight of Phillis Wheatley and other black women writers who followed her. Phillis Wheatley left a legacy that will survive through the ages. Her words and ideas cast a shimmering light that endures.

2

Sojourner Truth

c. 1797–1883

From Slave to Feminist Visionary

DURING A LONG LIFE rich in tragedy and triumph, Sojourner Truth helped change the way Americans viewed women and blacks. At a time when African Americans still lived in bondage to whites, Sojourner Truth spoke out publicly against the evils of slavery, one of the first black women to do so. Moreover, she startled the nation and the world by speaking out vociferously against gender inequality. Her speech to one of the earliest woman's rights conventions stands a century and a half later as a model of personal bravery and moral righteousness. In 1851, after having survived beatings, the selling of several of her children, and the hardships of servitude for much of her life, Sojourner Truth rose before a gathering of liberal white women in Akron, Ohio, and argued forcefully for a new way of thinking. It was a shocking, scandalous speech, primarily because in America at that time, no one— even in the supposedly "free North"—imagined that a black woman, a former slave, would have the gumption to speak publicly about the inequalities that existed then between women and men, black and white.

Now, more than one hundred years after her death, Sojourner's remarkable life is being examined anew by scholars and feminists. Nell Irvin Painter, a historian at Princeton University, wrote a comprehensive, thoughtful biography of Sojourner in 1997. And in classrooms and book groups across America, readers are learning the history of a strong black woman. "She made lots of enemies, and it wasn't unusual for her to receive threats on her life, to have rocks thrown at her while she spoke," said Laura Rasor, associate pastor at Church Street Methodist Church in Nashville, Tennessee. "But nothing could stop Sojourner from speaking the truth," Rasor said during a 1996 sermon.

Strong spiritual beliefs sustained the young Isabella Baumfree through the traumatic first half of her life. When, in her forties, she broke free from slavery, Isabella felt God's hand taking hold of her life. She renamed herself, and for the next forty years or so, the uneducated black woman dedicated her life to speaking out against man's transgressions. It was a startling transformation.

In a brutal era, Sojourner Truth was strong of body and spirit, and her life story remains one of the most vivid examples of black women's contribution to this nation. Born in Ulster County, New York, in the late seventeen nineties, Isabella was owned by a white slavemaster. By the time she was thirty she had worked as a field laborer for five different owners. At that time slavery helped drive America's economy. On farms and plantations from New York to South Carolina, hundreds of thousands of slaves worked from sunup to sundown gathering, tending, and manufacturing the goods and services that enabled the nation to grow quickly. But a new wind of antislavery sentiment began blowing in the early nineteenth century. In cities like Boston, Philadelphia, and New York, liberal religious groups, including Quakers and Unitarians, began arguing for an end to slavery in America. In 1827 slavery was ended in New York State. On the Fourth of July of that year, Isabella officially became a free woman.

Things wouldn't change overnight. For the rest of her long life Isabella carried the psychic and physical scars of slavery. In fact, when her owner, Master Dumont, refused to obey the antislavery law in New York State, Isabella ran away from his farm and took refuge with a white family. Isaac and Maria Van Wagener welcomed her into their home and let her live in their guest room. Isabella relished the time to recover, and she became fast friends with the Van Wageners. While a slave, she had borne thirteen children and had watched, heartbroken, as many of them were sold away to distant white masters. The void created by the loss of her children could never really be filled. But when Isabella learned that Dumont had sold her thirteen-year-old son Peter to a slave trader in Alabama after the New York antislavery law was passed, she was despondent. Encouraged by the Van Wageners and other white abolitionists, Isabella filed a lawsuit in New York to win him back. Months later, when a jury found in her favor, Isabella became the first black woman in the nation to win such a legal case against a white man.

After winning back her son and his freedom, Isabella moved to New York City and worked as a maid for the next few years. While there, she met several Methodists and began attending Bible study groups. She felt called to the ministry and became involved in a group called the Magdalene Society. A controversial group in its time, it worked to improve the lives of women prostitutes in New York. Isabella told her new Methodist friends that she felt a special kinship with the "fallen women," because, having been a slave, she knew the sting of shame and desperation that came with being owned by another person. She was sympathetic but somewhat critical of the prostitutes' plight, saying of them, "To be free and yet sell yourself to be used like a slave—this must be sinful indeed."

Always a deeply religious woman, Isabella felt a calling from God after her emancipation. She received a vision, she said, and a sharp, inexplicable sense that the Lord wanted her to put herself to His service. In 1843 she changed her name to Sojourner Truth. She told her friends and family that she now carried a "perfect trust" in God.

Setting out on foot from New York City, Sojourner traveled the countryside proselytizing and singing. Venturing through Long Island and Connecticut, the tall, straight-backed black woman possessed little more than the clothes she wore. But she stopped in villages and towns alike, speaking about her love of God with anyone who would listen. "Children, I talks to God, and God talks to me," she often told her listeners. Soon journalists began filling newspapers with accounts of the curious woman who visited rural churches and prayer meetings and transformed listeners with her forceful singing and plainspoken stories of the horrors of slavery.

She stunned churchgoers with her deep, resounding voice and her poignant stories of loss and religious redemption. She eventually made her way to the Northampton Association of Education and Industry, a unique community of abolitionists and other liberal-minded individuals in rural upstate New York. There she met such larger-than-life figures as former slave Frederick Douglass and white abolitionists William Lloyd Garrison and Olive Gilbert. To Douglass, a self-educated man and vehement abolitionist, Sojourner was a remarkable individual. He found her to be "a strange compound of wit and wisdom, of wild enthusiasm and flint-like common sense." At Northampton, Sojourner spent time talking and praying with like-minded people. She had never learned to read or write, but her ability to communicate was formidable. She began recognizing a link between the oppression of blacks and the oppression of women in America.

The Northampton group disbanded in 1846, but Sojourner remained in the tiny town of Florence. Thanks to a loan from Samuel Hill, a white abolitionist, Sojourner was able to buy her first home, a modest shelter on Park Street in Florence. There she worked with Olive Gilbert on her autobiography. *The Narrative of Sojourner Truth: A Northern Slave* was published in 1850. It contained searing accounts of the cruel reality of slavery, such as this:

> A cellar under the mansion was assigned to the slaves as their sleeping apartment. All the slaves he possessed, of both sexes, sleeping in the same room. Isabella carries in her mind to this day a vivid picture of this dismal chamber; its only lights consisting of a few panes of glass, through which she thinks the sun never shone.
>
> And the space between the loose boards of the floor, and the uneven earth below, was often filled with mud and water. . . . She

shudders, even now, as she goes back in memory and revisits this cellar and sees its inmates of both sexes and all ages sleeping on those damp boards, like the horse, with a little straw and a blanket.

The book created a sensation and made Sojourner a popular speaker on the religious and antislavery circuit. For the next several years, she traveled regularly and spoke out against slavery. In 1851, at an Akron, Ohio, gathering of the nascent woman's rights movement, she gave one of the most noteworthy speeches in American history.

As she took the stage, several audience members shouted angrily. The few men in the room protested loudly, but the conference organizers ignored them. Her face lined with the hardships she endured, Sojourner rose to make some of the most controversial comments ever chronicled in the nineteenth century.

"Well, children," she began, her head crowned by a cloth turban, her imposing body covered in a simple cotton dress. "Where there is so much racket, there must be something out of kilter. I think that 'twixt the Negroes of the South, and the women of the North all talking about rights, the white men will be in a fix pretty soon. But what's all this here talking about?" As some members of the audience stopped their grumbling and complaining, Sojourner continued:

That man over there says that women need to be helped into carriages, and lifted over ditches, and to have the best place everywhere. Nobody ever helps me into carriages, or over mud-puddles, or gives me any best place! And ain't I a woman? Look at me! Look at my arm! I have ploughed and planted and gathered into barns, and no man could head me! And ain't I a woman? I could work as much and eat as much as a man—when I could get it—and bear the lash as well! And ain't I a woman? I have borne thirteen children, and seen most of them sold off to slavery, and when I cried with my mother's grief, none but Jesus heard me! And ain't I a woman?

Finally, the crowd began to grow silent.

Then they talk about this thing in the head; what's this they call it? [An audience member whispered 'intellect.'] That's it, honey. What's that got to do with women's rights or Negroe's rights? If my cup won't hold but a pint, and yours holds a quart, wouldn't you be mean not to let me have my little half measure full? Then that little man in black there, he says women can't have as much rights as men, 'cause

Christ wasn't a woman! Where did your Christ come from? Where did your Christ come from? From God and a woman! Man had nothing to do with Him. If the first woman God ever made was strong enough to turn the world upside down all alone, these women together ought to be able to turn it back, and get it right side up again! And now they asking to do it, the men better let them. Obliged to you for hearing me, and now old Sojourner ain't got nothing more to say.

Brief and concise, the extraordinary speech set off a storm of controversy. With her clear, loud voice echoing in the convention hall, Sojourner had deftly told listeners why she felt women's rights and the rights of blacks were important to all humans. When Frances Gage, a feminist activist and one of the organizers of the early suffrage movement, recalled Sojourner's speech years later, she wrote: "When slowly from her seat in the corner rose Sojourner Truth, who, till now, had scarcely lifted her head, 'Don't let her speak!' gasped a half dozen in my ear. She moved slowly and solemnly to the front, laid her old bonnet at her feet, and turned her great speaking eyes to me. There was a hissing sound of disapprobation above and below."

But Sojourner finished her short address, and the crowd roared in applause. She returned to her corner of the hall, and Gage recalled, "I have never in my life seen anything like the magical influence that subdued the mobbish spirit of the day, and turned the sneers and jeers of an excited crowd into notes of respect and admiration. . . ."

It was a triumphant moment, and one that Sojourner likely considered simply another part of God's calling. After that stunning public speech, Sojourner became even more sought after by abolitionists and woman's rights activists. Because of her bearing—historians say that Sojourner was nearly six feet tall—and her deep voice and direct gaze, it was not unusual for white men to believe that she could not possibly be a woman. At one appearance, in 1858, a local doctor who advocated the continuation of slavery accused her of being a man. The men in the crowd actually demanded that she prove to them that she was not a man. Quietly, Sojourner unclasped the top buttons of her dress. Briefly revealing her brown chest, she told the group that she had "fed many a white baby" with her breasts. She had nursed white babies, she added, even while her own children, sold off to slavery, had been denied her breastfeeding. Then, further shocking the crowd, she asked the men if they, too, wanted to suckle at her breast. Humiliated, the men fell silent.

In the late eighteen fifties, after moving to Michigan, Sojourner continued traveling and speaking out against slavery. In Washington, D.C., she rode the public trolley cars and often was thrown off by angry conductors. Sojourner drew attention to the blight of segregation by insisting on being allowed to ride the Whites Only streetcars in the nation's capital. And after disrupting an important meeting of national leaders by demanding an audience with the president, Sojourner was finally invited to meet Abraham Lincoln. When she met him in 1864 after he signed the Emancipation Proclamation, the lean, serious president told her he had heard of her speeches and admired her strength. In Washington, Sojourner also worked with former slaves to form a township known as Freedman's Village.

Well into her late seventies, Sojourner continued speaking to groups and fighting against segregation. When the Civil War ended, Sojourner began crusading for a government program that would give former slaves their own land—land that they rightfully should have earned after so many years of working for free. Congress refused to enact such a redistribution plan, and Sojourner had to console herself with the "forty-acres-and-a-mule" plan that some states instituted. She continued making public speeches, even delivering another remarkable address to a Northern group while she was in her eighties. As always, her words were unsophisticated but carried the ring of a basic truth. As humans, we should work together to build a world that values the spirit we all share.

Sojourner said, in 1867, in one of her final speeches:

> I am above eighty years old. It is about time for me to be going. I have been forty years a slave, and forty years free, and would be here forty years more to have equal rights for all. I suppose I am kept here because something remains for me to do; I suppose I am yet to help break the chain.

Sojourner's last trip took her back to Michigan. There, in 1883, in her home in Battle Creek, she died quietly in her sleep, surrounded by friends, grandchildren, and admirers. She had indeed helped America break the bonds of slavery.

3

Harriet Tubman

c. 1820–1913

From Runaway Slave to Black Moses

HARRIET TUBMAN helped change American opinion on slavery and racism in the United States. She also personally engineered the freeing of hundreds of blacks from slavery in the Deep South.

For a time during the nineteenth century, Tubman was one of the most wanted women in the nation: Slave masters and law enforcement officials in the South knew that the former slave was orchestrating the escape of other blacks, and they wanted her stopped. But Harriet—who earned the nickname "Moses, the Deliverer"—made at least eighteen trips from the South to the North over several years, securing new lives of freedom for hundreds of blacks. Traveling by night and in often treacherous conditions, Harriet used a network known as the Underground Railroad. It stretched from the farthest reaches of the slaveholding states, many miles away to the "free" Northern states. In her time, it would have been remarkable for anyone to surreptitiously transport so many enslaved individuals successfully even once. But Harriet, imbued with a strong physical constitution and a notoriously tough will, did it time and time again.

"There was one of two things I had a right to—liberty or death," Harriet once said. "If I could not have one, I could have the other, for no man should take me alive." Her life was a roller coaster ride of danger and achievement, of incredible hardship and a strong-willed righteousness that made her fearless in the face of death. Yet after a long life that included friendships with former slaves like SOJOURNER TRUTH and Frederick Douglass and white abolitionists like William Lloyd Garrison, Harriet died alone in 1913.

In the years after her death, scholars and other American leaders took serious note of her extraordinary contribution to this nation. In 1914 a bronze plaque commemorating her life was placed on the wall of the Cayuga County Courthouse in upstate New York, near where Harriet had lived. In 1944, during the roiling days of World War II, Eleanor Roosevelt christened a U.S. liberty ship the U.S.S. *Harriet Tubman* in her honor. More recently, in the nineties the U.S. Postal Service issued a stamp bearing her likeness. And in uncounted elementary schools and university study halls, new generations of American youth pore over history texts and research documents to learn more about the woman known as "Moses, the Deliverer." Nearly a century after her death, Harriet's part in changing America is indisputable. By remaining true to her beliefs, by trusting in God, by outsmarting numerous white segregationists to free hundreds of slaves, Harriet Tubman is a striking example of black women's role in improving America.

Born a slave in Dorchester County, Maryland, in 1819 or 1820, one of eleven children. Harriet's real name was Araminta Ross. Because she reminded others of her mother, soon everyone began calling the young girl by her mother's first name—Harriet. Along with many of her siblings and her father and mother, Harriet and Benjamin Ross, little Harriet lived in a ramshackle, windowless shelter on a plantation on the Eastern Shore of Maryland. As with the lives of thousands of African Americans on hundreds of other farms and plantations in the South, the Ross family's environment was harsh and bleak.

By the age of five, she was doing housekeeping and other domestic chores in the big house of the plantation. When she outgrew those duties, she was sent to work in the fields, where ceaseless hours of hard physical work began strengthening her young frame. During these years, Harriet learned to be sharp of eye and keen of ear. She had to, in order to survive the hazards of plantation life. Harriet was a hard worker and an independent-minded young girl. Her father adored her and often took her with him to hunt in the surrounding woods. In her earliest years Harriet grew familiar with the ways of fishing, trapping, and outdoor life, valuable skills that would sustain her in later years.

All the same, her childhood on the plantation was by no means bucolic. By the time Harriet reached adolescence, she had been taken away from her parents several times—often for months at a stretch—to work at other plantations. It was a brutal, merciless existence, and Harriet's back showed welts and scars throughout her life from beatings she'd received as a child.

Deeply religious and possessed of a strong personality, Harriet learned to despise the ways of slavery. Physically slight, she nevertheless had a strong, wiry body which made her a dependable worker to her white owner. Many slaves, even strong ones, died young for any number of reasons: work-related injuries, fatal beatings, illness, poor diet. Harriet came close to death twice in her young life. When she was thirteen years old, a white plantation foreman slammed a heavy iron weight against her skull. Harriet had refused to follow the man's orders, protesting that the white man was wrongly punishing another slave. The iron weight fractured her skull, and her family feared that she would not recover. Remarkably, she survived the blow but forever after suffered severe headaches and occasional blackouts. On another harrowing occasion, Harriet contracted measles and bronchitis. She had been hired out to work as a weaver at a neighboring plantation, and her living conditions were even sparer than at the home she shared with her family near Cambridge, Maryland. For several days, Harriet was desperately ill. She eventually recovered, but her voice deepened into a husky low register that distinguished her for the rest of her life.

Harriet's early brushes with death helped to mold her into a strong, no-quit individual. Hired out to another farm, she overheard the slaves speaking of an "underground railroad." Harriet took note, paying close attention to their whispered comments about slaves who had escaped to "free" Northern states. Those few illicit bits of talk left an indelible mark on young Harriet: she knew that she had to try to escape someday.

In 1844 Harriet fell in love with a free black man named John Tubman. They married, and Harriet hoped in vain that his status as a freedman would be conferred upon her as well. They lived as man and wife for a few years, with Harriet officially a slave and her husband a hired worker on the plantation, free, but still beholden to the white slave master. Harriet tried to persuade John to attempt fleeing with her, but he refused. He argued that he faced death for helping a slave escape captivity and that Harriet should simply accept her fate.

In 1849 Harriet was sold to a far-off plantation. While traveling at night to her unknown destination with the slave trader who had purchased her, she slipped into the dense woods and disappeared. Like a whiff of smoke, she was gone from the Dorchester County plantation where she had lived with her family and husband for most of her twenty-four years. It was a bold, impulsive move, but Harriet decided she could no longer face the cruel uncertainty of being sold and resold again and again.

The next few weeks filled Harriet with terrible fear as she traveled alone through the backwoods and small villages. At first, she couldn't be sure whom to trust, but she did remember the words of the slaves whom she had heard speak about an "underground railroad." She carried with her a scrap of paper bearing the names of two whites who were said to be sympathetic to runaway slaves. When she arrived at the rural home of the first individual, she was hustled into the back of a wagon, covered with a burlap sack, and spirited to another location. There the silent routine was repeated. After many miles of traveling this way, Harriet was brought to a road and told which way to go to reach Philadelphia.

After that, she walked the quiet roads at night, darting into the underbrush at the first sign of a horse or carriage. She slept in barns and sheds on farms where she believed she'd be safe. After several weeks of living by her outdoor skills and praying to the Lord for guidance, she reached Philadelphia. She had traveled more than a hundred miles from Maryland to Pennsylvania, mostly on foot, and mostly by herself. It was a remarkable pilgrimage, but Harriet was strong, determined, and fortunate to receive some aid from a few blacks and sympathetic whites along the way.

Once she settled in Philadelphia, she worked as a cook for a year and became preoccupied with learning more about the shadowy network of whites and free blacks who made up the underground railroad. She eventually met a white antislavery activist named William Still, who was known as the Philadelphia "Stationmaster" of the Underground Railroad. He quickly became friends with Harriet, and together they planned and carried out dozens of secret trips into the South to free slaves.

Late in 1850 Harriet got word in Philadelphia that some of her family members had recently escaped from a plantation in Maryland. She hurried back down to the "Northernmost Southern state" to try to assist them. When she arrived, she rendezvoused with her sister, Mary Ann Bowley, and her two small children. They were thrilled to see Harriet, and relieved to learn that she seemed perfectly capable of leading them to freedom. It was a joyous reunion, one that invigorated Harriet's determination to free more slaves.

Over the next few years, Harriet made several more trips into Maryland, freeing her brother and many others. During one of these trips, Harriet learned that her husband still lived in Dorchester County—and that he had married another woman. But Harriet's faith in God had grown tremendously while she lived her first years of freedom, and she never spoke unkindly about him.

Like SOJOURNER TRUTH, Harriet believed that God had planned for her a special mission in life. And by following His lead—which she likened to the North Star, which guided her on her clandestine travels—Harriet felt she would always find the right path. For the next decade Harriet continued her secret work. She became well known to abolitionists in upstate New York and in Canada. She was also notorious among white slaveholders, who posted a $40,000 reward for her capture. It is estimated that by 1858 she had led more than three hundred slaves to freedom. Her nickname—"Moses"—was whispered and revered in slave quarters from Maryland to New Orleans. All the while, Harriet was a smart, cagey Underground Railroad conductor. Short and stout, she issued orders to her charges and expected them to be followed closely. Through streams and briars and meadows and forests, Harriet conducted dozens of frightened slaves on more than seventeen trips. While encouraging and friendly with those she led to freedom, Harriet also demanded strict obedience from them. Almost always, she carried a pistol to make sure that none of them would retreat. She vowed to shoot any runaway slave who caved in and tried to return to the plantation, saying, "If he is weak enough to give out, he'd be weak enough to betray us all, and all those who helped us. And do you think I'd let so many die just for one coward man?"

"All those who helped" included whites and blacks from towns and cities in Ohio, Indiana, New York, Pennsylvania, Maryland, and Virginia. With the help of Quakers, Methodists, and other groups that possessed the farms and services to shelter the runaways, Harriet and other conductors soon established a reliable route to freedom. Of course, there were close calls, and Harriet always felt that a higher presence was on her side. For William Still, Harriet was an inspiration. He wrote of her in his 1871 book *The Underground Railroad:*

> Her success was wonderful. Time and again she made successful visits to Maryland on the Underground Rail Road, and would be absent for weeks at a time, running daily risks while making preparations for herself and her passengers. Great fears were entertained for her safety, but she seemed wholly devoid of personal fear. The idea of being captured by slave-hunters or slave-holders seemed never to enter her mind. She was apparently proof against all adversaries.

On one of these journeys, Harriet met several white Quakers in Auburn, New York, a small upstate village. Here she encountered U.S. Senator William H. Seward. (He was also a former governor of the state.) Along with his wife, Frances, Seward became a dependable part of Harriet's network. When Harriet's cherished niece Margaret finally escaped from Maryland, the Sewards took her in. And in 1857 the couple gave Harriet a small home on their property. She lived there for many years, eventually purchasing the home from the Sewards for a small sum. Harriet even managed to relocate her parents to Auburn, and she used the quiet abode as her primary residence.

For the next several years, Harriet spent much of her time on the road. When she wasn't spiriting dozens of slaves to freedom, she could be found speaking to antislavery groups around the North and in Canada. Harriet moved confidently through the close-knit circle of dedicated abolitionists in upstate New York, including Douglass and the fervent antislavery activist, John Brown.

After the Civil War broke out, Harriet decided to help the Northern cause. She traveled to forts and encampments in the North, nursing the sick and caring for soldiers and slaves who had been wounded or captured in the fighting. In Port Royal, South Carolina, she was known for her herbal remedies and voluminous knowledge of the outdoors. By war's end Harriet had worked as a nurse, a spy, a cook, and a scout for the Union army. She had even led a battalion of blacks, the Second Carolina Volunteers, for a brief period during the war. Her mission was to infiltrate Southern black communities and collect information. Harriet did this expertly, providing military intelligence to Union colonel James Montgomery, resulting in successful Northern raids on many coastal Confederate towns in the mid-South region. When the war ended, Harriet triumphantly accompanied a Northern army regiment assigned to retrieve slaves from the South after Gen. Robert E. Lee surrendered. With the Emancipation Proclamation and the Thirteenth Amendment, Harriet knew that all her long years of working to free slaves had not been in vain.

She married a man ten years younger than she, Newlson Davis, and returned to Auburn. They built a home near the one she'd bought from the Sewards. In 1903 Harriet donated the original twenty-five acres to the African Methodist Episcopal Zion Church. It was her wish to see the property go to good uses, and along with the church, a shelter for wayward people and orphaned children was dedicated at the site.

Harriet endured several more battles during her remaining years, including a long and rancorous fight with the federal government over veteran's benefits. (She had received less than $200 from the Union army for more than three years of dedicated work.) But she also joined the cause of women's suffragists and became an important part of a community of feminists centered on the tiny upstate New York town of Seneca Falls.

Although bowed a bit by age, and missing several of her front teeth, Harriet was a valuable and forceful speaker at many women's suffrage events in her later years. At conventions and conferences with the likes of Susan B. Anthony and Elizabeth Cady Stanton, Harriet stood proudly and spoke plainly about her dramatic experiences with the Underground Railroad.

When she died on March 10, 1913, she was at least ninety-three years old. Her friends Sojourner Truth, Frederick Douglass, and William Still had passed on long before her. But Harriet was not forgotten by the nation. She was given a military funeral and buried in Fort Hill Cemetery, in Auburn. The woman who had helped so many others find their way to freedom was laid to rest close to the little building she called home. Her grave site is considered a local treasure and is a popular stop on tourist trips to upstate New York historic monuments.

4

Ida B. Wells Barnett

1862–1930

Fighting Injustice, Writing History

IDA B. WELLS BARNETT, journalist, civic leader, mother, and feminist, was a formidable woman who worked unceasingly to end the barbaric crime of lynching and to secure voting rights for women and blacks in the United States. From the late eighteen eighties through the nineteen twenties, Ida wrote hundreds of articles and tracts defending the causes of downtrodden people. The daughter of former slaves, she rose during her sixty-nine years to the estimable position of political candidate, newspaper editor, and community pillar in Chicago. Chronicler of an era fraught with tragedy and injustice—from the end of legalized slavery in America to the evolution of woman's rights—Ida forged a consciousness that helped undo centuries of inequality and cruelty.

By the time of her death in 1930, Ida had organized several important black women's civic clubs, and established the *Chicago Defender* as the leading black newspaper in the United States. Her accomplishments are especially noteworthy considering the era of racism, sexism, and economic inequality in which she lived.

Ida was born in the tiny hillside hamlet of Holly Springs, Mississippi, in 1862, the first of eight children. Her father, a carpenter and prominent citizen of the town, was a stern role model for his children. In Ida, a serious child, he saw early signs of a leader and encouraged her to do well in school. She took her parents' advice and became a star student at the local elementary school. She went on to be among the first of her town's citizens to attend Rust College, a liberal school for blacks in the region. Supported in part by "the more enlightened part of the white community," as Ida's daughter, Alfreda Duster, described them, Rust offered a range of subjects and top-notch teachers for its students. Ida, a quick study, soon distinguished herself. Her father and mother were very religious, and on Sundays she was permitted to read only the Bible. She flourished academically and made plans to attend a teacher's college. Ida's budding intellectual identity was significantly challenged, however, by a national health crisis. A yellow fever epidemic swept through the South in 1878, and Ida's family was not spared. In Holly Springs, a town of fewer than 4,000 people, 304 citizens succumbed, and nearly 2,000 of the townsfolk fled. Ida lost many friends and relatives, including her mother and father and three siblings. At age sixteen, she alone was left to care for three surviving siblings. Though relatives and neighbors offered to take them in separately, she was determined to hold the family together. Because her father had been prosperous, she was able to do so. (The local Masonic Lodge, where her father had been a member, helped out financially from time to time.)

Ida also continued her own education. She passed the state teacher's examination and took her first job in a rural schoolhouse six miles away from Holly Springs. In 1883, as her brothers began their own careers as carpenters, she was finally able to begin her own life. When an aunt in Memphis offered to let Ida live with her, she moved to the bustling river town and took a job teaching elementary school in Woodstock, an outlying village. The aunt, Fannie Butler, even promised to help care for Ida's younger siblings, and the grieving youngsters found some stability. A self-confident young woman by nature, Ida was fast becoming a responsible adult. She was a devoted teacher. Knowing that education was especially important for black children, she emphasized serious scholarship among her young charges.

All the while, the young teacher was becoming increasingly frustrated with the spread of Jim Crow laws throughout the Deep South. And in May 1884 she decided to take a stand. At that time in the Deep South, blacks were required to ride in separate cars on the railroads that served the region. One lovely spring morning in 1884, Ida went to board the segregated car of the Chesapeake and Ohio Railroad, which she rode each day to school. In the strained years of post–Civil War Reconstruction in the South, local laws required companies to maintain "separate but equal" facilities for blacks and whites. In the case of some railroad companies, black patrons were often relegated to seats in smoking cars. For Ida the humiliation had become unbearable. On this morning in May, she marched into the "white" railroad car, and took a seat. When train employees told her to go into the smoking car, she refused. As ROSA PARKS would do nearly a century later, Ida held up the trip. The conductor attempted to force her to go into the "colored car," but still she refused. Finally, Ida left the train at the next stop, furious.

For the rest of her life, Ida's vociferous protests would sometimes put her at odds with other blacks, who felt that her bold refusals to abide by discriminatory laws would endanger the well-being of other, less outspoken African Americans. But in May 1884 the young Ida knew only that she had had enough of being treated like a second-class citizen. She filed a lawsuit against the transportation company. It was a nervy move, and an early indication that Ida was not one to suffer racist humiliations gladly.

Near the end of the year, a local court returned a verdict in favor of Ida's right to sit in the nonsmoking (white) railroad car, and blacks around the Deep South rejoiced. Temporarily, her victory provided blacks with some hope that America's justice system could work for them. Later, however, the Tennessee Supreme Court overturned the lower court's decision, and Ida was dejected. On April 11, 1887, shortly after the court's unfavorable decision, Ida wrote in her diary: "I have firmly believed all along that the law was on our side and would, when we appealed to it, give us justice. I feel shorn of that belief and utterly discouraged, and just now, if it were possible, would gather my race in my arms and fly away with them." Her thoughts, expressed eloquently and with a hint of the writerly flair to come, turned toward finding solutions.

For the time being, she took a teaching job in the Memphis school district, a big step up from Woodstock. In the mid-eighteen eighties, Ida officially joined the largest public school district in the busy, mid-sized town and distinguished herself as a powerfully effective teacher. During her seven years in the Memphis school, Ida continued her own education, taking classes in drama and speech and constantly working to improve her own knowledge of the education process.

By the end of the decade, Ida had come upon another way of turning her considerable skill and energy to a worthwhile cause. At her local church she volunteered to write the story of her failed lawsuit for the congregational newsletter and in the process discovered that she had a knack for descriptive, journalistic writing. Over the next several months, Ida wrote numerous articles for the local church newspaper. In time her columns began to be reprinted in the black-owned and operated newspapers that were appearing in the South after the Civil War.

Like their counterparts in the North, the black newspapers in the South served a crucial role in the community. From editorials about civic issues to advertisements for black-owned businesses, these newspapers provided a way for African Americans to remain connected in a segregated world.

For Ida, catching the journalism "bug" brought a big change in her life. At last, she had found a way of using her sterling education and her strong belief in justice and fair play. By the late eighteen eighties, she had taken a part-time job writing for *Free Speech,* a small black newspaper in Memphis. She wrote several meaningful exposés of the horrors of racial discrimination, even penning an investigative story outlining the sorry conditions of the "colored" elementary schools operated by the Memphis school district. Eventually, Ida poured her savings into buying the newspaper. And after administrators at the Memphis school district fired her for her criticism of them in the newspaper, she turned her full attention to journalism.

In the spring of 1882 Ida traveled around the South reporting for *Free Speech,* describing in vivid detail the lives and tribulations of blacks living under segregated laws. When three black men were lynched in Memphis, she devoted several stories to the tragedy, placing the blame squarely on the whites who had killed the men and on the whites who turned a blind eye to such brutality. Shortly thereafter, an angry mob of white townsfolk set out to silence her. They stormed the small office of her newspaper and destroyed her printing press. Fortunately, Ida was reporting in Philadelphia when the mob descended on her newspaper. Friends sent word to her that she might be in danger if she returned.

Consequently, Ida embarked on a crusade to shed light on the cruel injustices done to blacks in the Deep South. For the next few years, she traveled and lectured in the Northeast, writing for black newspapers like the *New York Age* and other publications in Boston and Philadelphia. Her words were always plain, and her stories of lynchings were heartrending. Ida supplemented her income by lecturing to antilynching groups in the Northeast, and she soon came to the attention of human rights advocates abroad.

Ida spent much of the spring of 1893 traveling in Wales, Scotland, and England, speaking to supportive audiences. By the time she returned to the United States, she was buoyed by the organizing skills she had observed in the United Kingdom. The suffragist movement was just beginning, and Ida began advocating for the formation of women's groups in New England, among blacks and whites. Within a few years, Ida had a hand in organizing women's civic clubs in Boston and Chicago.

Her involvement brought about the formation of the nation's first black women's civic club, a Chicago organization that took on Ida's name by the end of the eighteen nineties. By constantly touring and writing, Ida had turned the issue of lynching into a cause célèbre among prominent liberals in America and England. And as her fame grew, so did Ida's commitment to addressing the poor conditions women and blacks faced in America. Ida moved to Chicago and began writing about the presence of racial discrimination in the supposedly "free" Midwestern hub.

When the World Exposition announced that Chicago would host its next world's fair, Ida began writing about blacks who were excluded from taking part. She published "The Reason Why the Colored American Is Not in the World's Columbian Exposition." In this booklet Ida pointed out the unfairness of white organizers excluding blacks from the huge fair. Black Americans, she argued, "have contributed a large share to American prosperity and civilization. The labor of one half of this country has always been, and is still being done, by them." Her appeal to the organizers of the fair failed, but Ida had turned the attention of prominent Chicagoans to the concerns of the city's black citizens.

Although she now called Chicago home, Ida retained deep feelings about the barbaric crime of lynching in America. Her two trips to England had encouraged her to keep closer track of lynchings in America and to work to document hangings throughout the nation. In 1895 she published *A Red Record: Tabulated Statistics and Alleged Causes of Lynchings in the United States, 1892–1894*. The book described graphically the hanging, burning, and mutilating of blacks. As Ida saw it, lynching showed the nation's tolerance of unspeakable cruelty: "It becomes the painful duty of the Negro to reproduce a record which shows that a large portion of the American people avow anarchy, condone murder and defy the contempt of civilization," Ida wrote. In 1894 alone, she pointed out, 132 Americans had been sentenced to death by law, whereas 197 mostly nonwhite citizens had been "put to death by mobs who gave the victims no opportunity to make a lawful defense." Ida added, "No comment need be made upon a condition of public sentiment responsible for such alarming results."

Ida's research into the terrible reality of lynching shocked white America. More than just a statistical roundup, the book became popular in Britain and in northeastern American cities as a detailed history of the inhuman practice. With the help of influential white Englishmen and politically connected Northerners, Ida hoped to put an end to lynching everywhere. Though her efforts did not prove successful, Ida had set in motion an antilynching movement that would ultimately succeed in turning the nation against the ritual.

Meanwhile, Ida continued writing for Chicago newspapers and organizing women's civic clubs. Along the way, she fell in love. Ferdinand Lee Barnett was a handsome and prominent member of Chicago's growing middle-class black community. A graduate of the Northwestern University law school, Barnett had founded the city's first black newspaper, the *Conservator.* He and Ida were a match made in heaven: She shared his love of and belief in the principles of democracy, while Barnett admired Ida's commitment to serious journalism and the role of a free American press. They married in 1895, and Ida became stepmother to Barnett's two young sons. (His first wife, Molly Graham, had died young.) Over the next several years, Ida gave birth to four children of her own and became a pillar of Chicago's burgeoning black community. Two of her sons were named after antilynching advocates Ida had met while traveling and lecturing abroad.

After the birth of their first child, in 1897, Ida decided she would give up her globetrotting for the time being. For the next decade she stayed at home and maintained a large, boisterous household in a fine Chicago neighborhood. Like her father before her, Ida made sure that her children were well educated. With one exception, all of Ida's four children graduated from high school, went on to college, and became successful professionals.

In 1901 Ida and her husband moved into a predominantly white Chicago neighborhood and suffered cold shoulders from some of their white neighbors. But being of sound religious principles as well as politically astute, the Barnett family did not fear reprisal for having broken the unofficial color barrier. In one instance, when a group of young white toughs followed one of Ida's sons home and lingered in front of the house yelling threats, Ida emerged and told them to get lost. She was fearless in the face of racial animosity, and assured the young cutups that she had a gun and was prepared to use it to defend her family.

Over the next few years, the Barnett home on Rhodes Avenue in Chicago became the center of black civic activism in the city. As time passed, and more and more blacks moved into the neighborhood, the Barnetts came to preside over a significant community of black working professionals.

During this time, Ida continued her work organizing civic groups. She also taught Sunday school at Grace Presbyterian Church and helped found the Negro Fellowship League, a group similar to the National Association for the Advancement of Colored People in that it fought injustices against black citizens. The league also opened an employment agency for blacks, as well as a boardinghouse for indigent black men. All of this work with less fortunate blacks created some tension between Ida and the upper-middle-class blacks in Chicago. Many of them, newly arrived in the middle class, didn't understand why Ida devoted so much time and energy to helping out "country Negroes" who flooded into Chicago seeking work. But Ida didn't listen to their protests, and even worked to open a settlement house that would serve as a central service provider for poor blacks in Chicago. Despite her political and social connections, the group did not really flourish. Yet Ida never relinquished her belief that as long as some blacks suffered economic and social hardships, all blacks should work to help them.

After her children entered their teens, Ida resumed her career in journalism. In the early years of the new century she covered the nation for the *Chicago Defender,* writing about race riots and other problems involving American blacks during the industrial age. Her stories of racial unrest in places like rural Illinois and Arkansas are classics of reporting.

After an illness in 1920, Ida once again turned to community organizing. After a thirty-year absence from the group, Ida was elected president of the black women's club she had founded in the eighteen nineties. It was now called the Ida B. Wells Women's Club, and she raised its profile by taking over the reins. Through this and other club affiliations, Ida worked to improve black-white race relations. Even after MARY McLEOD BETHUNE was elected president of the Ida B. Wells Women's Club, Ida maintained dialogues with white women in Chicago's liberal social groups, including the prominent Cook County Federation of Club Women. Throughout, Ida worked hard to encourage blacks to register to vote and to participate in the political process. In 1913, as the woman's voting rights movement was picking up steam, Ida organized the first black suffragist group in the nation—the Alpha Suffrage Club. Like millions of other American women, Ida and her group members celebrated when women were allowed to vote a few years later.

In 1930, encouraged by her supporters in local politics, Ida ran for state senator. Listing her political affiliation as independent, Ida came in third in the primary election, behind Republicans Warren B. Douglas and Adelbert H. Roberts. It was a bruising experience, but Ida never lost faith in the political process. At the Metropolitan Community Church, where Ida had been a member since 1920, she hosted political forums that became popular events in Chicago. Between 1928 and 1931, Ida wrote and rewrote her autobiography, working diligently with a secretary provided by her son, Herman K. Barnett, who by then was a prominent Chicago lawyer.

Unfortunately, Ida suffered from an undiagnosed kidney ailment. In March 1931 she fell ill. A group of doctors worked to save her but could not. She was dead at age sixty-nine. Thousands of Chicagoans mourned her passing, and the *Chicago Defender*—the newspaper that gave Ida a forum through most of her professional career—memorialized her as an "elegant" and "striking" woman.

Ida's diaries and the autobiography she had written were preserved by her family, and they were published in 1970 by the University of Chicago Press. In *Crusade for Justice,* Ida's daughter, Alfreda Barnett Duster, pays her mother perhaps the highest compliment possible: she recognized her as a shining example of black women's role in making America the preeminent nation in the world. "The most remarkable thing about Ida B. Wells Barnett is not that she fought lynching and other forms of barbarianism," Duster wrote. "It is rather that she fought a lonely and almost single-handed fight, with the single-mindedness of a crusader, long before men or women of any race entered the arena." And for that all Americans can rejoice.

5

Mary Church Terrell

1863–1954

A Pioneer of Democracy

THANKS TO HER LONG PRODUCTIVE LIFE of teaching, learning, and organizing, Mary Church Terrell played a crucial role in helping this nation develop into a world power. Like MARY MCLEOD BETHUNE and IDA B. WELLS BARNETT, Mary Church was the descendent of slaves. Determined to make the best of her parents' legacy, she began a long, proud tradition in which first-generation freedwomen devoted their lives to uplifting all black Americans.

In the late eighteen nineties, as a fresh-faced idealist from a Deep South homestead, Mary added her insights and knack for organizing to the growing suffragist movement. In addition to arguing boldly against *Plessy* v. *Ferguson,* the landmark decision of the U.S. Supreme Court that upheld the racially discriminatory separate-but-equal rule, Mary was a key member of a coalition that helped secure voting rights for women.

Like SOJOURNER TRUTH and HARRIET TUBMAN before her, Mary Church Terrell participated in a grassroots political organizing that overlapped considerably with the growing feminist and suffrage movements of the twentieth century. In small villages in Ohio and upstate New York, in Pennsylvania and Maryland and Massachusetts, abolitionists and suffragists had long crossed paths in their respective quests for freedom. For Mary, teaching would set her on a path to history, and her perseverance in poorly funded segregated public schools in the nation's capital remain a formidable example of dedication to overcoming immense obstacles. Mary was a well-bred intellectual with a big heart and an impressive sense of dignity. In an eventful life spent fighting for economic justice and educational opportunity on behalf of millions of black Americans, those attributes proved more than handy for Mary Church Terrell.

Mary Church was born in 1863, the year President Abraham Lincoln issued the Emancipation Proclamation, the document that broke the bonds of thousands of slaves. The Civil War, with its hundreds of thousands of dead and wounded and an uncounted number of displaced citizens, left a horrendous scar on the Southern landscape and the American consciousness. Mary never forgot the courage and bloodshed it required to bring an end to slavery in America: "If it had not been for the victory of the Union Army," Mary wrote in 1888, "I would be on some plantation in the South, manacled soul and body in the fetters of a slave."

Mary's parents, Robert and Louisa Church, worked as slaves on a farm near Memphis, Tennessee, and in the years after the Civil War experienced the turbulence and uncertainty felt by other African Americans in the Deep South. Seeking new opportunities and a safe environment for their bright daughter, Robert and Louisa sent Mary north for her education, to Yellow Springs, Ohio, where she attended public schools. A dedicated student with a keen mind and inquisitive nature, Mary excelled. After completing secondary school, she enrolled at Oberlin College, near Lorain, Ohio. There she received both an undergraduate and an advanced degree and decided to become a teacher. Indeed, during breaks from Oberlin, Mary had spent time teaching at a well-known black college, Wilberforce University.

Thereafter, Mary began a long climb to the top of the nation's growing community of dedicated black educators. She moved to Washington, D.C., where she began teaching at Washington Colored High School. In time, Mary's fine eye for detail and her calm expertise helped her to become principal of the large segregated high school on M Street.

As in hundreds of other all-black public schools throughout the nation, resources were meager. Mary grew frustrated by the lack of funding for her eager but needy young pupils. Realizing that black Americans were required to improve themselves without the benefits of a government they helped support planted the seed of activism within her. She resolved then to "keep on moving, keep on insisting, keep on fighting injustice," Mary told an interviewer in 1938.

When, in 1896, the Supreme Court voted to uphold a controversial law that allowed "separate but equal" public facilities for blacks and whites, Mary grew even more determined to right the inequitable distribution of political and social power in America. She helped found the National Association of Colored Women, a group related to the National Federation of Afro-American Women and to the Colored Women's League. The early nineteen hundreds were a remarkable time for women activists both black and white. Mary's involvement in the historic Niagara Movement as well as with the powerful women's organizations would facilitate two major developments in twentieth-century American history: the formation of the National Association for the Advancement of Colored People and the ratification of the Nineteenth Amendment, which at long last guaranteed full voting rights for women.

Gaining voting rights for women was a triumphant moment for Mary. She had passionately advocated woman's suffrage in years of lecturing and writing: "If we fight, we get our rights," Mary wrote confidently in 1910. "We're second class citizens because we sit idly by."

As an educator Mary became a familiar and impressive figure in Washington, D.C. With a regal bearing and a fabulous sense of the day's fashions, she was a striking addition to the network of community organizations and educational groups that revolved around the federal bureaucracy. By the twenties Mary was a force to be reckoned with on the issue of public education. She had married a promising lawyer, Robert Herberton Terrell, in 1891. Together, they made a dynamic pair, and Robert Terrell earned a reputation as a hardworking, intelligent judge. In his later years he became one of the first African Americans to serve as a municipal court judge in Washington, D.C.

Mary continued to seek better schools for black students in the nation's capital and around the United States. As testament to the trust and respect accorded Mary by her collegues, she was appointed to the board of education in Washington, D.C., in 1895, the first African American ever named to that august board. Mary took her responsibilities extremely seriously and was outspoken about the disparities that existed in America. She railed against the dominant press for its insensitive, inaccurate, and damaging coverage of African Americans: "There is a 'Conspiracy of Silence' in the American press so far as the colored American side of the story," Mary wrote in 1907. "Anybody who makes him ridiculous or criminal can get a hearing, but his struggles and heartaches are tabooed."

Indeed, Mary would spend the rest of her life writing, organizing, and working as an educator. All the while, her goal was to secure improved conditions for all African Americans. She cofounded a District of Columbia task force to eradicate racial discrimination and became friend and mentor to many political and social activists, including Adam Clayton Powell Jr. and the great union organizer A. Philip Randolph. Through her work in women's clubs and political groups and in the educational arena, Mary helped foster a revolution in popular thinking.

A few months before her death, in 1954, the Supreme Court had handed down another landmark decision involving racial discrimination. Known as *Brown* v. *Board of Education,* the decision effectively did away with the separate-but-equal doctrine that had originally set young Mary Church on the path of activism so many years earlier.

It was a full circle, one that Mary fortunately was able to see come to a close before her life ended. And as she remarked in 1920, the success of America will continue to depend on the legacy we leave for our children—and on how well we prepare them to lead: "Students in our colleges and universities can do much to eradicate prejudice by starting a crusade which has for its slogan, 'Down with discrimination against human beings on account of race, color, sex, or creed.'"

6

Madame C. J. Walker

1867–1919

Defining African-American Beauty

WHETHER SPRUCING UP for a day at the office or dolling up for a night on the town, millions of black American women owe thanks to a sharp businesswoman who came to be known as Madame C. J. Walker.

Sarah Breedlove rose from humble beginnings in the Deep South to command one of the largest beauty-care companies in the world. She became the first black woman in American history to amass a fortune of more than one million dollars. During her illustrious entrepreneurial career, Madame Walker provided jobs for thousands of black women and with her products secured and enhanced their self-esteem. As the legendary black writer James Weldon Johnson saw her, C. J. Walker helped black American women to learn to love their own special brand of beauty. "She taught the masses of colored women a secret age-old, but lost to them—the secret every woman ought to know," Weldon wrote. "She taught them the secret of feminine beauty."

Although an object of some social controversy during her lifetime—notably from blacks who felt she was encouraging African Americans to try to "look white" with her products—she persevered. Eventually, her cosmetology schools and beauty products businesses held forth in many large American cities. It may have seemed an unlikely calling, but C. J. Walker saw an immense need for ways to improve the personal self-esteem of black American women; and in her able hands, the issue of grooming and personal hygiene earned a place in the nation's fabric.

Indeed, young Sarah Breedlove came of age when few black American women could afford to make their physical appearance a priority. Born in Delta, Georgia, shortly after the Civil War ended, C.J. (as she came to be known), like thousands of black American girls, faced a bleak future.

During the eighteen seventies, blacks in the Deep South struggled to carve out a place for themselves. It was the Reconstruction era, and the "official" end of slavery had not brought financial independence for most African Americans. Her parents, Owen and Minerva, former slaves, died when she was young, and C.J. was raised by her older sister. As often was the case during this period, girls barely of high school age got married. For C.J., her marriage took place when she was fourteen, to a man several years older than she. By the time she had turned twenty, her husband had died, and she was left to fend for herself and her infant daughter, A'lelia. With pluck and determination, young C.J. headed north, like thousands of other Southern blacks fleeing the devastating effects of slavery.

In East St. Louis, Illinois, she found work as a laundress. For the next several years, she worked long hours. She found the bustling, industrial city a haven for women like herself—the descendents of slaves who were trying to establish their own financial independence. Gifted with resourcefulness, ambition, and a strong will, C.J. soon came to realize that she held the power over her own destiny. While making money on the side by dressing the hair of other black women in St. Louis, she invented a metal comb that could flatten curly hair. In 1905, by experimenting with existing products, she also invented a chemical compound that conditioned blacks' hair. Prior to this, black women had few options for styling their hair. C.J. found that her pioneering treatment solution, combined with the hot comb, offered black women new choices for styling. She was able to leave her job at the laundry and concentrate on hairdressing for the growing numbers of professional blacks in St. Louis.

To the uninitiated, her hair-treatment products appeared to allow black women to "whiten" their tresses by straightening them with the special comb and a chemical solution. But C.J., who was proud of her Southern roots and of her ethnic heritage, would not hear of such talk. As her empire grew, she forbade her workers to use the term *hair straightener.*

Over the next decade, C.J.'s business enterprise grew tremendously. She had married Charles Walker, and he supported her efforts to expand her business. After her initial success in St. Louis, she set out to establish her company in the region. From the beginning, she traveled about the Northeast and Midwest selling her conditioning solution. Over time, her list of products grew to include facial products, hair adornments, and etiquette tips.

In Chicago she established one of the largest and best-known beauty schools in the nation. It was a large, prosperous business, one that drew enthusiastic young black women from across the nation seeking work and instruction. As C.J. designed the business, she allowed her eager young saleswomen to claim a part of the enterprise through franchises. In this manner, the Madame C. J. Walker School of Beauty became synonymous with pride, prosperity, and self-esteem among black women during the early part of the twentieth century.

In 1910 she oversaw the construction of her own factory in Indianapolis, an impressive development that coincided with an industrial boom. Her image—with her strong features and carefully coiffed hair prominently featured—became known around the world, as she expanded her customer base to include black women in the Caribbean. An astute businesswoman, she maintained a firm grip on her growing enterprise and soon became one of the wealthiest women in America. This achievement was even more impressive considering that few black women during this period were fortunate enough to find jobs that allowed them to do more than keep their families together.

But C.J. was visionary, and uncounted black women owed their personal and financial independence to her unique example. At her death, in 1919, she had established a legacy of entrepreneurship that was almost mythical in black America. She had bought a beautiful home in Irvington-on-the-Hudson in New York and commanded the respect of businessmen and local townspeople alike.

Some eighty years after her death, a new generation of Americans is learning the story of the phenomenal Madame C. J. Walker: in 1998, the United States Postal Service issued a stamp with her face on it. And in tiny villages and big cities from California to Maine, her strong features could be seen peering from post offices and the bags of letter carriers. It was a supremely poignant tribute to the woman who first put a stamp of beauty on the black woman's experience in America.

7

Mary McLeod Bethune

1875–1955

Advocating Freedom From Schoolhouse to White House

BY THE TIME Mary McLeod Bethune died in 1955, much of her life's work had begun to bear fruit. The college she founded in 1904 had educated thousands of young black women; the National Association for the Advancement of Colored People (NAACP), where she once served as vice president, had become the leading civil rights organization in America. And, perhaps most important, her work in the highest levels of the U.S. government—during several administrations, including the long Franklin D. Roosevelt presidency—had sown the seeds for educational and economic gains that black Americans would reap during the rest of the twentieth century.

In the annals of U.S. history, the rags-to-riches story is familiar and emblematic of our national spirit. Like dozens of other prominent black women, Mary McLeod Bethune embodies the essential elements of the American Dream: hard work, strong faith, and equal opportunity can turn a pauper into a prince in a democratic society. Mary McLeod Bethune's version of the classic story spans the Reconstruction era and our modern era, from the official end of slavery in American to the dawn of integration and black nationalism.

Armed with a hefty sense of personal dignity, a sharp intellect, and a legendary ego, Mary McLeod Bethune rose from the muddy streets of a tiny South Carolina village to the rarefied sphere of national leaders and international heads of state. She served as a key advisor to presidents on matters of race and women and helped the world community devise the United Nations charter during a historic week in San Francisco in 1945. She received honors from governments in Haiti, Switzerland, and Africa. She helped set an agenda for the educational and economic advancements of generations of African Americans to come. "She is a public institution," said writer Edwin Embree during the nineteen forties.

While she stepped on a few toes along the way, earning criticism from black leaders and white leaders alike, Mary remained commited to uplifting millions of blacks and women in America at a time when few official advocates for either group existed. "I thought I was so unselfish," Mary said in 1954. "I was applauded into the belief that I was a great leader—just and pure and honest and loved. But, now I realize how much of what I did was for my own glorification. . . . I want to do all I can now to make right all of the wrong things."

As history has shown, few leaders have been without personalities and idiosyncracies that some of their peers found problematic during their eras. For Mary McLeod Bethune, her rich legacy of activism on behalf of women and minorities certainly deserves to overshadow any lingering controversy surrounding her brusque personal style. A black girl growing up in the Deep South after Reconstruction had to develop a thick skin to survive.

Mary Jane McLeod was born in South Carolina on July 10, 1875, the fifteenth of seventeen children. Her parents, Samuel McLeod and Patsy McIntosh McLeod, had been slaves on a cotton plantation in Maysville. For the McLeod family, the lush, fertile land surrounding the plantation where they had worked for decades provided a suitable home, and Mary Jane grew up in a poor but loving household. In the years following emancipation, Samuel succeeded in reuniting his family, locating and arranging the return of several of his children who had been sent to work on distant plantations. He was a resourceful provider for his large family, and Samuel McLeod eventually bought five acres where he built a home and business. In Mary Jane's youth, hard work in the cotton fields her father owned ruled the day.

She was discouraged by her peers from attending the local one-room schoolhouse for blacks in Maysville, but young Mary Jane insisted that she wanted to learn to read. Along with numerous other negative effects of slavery, the absence of reading and writing skills among many former slaves was a troubling fact. During her formative years, Mary Jane obeyed her parents wishes that she help her family in the cotton fields. The work was backbreaking, and at an age when most other American children were learning the alphabet, Mary Jane toiled under hot sun and thick humidity, a rucksack tied around her waist, her hands pricked and bloodied by the chore of pulling cotton.

At every opportunity Mary Jane pestered her parents to send her to school. She yearned to read and write; she felt the Lord had given her an inquisitive, ambitious nature because He intended for her to use it to help blacks. Eventually, Samuel and Patsy capitulated, and Mary Jane was allowed to study with Emma Jane Wilson, the stern but fair teacher at the local school for blacks. It was a triumph for young Mary Jane, and she was determined to make the most of it. Soon her parents realized they had made a wise decision, for Mary Jane became a star in the classroom. Wilson praised the girl's diligence and her keen appreciation of diction and comportment lessons as well as the basic elements of education—reading, writing, 'rithmetic and history.

Indeed, it was Emma Wilson who set Mary Jane on a path that thousands of black women would want to follow. The dedicated teacher saw in her promising young student the signs of a leader, and she wanted her to have the chance to learn all that she could. She gained Mary Jane a coveted scholarship at an established educational academy. For the first time in her life, Mary Jane left her family's sprawling "homestead" and lived a new life. At the respected Scotia Seminary outside Concord, North Carolina, Mary devoted all her energy to mastering her studies. From Shakespeare to Emerson to Poe, Mary learned to read and interpret the classics of literature. With a work ethic forged in the harsh discipline of agriculture, Mary applied herself wholeheartedly to education.

In 1894 her dedication paid off. Mary learned she had received another scholarship, at the prestigious Dwight Moody Institute for Home and Foreign Missions. She set off for the college in Chicago believing she would become a missionary in Africa. Mary enjoyed the bustle and activity of metropolitan Chicago. She often visited the local jails to sing and minister to the black inmates. She volunteered at the Pacific Garden Mission, where she fed the homeless and down-and-out members of the city's black community. An interest in women's civic clubs also took root in Mary's burgeoning political outlook during this time, and she eventually founded several prominent clubs—including the National Council of Negro Women—whose members worked to improve the black community. Yet when a college advisor informed Mary that few, if any, black missionaries would ever be sent to work in Africa, Mary decided to leave school.

Far from being discouraged at seeing her dream of being a missionary in Africa thwarted, Mary chose to keep pushing ahead. Her work in the jails and poorhouses of Chicago had convinced her that "Africans in America needed Christ and school just as much as Negroes in Africa," Mary recalled years later. "My life work lay not in Africa, but in my own country."

A few years later she returned to South Carolina, where her old mentor, Emma Wilson, offered her a job teaching. It was a joyous homecoming for Mary, who had first begun to find her identity so many years earlier in the very school where she now would teach. As Mary saw it, she was putting her "missionary spirit—the spirit of doing for others" to good use. Within a few years, restless and wanting to extend her teaching to more students, Mary McLeod sought and received an appointment to a large school in Georgia. At the Haines Institute, operated by the Presbyterian Board of Education, Mary learned plenty about entrepreneurship and personal responsibility. The institute was presided over by a notorious autocratic educator named Lucey Craft Haney. Haney was a devoted civic activist, and she even founded a hospital for blacks at a time when medical and other social services were limited for nonwhites in the Deep South. Haney demanded of her teachers and pupils a high degree of scholarship and dedication and used a rigid, programmatic model to get it. Mary flourished in an atmosphere where women educators set the curriculum, the tone, and the spirit of the growing school.

After four years Mary was transferred to another Presbyterian school, this one in Sumpter, South Carolina. At the Kendell Institute Mary continued her education and improved her teaching skills. There she met Albertus Bethune, a former schoolteacher who had opened his own business. He was a confident, prosperous man, and Mary was smitten. They married in the spring of 1898 and had a child soon thereafter. By the end of the decade, the couple had moved to Savannah, and Mary decided to spend more time at home so she could concentrate on raising her son, Albertus McLeod Bethune Jr. The next few years were productive and enlightening for Mary and her new family.

In Savannah Mary returned to the community work that had so occupied her before the birth of her son. When a visiting minister, the Rev. C. J. Uggans, asked Mary if she could help him establish a school in north central Florida, she decided to take the assignment. In Palatka, a small, agricultural town, Mary founded a community school, did volunteer work in local jails, and recruited the young townsfolk into civic clubs. In five years, under the tutelage of Uggans and his church, Mary transformed the black community, establishing a network of educational and civic groups that benefited blacks in the isolated region.

It was perhaps inevitable that Mary would ultimately found her own school. In 1904, in the seaside town of Daytona, Florida, Mary opened the Daytona Literary and Industrial Institute for Negro Girls. Now, after many years of immersing herself in the cause of education, Mary controlled a vast resource. It would become a beacon to thousands of blacks as, for the next two decades, she presided over the school. (It eventually merged with another local black school to become Bethune-Cookman College.) Drawing on the methods and philosophies of the teachers and scholars who had helped her, Mary shaped the school into a place where students could grow intellectually and spiritually. Along with "book learning," the college also offered a range of vocational courses, an important addition since boys were soon allowed to attend the formerly girls-only school.

By the 1920s Mary was known around the nation as a formidable advocate for black empowerment. The two-story white frame house that Albertus Bethune built for his family in Daytona in 1914 became a center of activity in the black community. When Mary helped lead a voter registration drive for blacks, her effective organizing and vocal denunciations of the "separate-but-equal" Jim Crow laws of Daytona Beach earned the ire of the local Ku Klux Klan. When hooded Klansmen showed up at the Bethune property to intimidate the family, they were faced down by local black villagers.

Through her post as president of the State Federation of Colored Women's Clubs, Mary helped rally black women throughout the Southeast to begin demanding adequate health and education facilities for children. Many years passed before the health care and educational opportunities for blacks would come to approach that of whites in the Deep South. In 1924 Mary was elected president of the most elite black women's civic group in the nation, the National Association of Colored Women's Clubs (NACWC). During her four-year term, she became a dynamic leader, a fund-raiser beyond compare, and a consultant to national education experts.

Mary spent much of the next few years in Washington, D.C., even succeeding in opening a headquarters of the NACWC in the nation's capital. In 1928 she took part in a national child health and education initiative organized by President Calvin Coolidge's Committee on Child Welfare. It was the beginning of a long association with the White House. Mary pressed the concerns of blacks, women, and children through succeeding presidential administrations, including Herbert Hoover's and Franklin Delano Roosevelt's. During his twelve years in the White House, Roosevelt instituted many social and welfare programs that were revolutionary. His wife, Eleanor Roosevelt, came to rely on Mary to help her devise social welfare policies that addressed the needs of poor and rural Americans, including blacks and women.

As Mary's biographer, Rackham Holt, described it, Mary had become "the expert on educational boards, able to supply the facts on 'Negro institutions' that received federal funding." While Mary's sometimes abrasive personal style drew criticism from some other black educators, she stuck to her conviction that advising the top white elected leaders was an important and valuable task. Throughout the thirties and much of the forties, she served on dozens of boards, committees, and panels dealing with educational and economic policy issues affecting blacks. When Eleanor Roosevelt invited Mary to participate in a luncheon for leaders of the National Council of Women at her fabulous Hyde Park home, history was made: For the first time, a black woman had been invited by the Office of the President to join with socially and politically prominent white women who were in the vanguard of a growing feminist movement in America. And following the historic afternoon meeting, Mary was appointed to the National Youth Administration. Thereafter, she developed a strong friendship with Eleanor Roosevelt and with Franklin's mother, Sara Delano Roosevelt. Politically moderate and socially liberal, they shared Mary's firm resolve that government could play a positive role in improving the conditions of masses of overlooked citizens.

Through her appointment as advisor on minority affairs at the National Youth Administration, Mary pulled together a coalition of black educators and community and church leaders. Their vision was only partially fulfilled, however, because the Great Depression made jobs scarce for all Americans. Nevertheless, when Mary returned to Daytona in 1944, she was hailed as a local heroine.

Over the next decade, Mary went about the administration of her college. She also oversaw her many interests in black-owned businesses in Florida and in Pittsburgh, where she held stock in one of the nation's preeminent black newspapers, the *Courier*. During World War II, she lobbied the U.S. War Department to allow black women to serve as officers in the Women's Army Corps, and helped captain the Women's Army for National Defense. It was a busy, productive time for Mary, who had matured into an imposing figure with snowy white hair, rigid posture, and a serious demeanor.

In 1945 she was sent by President Harry Truman to San Francisco, where she consulted with organizers of the United Nations. Along with the great educator and sociologist W. E. B. Du Bois, Mary represented the concerns of black Americans in the coalition of world leaders who included people of color from Europe, Africa, and the Caribbean. Together, this contingent argued for increased attention to the plight of minorities worldwide in the wake of colonialism. While their agenda was received coolly by white members of the nascent United Nations, Mary stood firm. At the end of the conference, Mary declared that the gathering in San Francisco "is not building the promised land of brotherhood and security and opportunity and peace. . . . We still have a long way to go."

Nonetheless, her place as a staunch and reliable expert on the needs of black Americans was cemented. During the next decade, Mary continued to oversee many civic clubs and to be involved in the administration of her college. Although a board of directors now existed and she no longer held the absolute last word over the day-to-day operations of Bethune-Cookman College, Mary established a foundation in her name that was attached to the school. It was to be a monument to her perserverance and accomplishments, a "living museum" that would house her large collections of papers, artifacts, and commendations from her long and fruitful career. Located near the school, the foundation today includes a treasury of personal history housed in the very building that Albertus Bethune had built for his wife in 1914.

When Mary McLeod Bethune died unexpectedly of a heart attack in 1955, the nation mourned. Her years of devoted service did not go unnoticed, and private and government organizations pitched in to help keep the college and the Mary McLeod Bethune Foundation alive. In 1975 the two-story home where Mary launched her long career of public service was declared a National Historic Landmark. And to this day a stream of scholars, fans, history buffs, and other interested Americans trek to the modest, whitewashed building to experience up close the world of a black woman who dedicated her life to the betterment of her nation.

8

Zora Neale Hurston

1891–1960

A Rural Road to Writers' Renaissance

FROM A FORMER SLAVE in the eighteenth century named PHILLIS WHEAT-
LEY to a twentieth-century Nobel laureate named TONI MORRISON, black
American women have played a significant part in this nation's formi-
dable literary tradition. Zora Heale Hurston bridges the generations.
She was a woman whom Harvard black studies scholar Henry Louis
Gates Jr. calls "a metaphor for the black woman writer's search for tra-
dition." Her life and times provide abundant material for reflection.

After a precocious childhood in a small Florida town, Zora arrived
in New York during one of the most creative eras black artists in America have ever experienced. A prolific life of writing won her international acclaim—including two Guggenheim Fellowships—and the praise
of contemporaries like Langston Hughes and Alain Locke. She wrote of
folk legends and lost loves, of ancient rural beliefs and the struggle for
identity in the modern swirl of twentieth-century America. She also
endured uncounted racial humiliations and worked menial jobs to support herself toward the end of her life, including a stint as a maid.

When Zora died in Florida, in 1960, her remarkable work was all
but forgotten by American readers—until the early seventies, when a
conscientious fan named ALICE WALKER began writing about her love of
Zora's work. Walker's attention sparked renewed interest in a woman
who had died penniless and alone. All the same, "Her books and folktales vibrate with tragedy, humor, and the real music of black American
speech," wrote MAYA ANGELOU in introducing the 1991 reissue of
Zora's autobiography, *Dust Tracks on a Road.*

Although she liked to say she was born in Florida, Zora Neale
Hurston was actually born in the tiny Alabama village of Notasulga, on
January 7, 1891. Her father, John Hurston, was a carpenter and Baptist preacher. Her mother, Lucy Potts Hurston, had been a schoolteacher. A year after her birth, Zora's father moved his family to
Eatonville, Florida, a tiny community distinguished as the first-ever all-
black town in the country.

Made up of self-supporting blacks who farmed their own land and operated their own businesses, Eatonville became a rich source of stories for Zora later in her life. But when her mother died in 1904, nine-year-old Zora despaired. The inquisitive girl had had mixed feelings about her mother, a woman she "seemed to have pitied but only glancingly loved," according to Maya Angelou. John Hurston remarried after Lucy's death, and Zora soon found herself at odds with her new stepmother. "If I died," Zora wrote years later, "let me die with my hands soaked in her blood. I want her blood and plenty of it." While those words might seem frightening in their violent imagery, the strength of Zora's writing lay in her keen ability to translate raw, uncensored emotion into equally raw language. Few critics of Zora's work ever complained that they found her writing stultifying or falsely sanitized.

It wasn't long before Zora fled her tiny Florida village for the North, finding work with a traveling theater company that had come through the South. She attended the Morgan Academy in Baltimore and graduated in 1918. She worked a series of odd jobs to support herself, including as a waitress in a nightclub and as a manicurist. Zora enrolled in one of the best-known black colleges in the nation, Howard University, in 1920. She was an erratic student and shocked some classmates with her independent and self-confident nature. She received an associate's degree from Howard and had her first piece of serious writing, a story called "John Redding Goes to Sea," published in the university's literary magazine in 1921. Three years later she wrote a short story that appeared in *Opportunity*, a literary magazine published by the National Urban League. It was during this period that she met and was befriended by a young man who would also leave his mark on Harlem's celebrated artistic world: Alain Locke. She won second place in a writing contest sponsored by *Opportunity*, and Locke convinced Zora that she should move to New York.

Harlem in the early twenties was pulsing with excitement. Intellectuals like W. E. B. Du Bois and Charles S. Johnson led a vanguard of political activists, painters, writers, and educators who produced some of the most stunning works in American culture. For Zora, it was like finally coming home. She eagerly joined the creative crowd, a group that collectively became known as the New Negro Movement. She attended many parties and took up the controversially snappy fashions of the day, including wearing pants and smoking cigarettes in public. Photographs of her during this period show a confident young woman, her face laughing and open, her head topped by dashing hats. Zora spent hours with other writers like Langston Hughes, arguing, telling downhome stories, and drinking in the cosmopolitan air of New York in the Jazz Age.

In 1924 she enrolled at Barnard College, an exclusive liberal arts school for women. Zora landed a job as an assistant to popular writer Fannie Hurst and began studying anthropology at Barnard with Franz Boas, the "father of American anthropology." Boas believed in a theory that was radical for its time: "cultural relativism." This theory held that differences in populations are the result of social, historic, and geographic conditions and not predetermined by genetics alone. His work appealed to Zora, who began to explore the value of folklore and mythology among African Americans.

In 1925 Zora wrote a short story called "Spunk" and a play called *Color Struck*. For these, she won *Opportunity*'s top award that year and earned the attention of prominent white writers like Eugene O'Neill. Although she couldn't actually type, Zora worked as a secretary for Hurst and began making a name for herself amid the literary world in New York. The next few years were a whirlwind of activity for Zora. She published numerous essays and short stories, many of them about life in rural Eatonville and the amazing characters who populated her small Southern town during her childhood.

Encouraged by Boas, Zora returned often to Florida to collect research for anthropological studies, as well as material for her writing. She cowrote a play with Langston Hughes, but eventually fell out with him over ownership issues. The play, *Mule Bone*, was a comedic look at black folk culture. It was not performed and was only published in its complete form some seventy years later, long after Zora and Hughes had died.

Still, the decade between 1925 and 1935 was spectacularly productive for Zora. Her works were published in popular magazines and serious literary journals alike, including *Ebony* and the *Journal of Negro History*. In May 1927 she married Herbert Sheen, a man she'd begun dating while an undergraduate at Howard University. That year, too, she found a wealthy benefactress, Mrs. Charlotte Mason, who was willing to bankroll her research, and continued gathering stories and legends from blacks in rural Florida. Zora received an undergraduate degree from Barnard, in 1928, and promptly filed for divorce from Sheen. Her divorce wasn't finalized until 1931, the same year that Zora wrote short sketches and monologues for a theatrical review called *Fast and Furious.*

Zora's growing interest in theater took her back to the South again, in 1934, when she traveled to Bethune-Cookman College in Florida. There she established a school of dramatic arts, a place where works "based on pure Negro expression" could flourish. She also published her first book that same year, *Jonah's Gourd Vine,* a fictional account of a small Florida town. Populated by characters who strongly resembled the family and friends of Zora's youth, the book earned some critical acclaim and was a selection of the Book-of-the-Month Club.

In 1935 Zora spent a few months at Columbia University in New York, where she planned to study for a doctorate in anthropology. But her other interests—including writing, anthropological field work, and nightclubbing—left little time for poring over textbooks. So Zora continued doing what she loved most, chronicling the ways of the country folk she knew so well. She worked on a folk music collection for the Library of Congress and joined the WPA Federal Theatre Project as a drama coach. Although the Great Depression had rendered many Americans jobless—especially unskilled blacks in the northern cities—Zora found no shortage of work during much of this period.

Her second book was published this same year. *Mules and Men* was a highly regarded collection of stories and folktales from her upbringing in Florida. With vignettes, short scenes, and vivid portrayals, she brought to life the people of Eatonville and the surrounding region. Her eye and ear were sharp, and Zora dazzled the literary world by recreating the front porches and backwoods and Sunday sermons of the black men and women of rural Florida. While some critics found fault with her work because it did not focus explicitly on racial inequality, Zora held fast to her belief that shedding light on the lives and culture of rural blacks would go a long way toward breaking down racist stereotypes. Behind the colloquial speech of her characters were complicated individuals who possessed the smarts and initiative, the faults and ambiguities, of all human beings, qualities which were rarely attributed to blacks by whites.

In 1936 she stunned the academic and artistic worlds by receiving a Guggenheim Fellowship. It was a grand honor, carrying international legitimacy as well as a hefty financial award. Zora's plan to study ancient West Indian voodoo practices had impressed the fellowship committee, and soon she traveled to the Caribbean for field research.

While in Jamaica, Zora learned of the troubling presence of interethnic racism. Darker-skinned blacks were shunned by lighter-skinned blacks; the lighter-skinned "mulattos" were often cruel arbiters of power on the scenic island.

Their Eyes Were Watching God, a heartfelt novel about mythology, self-discovery, and gender and age divides, appeared in 1937. Through the eyes of Janie Crawford, Zora spun a story of myth and folktelling that revealed rifts and uncertainties in her community. Her heroine is illiterate and flawed, but she manages to find and protect her moral center amid a male-dominated, white-dominated world. This book is now widely viewed as one of the finest examples of storytelling in modern literary history, a rich detailing of a part of American life that had been overlooked by mainstream publishers. In its day, it was well received by the literary establishment.

But Zora's use of "down-home speak" was not always popular with African Americans (particularly in northern cities) who were struggling to overcome prejudices and stereotypes. For many blacks who had emigrated to the North, it was vitally important to overcome the widespread perception held by whites that they were uneducated and unsophisticated. All the same, *Their Eyes Were Watching God* had made Zora one of the best-known writers of the thirties. Not content to rest on the success of this book, Zora traveled to Haiti in 1937, after the Guggenheim Foundation renewed her award for another year.

Between 1938 and 1942 Zora traveled extensively and kept busy in a number of artistic and academic arenas. She seemed to have found a workable balance between the social, academic, and literary sides of her life. In 1939 she married Albert Price III, in Florida, where she had returned a year earlier to put together a play for the Federal Writer's Project. Zora continued writing, and was published in popular magazines and academic journals; she received an honorary degree from Morgan State College and collected oral histories and folklore in South Carolina; she wrote an unsual work called *Moses, Man of the Mountain,* a version of the biblical Exodus story written in "Negro vernacular." By the time her autobiography, *Dust Tracks on a Road,* was published in late 1942, Zora was widely viewed as a controversial, talented American writer. She had enjoyed enormous critical success, even if her books and essays didn't always provide her a substantial income.

For a few months in 1941 Zora went to Hollywood and worked as a story consultant for Paramount Pictures, where she was one of the few black American women doing nonacting work in the motion picture industry during its golden era. She returned to the East Coast in 1942 and published numerous short stories and essays in a variety of journals, including the lyrical "Cock Robin, Beale Street," and the intriguing "Story in Harlem Slang."

In 1942 Zora wrote for the popular *Saturday Evening Post* and won the prestigious Anisfield-Wolff Book Award for *Dust Tracks on a Road.* When her distinctive image appeared on the cover of the lofty *Saturday Review of Literature,* few in the literary world could doubt that Zora's was an enormously important voice. She was at the zenith of her personal and professional powers, receiving Howard University's Distinguished Alumni Award and publishing provocative essays in respected journals. Yet as one of her village characters might have guessed, the fates don't always let the good times roll.

Divorced from her second husband in 1943, Zora spent the next year living on a houseboat along the winding, isolated rivers of west Florida. Although she wrote essays and short stories from time to time, and saw them published in a host of serious journals, her next novel was rejected by her publisher, J. B. Lippincott.

Zora returned to New York in 1946 and worked to help elect a Republican political candidate. Politically conservative, Zora had devoted much time and energy over the years to supporting Republican candidates. Some other emerging black writers of this era decried her political conservatism. But ever self-assured, Zora maintained her own position and was unafraid to flout convention. Her unpopularity with the burgeoning black intellectual community—including a promising young writer named Richard Wright—made her something of a literary outcast. For a few months in 1946 and 1947, Zora was so strapped financially she had to live in an unheated apartment in Harlem.

Over the next decade, Zora's fortunes rose and fell. She published several unique, thoughtful works in publications like the *Journal of American Folklore, Saturday Evening Post,* and *American Mercury.* Zora continued traveling when she could afford it. She went to British Honduras and lived there until 1948. She was arrested for allegedly molesting a schoolboy in New York, but the charges were later dismissed as groundless. Thereafter, Zora retreated into herself. She felt she was the target of political persecution and became depressed and suicidal.

One of her last books was *Seraph on the Suwannee,* a novel about the life and marriage of a white couple. To many of her readers, she seemed to have lost her special touch. She returned to Florida, where she supported herself by working as a maid in resort villages in Miami and on Rivo Island. Though short of money and job stability, Zora continued writing. In 1950 the *Saturday Evening Post* published her controversial essay "What White Publishers Won't Print." Later that year Zora drew even more criticism for her essay in *American Legion* magazine called "I Saw Negro Votes Peddled."

Zora moved around Florida quite a bit over the next few years, working as a librarian in Fort Pierce for a time and picking up occasional work from newspapers. By 1958 she was a substitute teacher at the Lincoln Park Academy in Fort Pierce, her literary genius tarnished by bad luck, changing times, and ill health. Zora suffered a serious stroke in 1959. Lacking money, she had to be taken to a county "welfare home" in Fort Pierce.

Her once shining spirit was dimming. Few besides a handful of loyal scholars and historians knew or cared that Zora Neale Hurston, one of the brightest lights of the Harlem Renaissance, was financially bereft and virtually alone. On January 28, 1960, Zora died of heart disease at the St. Lucie County Welfare Home. She was buried at the local "colored" cemetery in an unmarked grave.

Thirteen years later, Alice Walker wrote an homage to Zora Neale Hurston for *Ms.* magazine. The essay, a wholehearted tribute and poignant reminder of Zora's legacy as a writer and individual, touched off a flurry of interest in Zora's work. In 1991, Henry Louis Gates Jr. presided over the reissuance of her autobiography, *Dust Tracks on a Road.* Earlier, in the seventies, scholar Robert Hemenway had published a biography of Zora. Between 1990 and 1995 Zora's seminal work, *Their Eyes Were Watching God,* sold more than a million copies. Officials in Fort Pierce opened the Zora Neale Hurston Public Library, and her work was included in the distinguished Library of America series.

In classrooms across America her work is now read by millions. For a rebellious soul from a small Florida town, the road to recognition was long, difficult, and filled with surprises. For a long list of black women writers who followed her—including ALICE WALKER, MAYA ANGELOU, and TONI MORRISON—Zora Neale Hurston walked that road so that they might follow.

9

Alberta Hunter

1895–1984

An Entertaining Life

ALBERTA HUNTER was the godmother of blues and jazz singers. Her legacy of songwriting and her snappy performance style were passed on to a long line of women singers—from BILLIE HOLIDAY to LENA HORNE to ARETHA FRANKLIN—and remain benchmarks of excellence in modern popular music. Like other black women popular singers, Alberta learned her craft in a time-tested manner: performing in clubs and saloons around the nation. She came of age as a singer at a time when no respectable woman was supposed to work in entertainment, and she had to bear the stigma of performing popular music in places of low repute. Yet the diminutive woman showed a strong artistic determination and a keen understanding of what she wanted. Known for her saucy renditions of several blues classics, Alberta struggled and toiled for years in near obscurity before experiencing a renaissance during the seventies.

After having been absent from the stage for several decades, Alberta appeared at Carnegie Hall for the first time in 1978 and opened the Newport Jazz Festival that same year. The performances capped a magnificent comeback for a woman who had pioneered the art of jazz and blues singing but who had dropped from sight.

Eubie Blake, the great Tin Pan Alley piano player and composer, reunited with Alberta in 1977 for a series of classic shows that drew thousands of fans to the Cookery, a New York nightclub. He called her "the showstopper," and fans agreed. The lyrics of "My Man Ain't Handy No More," "Downhearted Blues," and other songs were somewhat risqué, but Alberta simply sang about life as she knew it—with a light, realistic touch that enraptured her listeners. "Sex is only a condition of the mind," Alberta told an interviewer during the seventies. "It's like age: Drink some lemonade and forget it."

Born in Memphis, Tennessee, on April 1, 1895, Alberta Hunter was the frail and sprightly daughter of Charles and Laura Hunter. She had been exceptionally small at birth, and her mother carried baby Alberta around on a tiny pillow for many weeks. Yet as she grew, she was filled with enormous energy, and little Alberta soon came to delight her mother by showing early signs of being quite a character. "She may have started out weak," wrote Frank C. Taylor in his 1987 biography *A Celebration in Blues*. "But there was never anything dainty about Alberta. As soon as she learned to get up and around on her scrawny legs, she was always a mess. Miss Laura kept their house clean as a pin, but there wasn't anything she could do to keep Alberta neat. She was always so dirty that family and friends called her 'Pig,' a name that stuck to her for the rest of her life like cold grits to a breakfast plate."

Alberta's first brush with adversity happened when her father and mother separated. Her father had worked as a Pullman porter and didn't spend much time in Memphis, but Alberta's first years were spent in the happy, secure environment provided by her hardworking father. Now Laura, desperate to keep Alberta and her oldest daughter fed and clothed, took a job as a maid in a local bordello. Alberta's mother never spoke about the goings-on she may have witnessed at her job. She kept her two impressionable daughters in the dark about certain aspects of "the sporting life," according to Taylor's biography, and encouraged them to have strong constitutions and to work hard. "She wasn't the crybaby type," Alberta said. "I guess that's the reason I'm so strong. She'd say, 'If something's gotta be done, let's get it done.' Don't feel sorry for yourself or anybody else" is how Alberta recalled her mother's early advice.

Over the next several years, young Alberta thrived in her mother's strict but loving household. In the early twentieth century, Memphis was a buzzing town with a dynamic black social and business structure. All along Beale Street music clubs, gambling halls, saloons, and other night spots gave the downtown an exciting, somewhat dangerous air of glamour and intrigue. W. C. Handy, one of the founders of a Mississippi-born style of musical expression known as the blues, lived in Memphis. Along with other black musicians from juke joints and roadhouses in the nearby Delta, Handy helped make Memphis one of the cradles of jazz and blues performing in America. For young Alberta, who loved the twanging sound of guitars even as an infant, the atmosphere made for a perfect early learning environment. At Dixie Park, a local gathering spot for blacks in segregated Memphis, Handy and other musicians would gather several times each year and mount free concerts. "We'd hear that 'ta-da, ta-da' of the band, and Lord, we'd be out that door so fast," Alberta remembered many years later.

Her mother saved as much money as she could from her job as a maid, and over several years Alberta's family moved to better homes around Memphis. They eventually moved into a small, neat house on the property of a white woman named Nellie Hunter. The older woman hired young Alberta to run errands for her and paid the energetic young girl twenty-five cents a week. It was a grand way to make a living, as Alberta saw it, and she used her money to buy treats for herself and her sister. Unfortunately, Nellie Hunter's husband took a liking to young Alberta and began expressing an inappropriate interest in her. "He was a dirty dog," Alberta told her biographer many years later.

Nonetheless, Alberta did well in school and especially enjoyed singing in the choirs at church and school. Neighbors and family members seemed to enjoy her lively renditions of popular hymns and songs of the day, and soon Alberta decided she might like to sing professionally. Her mother frowned on such notions, but Alberta persisted. In 1911 she boarded an Illinois Central Railroad train in the company of a former school teacher and her husband, and lit out for the big time—Chicago.

Although still in her teens, Alberta was determined to make it as a singer. Unbeknownst to her at the time, she would make her mark as a uniquely talented songwriter as well. In Chicago Alberta was thrilled and astounded by the look and feel of the big city. She knew that her mother had an old friend, Ellen Winston, who lived in Chicago. Alberta wasn't exactly sure of Winston's address, but she was confident she could find her. As fate would have it, however, one of the first places young Alberta went in to ask for directions was a saloon. "I could hear the music from one of those old-fashioned pianos you pump with your feet, a player piano. And they were playing, 'Where the River Shannon Flows'," Alberta told her biographer.

It was an auspicious introduction to the sound of what would come to be known as the Chicago blues. Eventually, Alberta found Ellen Winston working as a cook for a wealthy family in Chicago's Hyde Park neighborhood. She secured a job for Alberta peeling potatoes. It was hard, hot work, and Alberta vowed to get a job singing as soon as possible. After a few months of hanging around a jumping nightspot called Dago Frank's, Alberta convinced the musical director there to let her sing. Soon she was taking popular songs of the day and reworking them in her own humorous fashion.

From there, she realized she had a knack for word-play and gradually began to write her own songs. For the next several years Alberta played at popular nightclubs up and down State Street, including a famous establishment called Hugh Hoskins. Amid pimps, prostitutes, gamblers, and pickpockets, young Alberta developed a thick hide and keen sense of humor. Usually the youngest in the crowd, she had to be quick on her feet to avoid the advances of some of the older clientele. By 1915 Alberta was singing at one of the swankest nightspots in Chicago, the Panama Cafe on South State Street. It was an exuberant time, as Chicago underwent an amazing industrial growth.

In the next several years Alberta rose to the top of the burgeoning blues scene in Chicago. She worked with musicians like King Oliver and Louis Armstrong and earned a reputation as a tough, inventive singer. At that time some Americans, black and white, considered jazz and blues music sinful, although Alberta found that kind of thinking hypocritical. "Blues aren't sinful," Alberta said. "You're telling a story. Blues are songs from your soul. When you're singing the blues, you're *singing*."

Sure enough, over the next decade, Alberta would ride the crest of a wave of interest in jazz and blues. In 1917 Alberta was one of the hottest singers in Chicago, earning almost $20 a week—a veritable fortune back then—as a popular singer at the well-known Dreamland nightclub. By the early twenties, her salary had climbed to $35 a week, and Alberta was at the top of her game artistically. She made her first recording in 1922. Most of the songs were written by other tunesmiths, but Alberta managed to record one of her own numbers. "Downhearted Blues," a slow, insinuating number with zesty lyrics and sharp commentary about love relationships, became a classic. In New York she also made recordings with a promising young piano player and composer named Eubie Blake. The two hit it off famously, and Alberta would always name these sessions as her favorite.

Over the next several years, she recorded and performed several notable blues standards, including, "T'Aint Nobody's Business" and "You Can't Do What My Last Man Did," with the great musician Fats Waller, and her own composition, "Chirpin' the Blues." She put together her own band and set out on the road to play dates from Chicago to New York to Virginia and the Deep South. Billed as "Alberta Hunter and Her Boys," she was a popular and exciting entertainer, a tiny woman of enormous presence and stunning vocal inventiveness. They worked vaudeville houses and blues joints for many years before she decided to move permanently to New York. By the late twenties, she was known as one of the most sophisticated women in Harlem. At the Apollo Theater and the Cotton Club audiences cheered and laughed at Alberta's expert singing and playful stage patter. She was brash and bold, and greatly impressed young writers like Langston Hughes and DOROTHY WEST.

Alberta traveled to Europe for the first time in 1927 and became a sensation in Paris. "Well, I became very popular," Alberta said in 1987. The French clubgoers loved her salty renditions of songs like "Organ Grinder" and "I Can't Give You Anything but Love," and Alberta in turn adored cosmopolitan Paris. She became a well-regarded presence on the popular music scene in Europe, traveling frequently to London to perform, including one thrilling concert with the great singer Paul Robeson. Unfortunately, her return to the United States in 1929 coincided with the Wall Street stock market crash. For the next two decades, work became increasingly difficult for Alberta to find. During World War II, she toured with the USO and entertained black troops around the United States and in Europe. After the war, however, musical tastes were changing, and Alberta found her unique brand of blues singing somewhat out of favor.

In the late fifties Alberta decided she needed a full-time day job in order to support herself and talked her way into a training program at Goldwater Hospital in Harlem. For many years she worked there as a nurse. Always quick with a funny story or a kind remark, Alberta worked hard to care for her patients. But a diamond does not go long unrecovered, and eventually music scholars and fans rediscovered Alberta Hunter. Her career saw a remarkable rejuvenation in the late seventies when she reunited with Eubie Blake and the handful of other pals who had survived those early days in Chicago.

President Jimmy Carter invited Alberta to sing at the White House, and she enthralled the concertgoers with her classic renditions of many long-forgotten blues standards. Once again Alberta traveled the world singing songs that had suddenly found a new, fervent audience. "Grown men were seen to have tears in their eyes," the *New York Times* observed after one of Alberta's concerts in 1977. She sang regularly at the Cookery in Manhattan and drew hundreds of loyal fans with every performance. And when the CBS television program *60 Minutes* aired a segment in the mid-eighties on Alberta's comeback, she experienced a resurgence of public interest in her performing and songwriting. At last, the public agreed on her importance in the history of popular music.

Alberta spent the last few weeks of her life in good spirits, dictating the details of her experiences to Franklin Taylor, her biographer. Not surprisingly, the eternally feisty Alberta offered some valuable advice before she slipped away on October 17, 1988: "If a man looks like he has doubt in his mind, like he doesn't believe in God, I'll say, 'You're thinking the wrong way.' I'm an example of God's goodness. I'm eighty-nine years old. I'm an example of one of God's people. Keep me in mind . . . and remember, it's God, not me. That's right."

10

Bessie Smith

1894–1937

Breaking New Ground in the Blues

BESSIE SMITH SANG THE BLUES like no one before her. And in more than fifty years since her death, few other blues singers are so revered. Amid early twentieth-century songwriters, like ALBERTA HUNTER and Fats Waller, to modern jazz singers, like Cassandra Wilson and Ruth Brown, Bessie Smith is a towering example of the rich blues tradition handed down through generations of black American women. "Can't nobody bake a jelly roll like mine," Bessie sang teasingly in one of her big hits from the twenties.

Bessie's mixture of heartfelt expression and strong personal determination were unique. Between 1920 and her death, from Chicago to Memphis to New York and Kansas City, Bessie Smith made an indelible impression on the nascent popular music scene. She was born in the daunting years of post–Civil War reconstruction and rose to the heights of fame and fortune as a saloon singer of formidable presence and vocal range. She cut a dashing figure in nightclubs in the cities where the blues flourished in the early twentieth century, including the Cotton Club in Harlem, Dreamland in Chicago, and the smoky backrooms of juke joints on Beale Street in Memphis. Her untimely death robbed the world of a significant singing talent, one that was just beginning to blossom when Bessie died. Nonetheless, through the admiration and respect of a whole new generation of jazz and blues singers—not to mention several reissued recordings of her work— Bessie's sassy singing style and sensible outlook on life is preserved for all time.

During a hardscrabble childhood in the rural South, Bessie learned to emulate the singing style of the older black women she knew. Her exact birthday is unknown, although some historians and musicologists date the year of her birth as 1894. What we do know is that Bessie was born in Chattanooga, Tennessee, in a region steeped in American folk and gospel music dating back more than two hundred years. In the Baptist and African Methodist Episcopal churches all around Bessie's Chattanooga home, gospel music and centuries-old spirituals could be heard. From there the step into performing popular music was inevitable. Indeed, one of Bessie's early mentors was the famous Ma Rainey, and Bessie honed her singing craft by performing in dozens of juke joints around the Deep South during the early years of the twentieth century. From Atlanta to Memphis to Birmingham and Shreveport, Bessie sang the slow, sometimes agonizing refrains of love gone wrong and men gone bad, and expressed in highly personal, gospel-inflected songs the heart and soul of the black experience.

All around her, poverty, broken relationships, and unemployment made the lives of thousands of blacks difficult and bleak. Yet, like Rainey, Alberta Hunter, and BILLIE HOLIDAY, Bessie turned her experience of this shattered environment into the core of her artistic expression. After making a name for herself locally, Bessie was discovered by a well-known pianist and composer, Clarence Williams. Over the next several years she began recording some of the earliest blues standards. She would sometimes disdain the use of a microphone in live performances, believing that her rich voice and peppy personality could carry her message across the footlights. At Columbia Records, she became a powerful artistic presence, recording more than a hundred songs that endure today as blues classics.

Throughout her eventful career Bessie shocked listeners with her frank references to personal relationships. She was among the first popular female singers to allude to a woman's desire for sexual gratification. Like Alberta Hunter, and another blues singer, "Big Mama" Thornton, Bessie believed she was simply portraying life as she knew it. And while some people found the down-home feel of blues music too raw, Bessie thrived on the honest emotion and heartrending truths found in the words that she sang.

By the late twenties, the "Empress of the Blues," as executives at Columbia had dubbed her, reveled in the expensive trappings of a performer's life. Photographs from the early thirties show her confident and stylishly turned out in the sharp fashions of the day. By the mid-thirties she was known worldwide for her recordings with Louis Armstrong, Fletcher Henderson, and Benny Goodman.

Like many other world-class black musicians, Bessie was frustrated by the Jim Crow laws that forced her to perform in blacks-only clubs and to enter and exit through the kitchens of the glamorous white nightclubs where she occasionally sang. It was a life that defined the "duality" of the black experience so eloquently described by the great African-American philosopher W. E. B. Du Bois. In her public life Bessie, like other black women singers, soared to the heights of artistic success in her home nation, yet in her private life she was unable to enjoy the fruits of success.

Nonetheless, Bessie stood tall throughout her short career. By 1936 she was at the pinnacle of the music industry, and had even made a valuable impression on a new medium—major motion pictures. Beginning in 1929, Bessie went to Hollywood and performed in several lively short films. At that time, theater-owners required Hollywood studios to provide short films lasting ten to fifteen minutes to fill out their feature-film double bills. Moviegoers came to look forward to the extra treat of a small slice of culture served up in between the longer films. Bessie was a natural for the big screen. She was tall and blessed with a regal carriage, a broad, attractive face, and a powerful singing voice. Indeed, her performance in *St. Louis Blues,* a short made in 1929, was so candid and moving that industry censors banned the film from the nation's theaters. At that time, the troubling state of race relations in America was considered taboo, and Bessie's poignant portrayal of a troubled singer frightened the movie industry watchdogs.

Then, suddenly, Bessie Smith was gone. She died an untimely death in September 1937 from injuries she received in a car wreck near Clarksdale, Mississippi, but her unique talent, keen intelligence, and personal integrity live on. They are preserved on vinyl records, compact discs, and film to delight all future generations. Bessie's legendary recordings of "Downhearted Blues" and other standards remain to provide vivid, soulful evidence of all that black American women have contributed to this nation's sterling cultural heritage.

11

Hattie McDaniel

1895–1952

Confronting Cinematic Stereotypes

HATTIE MCDANIEL was the first black American ever to win an Academy Award. Her poignant performance in *Gone With the Wind*, the greatest film epic of all time, thrilled audiences around the world and remains a vivid chronicle of history and a romanticized ideal of the Old South.

At the height of Hollywood's Golden Era Hattie was one of the best-known black actors in America. She had learned to sing and act by appearing in numerous stage productions and musical reviews in the nation's vaudeville theatrical network. Hers was a formidable presence, and Hattie was a versatile performer. A trooper of the first rank, she was an uncomplaining, strong-minded player on the movie industry scene.

Arriving at a time when few African-American women were cast in major motion pictures, Hattie was usually relegated to playing the parts of maids and Mammys. All the same, she never failed to infuse her characters with humor and dignity. In the process, she stood as one of the strongest examples of all the composure, grace, and professional skill that black Americans have contributed to this nation's cultural development.

"I'm so proud to be a credit to my race," Hattie said during the Oscar ceremony in Los Angeles in 1939. At the time, few other prominent black Americans had managed the tough ascent to the top in Hollywood. Today the words of Hattie's Oscar acceptance speech may seem sad, but they marked an epochal turn in the late thirties: she had infused her roles with such dignity and pride as few other blacks had succeeded in doing. By her accomplishment Hattie had shown the nation that she and other black American actors merited recognition and respect.

Born in Wichita, Kansas, on June 10, 1895, Hattie was an easygoing and dedicated student. Her hardworking family moved around the West in the industrial boom of the turn of the century. Hattie first got a taste of the stage, thanks to her older brother, in Colorado. By the time she became a regular bit player in Hollywood films, she had spent much of her life in the theatrical community. "I was little more than a kid, but I was old within show business," Hattie said in an interview in the late thirties. Hattie recalled her first encounter with the theatrical life, in the dusty town of Denver. She was still in grade school when her older brother told her he planned to become a performer. "I had already won a medal in dramatic arts, when I was fifteen," Hattie said. "But then, one year later, my older brother, Otis, wrote his own show and songs, and persuaded my mother to let me go on the road with his company." Touring the country with Otis, Hattie began learning the theatrical ropes.

By her early twenties, Hattie had graduated to the more established performance venues across the nation. In Chicago, New York, Baltimore, Kansas City, Denver, and Philadelphia, enormous theaters offered residents nightly bills of a wide range of acts: jugglers and comedians, minstrels and jazz bands. Vaudeville was the place to go for lively stage entertainment. And in the days before television and motion pictures, actors and actresses around the nation had few other outlets in which to display their craft. For Hattie, the vaudeville circuit was a dream come true. Theatrical show places with illustrious names—the Orpheum and the Palace—were played by famous singers and hoofers, Eddie Cantor, Fannie Brice, Bill "Bojangles" Robinson, and a host of others. "I loved every minute of it," Hattie recalled following her rise to the top, "the tent shows, the kerosene lights, the contagious enthusiasm of the small-town crowds."

Hattie distinguished herself as a reliable and innovative actress. With the addition of the new, exciting medium of radio to the nation's cultural fabric, she found regular work. She was one of the first black American women to appear regularly on radio programs, singing popular standards of the late twenties and early thirties on a number of hit shows. Hollywood soon came calling. As the industry moved from producing silent pictures to sound extravaganzas, Hattie began working in films. From the early thirties through the fifties, she appeared in dozens of films, among them *The Little Colonel* (1935), *Nothing Sacred* (1937), and, the most romantic Hollywood epic of all time, *Gone With the Wind* (1939).

With her clear voice and appealing persona, Hattie became a favorite of film directors and producers. Initially she found the work thrilling and challenging. Although she was often cast as a sullen maid or a kerchief-wearing Mammy, she worked hard to prevent her stereotypical characters from becoming completely degrading to black Americans. Like fellow black actors and performers Ethel Waters, Bill Robinson, Eddie Rochester, and others who were offered only the roles of maids, porters, chauffeurs, and stable hands, Hattie often refused to act the more egregiously racist scenes that some filmmakers wanted during this era. Nevertheless, throughout her long career, she sometimes caught criticism from members of the black political community. They urged her not to continue accepting maids roles. Hattie responded by saying she understood their concerns, but that she had family members to support. Furthermore, she believed that she abided by her own rules of what roles and scenes were appropriate. With strong faith in herself, Hattie worked consistently and usually graced her two-dimensional characters with dignity and humor.

Indeed, her persistence paid off famously in late 1938, when she learned that she had been cast in the biggest motion picture of all time—David O. Selznick's production of Margaret Mitchell's tale of love and war in the Old South, *Gone With the Wind*. As the heroine's watchful and resourceful chaperone, Hattie gave her character a wise soulfulness. It was a stereotypical role, but Hattie brought such force and integrity to the part that she impressed black and white filmgoers alike.

Her work in a pivotal role helped propel that four-hour-long Technicolor spectacular into the history books as one of the most critically and commercially successful motion pictures of all time. In scene after scene Hattie took the potentially embarrassing character of Mammy, Scarlett O'Hara's maid, and invested her with amazing depth and strength. Critics hailed her performance as one of stunning power. In late 1939 Hattie became the first black American ever to win an Academy Award.

In the years following this success, Hattie continued to play maids and chaperones to leading white actresses. By the late forties, however, she was beginning to be increasingly troubled by these roles, and she turned to work in radio shows and in other theatrical arenas. When Hattie died unexpectedly from a heart attack in 1952, she had just completed a television series called *Beulah* and was taking fewer and fewer parts, content at last to begin enjoying some of the fruits of all her years of hard work.

In the annals of modern motion picture history, Hattie left a legacy of excellence and dedication that remains a high standard for all American actors. Indeed, some fifty years passed before WHOOPIE GOLDBERG became the second black woman to take home the prestigious Oscar. At that Academy Award ceremony, in 1991, Whoopie singled out Hattie as a unique source of inspiration for her own spectacular career.

12

Marian Anderson

1902–1993

Singing Freedom's Song

THE MODERN WORLD of classical musicians is small and competitive, a diverse community of men and women who fill concert halls and operatic theaters around the globe. In La Scala in Italy and the Metropolitan Opera in New York, opera lovers thrill to the sights and sounds of stars from a wide range of ethnic and economic backgrounds as they deliver the most beloved operas of all time, *Aida, Carmen,* and *La Bohème.* Early in the twentieth century, few black Americans have stepped up to those exalted stages or performed publically in those time-tested operas. Paul Robeson was the best-known exception. But by the end of 1939 a new virtuoso classical singer arrived to delight millions of music lovers worldwide—and that performer happened to be an African American.

In Marian Anderson, the daughter of humble Philadelphia laborers, classical music received a new kind of expression. With perfect pitch in an amazing vocal range, Marian Anderson rose from being a precocious star of an inner-city church choir to the zenith of international classical music performance. Through pluck and determination, as well as a mature and dignified personality, she overcame the powerful force of widespread discrimination that faced blacks and women in the United States during the first half of the twentieth century. Excelling in a highly specialized artistic field at a time when many black American women struggled daily for basic necessities, Marian Anderson ultimately emerged as a leading light in the glittering world of high culture. Through hard work, good timing, strong religious faith, and self-confidence honed by years of training and introspection, she established a new standard of operatic greatness, a yardstick by which all other American women classical singers will forever be measured.

During a long, remarkable life of artistic achievement, Marian also devoted her formidable intelligence and well-earned social position to fighting for human rights. After breaking down racial barriers at segregated performance halls during the thirties and forties and establishing herself as an operatic diva, she became the first black woman to sing a leading role with the Metropolitan Opera. Later, Marian served as a cultural delegate to the United Nations, and after her retirement from the concert stage, she turned her attention to teaching and lecturing.

During more than fifty years in the spotlight, Marian received dozens of humanitarian and artistic awards, including the National Medal of Arts. When she turned seventy-five in 1977, the United States Congress voted to have the Treasury Department mint a special gold medal in her honor. It was a fitting way of recognizing a black American woman who was a national treasure—an acclaimed performer with all the dignity and grace of historic figures like IDA B. WELLS BARNETT, HARRIET TUBMAN, and MARY MCLEOD BETHUNE.

The only difference between Marian and those other important, politically active women is that she turned her soothing, melodious voice into an instrument for social change. In 1939, when First Lady Eleanor Roosevelt resigned from the Daughters of the American Revolution, which had refused to let Marian sing in Constitution Hall, the public recoiled at the cruelties of segregation and the legacy of slavery that cast a shadow over the nation. But by staying focused on her craft and coolly persevering, performing only in integrated halls, Marian made a brilliantly effective stand for justice. She brought the talent and majesty of all black American women into the worldwide cultural arena. For even as a timid young girl from a working-class Philadelphia neighborhood, Marian showed strong indications that she had been singled out by a higher power for her illustrious gift.

Born in Philadelphia, on February 27, 1902, Marian Anderson grew up in a close-knit community of white- and blue-collar workers. Her mother worked as a janitor in a local department store, and her father was a laborer in the Reading Terminal Market. Marian's parents aspired to the better things in life, and a strong network of African-American businesses and civic organizations made it seem that anyone willing to work hard enough could move upward. The eldest of three girls, Marian had a secure, safe childhood. She enjoyed her schoolwork and the church activities her staunchly religious mother required of her.

When she was two years old, Marian's father died unexpectedly, and her mother decided to move with her three daughters into her mother's large home in South Philadelphia. Her father had been a dedicated volunteer at the Union Baptist Church, and Marian and her sisters continued their father's tradition of regular church involvement. A quiet, thoughtful girl, Marian was very close to her mother and grandmother, whom she lived with in a large home. When she was six years old, she joined the junior church choir, and within the next few months she began to discover that she might hold a key to prosperity for her struggling family.

By the time she was a teenager Marian had become a phenomenon, singing alto (or mezzo) parts because it suited the needs of the choir, though she was capable of singing a high soprano, too. Lacking formal training, her voice nevertheless created a sensation, and she earned a reputation in the close community of black churches as a supremely talented singer and impressive interpreter of gospel hymns and spiritu- als. In time, she became a featured soloist at other prominent black Philadelphia churches, eventually branching out to sing at local social functions and colleges. Imbued with a quiet elegance and uncanny maturity, Marian carried herself with the utmost professionalism. She regarded her voice as a precious gift and recognized its potential for uplifting herself and others.

In her teens Marian began visiting churches in regional Pennsylvania with the Union choir, earning her first taste of the performer's life on the road. During these years, Marian made her first trip to New York and was wide-eyed at the immense splendor of the famous Abyssinian Bap- tist Church in Harlem. Led by the dynamic minister, Adam Clayton Powell, Abyssinian played an important role as a lynchpin of secular and religious power in black America during this period. At this appear- ance, as at many other important black churches in the Northeast, Marian left hundreds of devoted fans in her wake. Additionally, Marian received her first glimpse of deep racial inequality. During a trip to a church in the nation's capital, Marian and the members of Union's choir were stunned to experience the humiliation of Jim Crow segregation.

In the twenties Washington, D.C., was still very much a Southern town, and blacks were required to use segregated public facilities. When Marian and the other choir members reached Washington, they were shunted into the "colored" railroad car. For the first time, Marian found herself stung by the poor conditions and gloomy atmosphere of their segregated environment. Perhaps more important, Marian's first exposure to the injustices of racial discrimination showed her how debilitating the Jim Crow laws were to the spirit of those black Amer- icans who were subjected to them.

Yet thanks to her mother's firm grounding and constant support, Marian endeavored to seriously explore her artistic potential. With financial help from parishioners at Union Baptist Church, Marian joined the prestigious Philadelphia Choral Society and began taking lessons with a noted classical singing coach, Giuseppe Boghetti. As her lessons with him progressed, Marian began expanding her repertoire, adding songs by Schubert, Brahms, Rachmaninoff, and other classical composers. It was difficult, strenuous work, but Marian pressed on, her fluid voice growing stronger, clearer, and more sonorous with each passing year. In concerts in Philadelphia and New York, Marian

enchanted audiences with her remarkably polished versions of complicated operatic selections, as well as of familiar and touching Negro spirituals and gospel standards. William King, a pianist from Philadelphia,
became her full-time accompanist, and Marian embarked on tours of
historically black colleges in the Deep South, including Morehouse College in Georgia and Fisk University in Tennessee. By the thirties
Marian's dedicated work and expanding skills were drawing notice
from outside of the black community. She had sung at many large, predominantly black churches and colleges from Savannah to New York.

Marian had also begun earning enough money from her singing
engagements to help her mother achieve the long-standing dream of
buying her own house. With pride and optimism for their future,
Marian gave her mother $600 she had saved to help buy a small house
on South Martin Street in South Philadelphia. Soon after that, Marian
helped facilitate another big change in her family. Her mother, who had
worked uncomplainingly for years as a housekeeper in Wanamakers
Department Store, came down with a virus one day; too ill to leave the
house, she nevertheless insisted on going to work. Almost on a whim,
Marian phoned the supervisor at the store and told her that her mother
would no longer work there. It was a risky move, but Marian was
determined to give her mother a rest after so many years of tireless
work. And now, of course, Marian would become the primary bread-
winner in the family. It was a task she felt prepared to assume.

Marian continued to concertize, sending most of her money home
to her mother and sisters in Philadelphia. With the wise advice of a
new manager, Arthur Judson, and her faithful pianist, William King,
Marian set her sights on the international world of classical music. For
the first time she traveled to England, and was received by the legendary
operatic master teacher, Raimund von Zur Mühlen. She wanted to
improve her delivery of the classics, and von Zur Mühlen was the preeminent expert of the day. After two lessons with her, the great master
teacher declared that Marian had to learn to speak German if she ever
hoped to succeed as a classical singer. Marian was temporarily disappointed, but she quickly recovered; she agreed to study with one of von
Zur Mühlen's star pupils, Mark Raphael.

She also became acquainted with the well-known British arts patron
Roger Quilter, who helped smooth her way into the European classical
music community. Thanks to Quilter's entrée, Marian performed at
regional concert halls around England, and her name began to circulate

in the upper reaches of the classical performance realm. Marian sang for audiences in London, Oslo, and Berlin, soaking up the new languages and cultures. In Copenhagen and Helsinki, she enthralled audiences, and thereafter was a huge star in these cities. At many of these concerts, Marian was accompanied by some of the foremost classical music conductors and composers of the era, including Kosti Vehanen and Jean Sibelius, Finland's greatest composer.

During the early thirties Marian toured Europe, eventually becoming fluent in several operatic languages, including Italian, German, and French. While on an extended trip to Paris, she made such a favorable impression on the legendary impresario Sol Hurok that he agreed to represent her.

Thereafter, Marian's career followed an upward trajectory. In New York she competed in a prestigious classical music competition for amateur performers at Lewissohn Stadium and came away with first prize. Between 1935 and 1939 she gave some of the most technically brilliant and emotionally powerful concerts of the era, in halls from Boston to San Francisco to Chicago. Along the way she reluctantly played venues where blacks were not allowed. Marian always made it a point to protest the segregated conditions; eventually, she refused to perform in segregated halls altogether and stunned the artistic community by turning down many prestigious engagements because of her strong belief in racial equality.

Then, in 1939, her ambitious manager decided that Marian should play one of the most revered concert venues in the world—Constitution Hall in Washington, D.C. The grand, stately hall was administered by the Daughters of the American Revolution, a socially prominent group of blue-blooded society matrons with familial ties dating back to the founding of the United States. Marian was unaware that the DAR was a segregated organization and that it had a history of refusing to allow blacks and other minorities access to Constitution Hall. In February 1939 Hurok learned that the group had turned down Marian's booking at Constitution Hall. The press caught wind of the situation and began writing stories about the great American operatic singer who had been turned away from one of the nation's great performance halls.

Marian remained silent about the brouhaha. She was giving a concert at the San Francisco Opera House when she learned some startling news: Eleanor Roosevelt, wife of the beloved president Franklin Delano

Roosevelt, had publicly lambasted the DAR for its refusal to let Marian sing in Constitution Hall.

"Mrs. Roosevelt Takes Stand" blared a newspaper headline Marian read while standing outside the beaux-arts opera house in San Francisco. As she recalled, "I was in San Francisco, when I passed a newsstand and my eye caught that headline. . . . I honestly could not conceive that things had gone so far." But indeed they had. The First Lady had sent a letter of resignation to the DAR: "I am in complete disagreement with the attitude taken in refusing Constitution Hall to a great artist," Mrs. Roosevelt wrote in her stinging rebuke. "You have set an example which seems to me unfortunate, and I feel obliged to send in to you my resignation. You had an opportunity to lead in an enlightened way, and it seems to me that your organization has failed." The eloquent letter set off a flurry of public debate about racism in America and the archaic tradition of segregation.

In the most unlikely way, Marian had become the center of a storm of political and social turmoil. The modest young singer was somewhat bewildered by all the sudden attention. Yet the unfortunate situation became a creative triumph for Marian—and for the generations of black women classical singers who followed her. For Eleanor Roosevelt was determined to make amends and to show the world that America was indeed a democratic nation, for blacks and whites, men and women. She personally invited Marian to sing at the annual Easter morning concert on the steps of the Lincoln Memorial.

On the cool morning of April 9, 1939, Marian stepped before a crowd of several thousand well-wishers and sang like an angel. "All I knew then was the overwhelming impact of that vast multitude," Marian recalled later. "I had a feeling that a great wave of goodwill poured out from those people" in the audience. In thanking the wildly applauding crowd, Marian gave little hint of bitterness at the embarrassing Constitution Hall imbroglio. "I am overwhelmed," Marian said, after she'd finished a stunning program that included domestic standards like "America," classical selections like "Ave Maria," and three spirituals. "I just can't talk. I can't tell you what you've done for me today. I thank you from the bottom of my heart, again and again."

It was a breathtaking performance, made even more so by Marian's cool professionalism and the energetic support of powerful politicians in attendance, including the secretary of the treasury, Supreme Court justice Hugo Black, and New York State representative Caroline O'Day. With admirable aplomb and a remarkably calm demeanor, Marian had succeeded in knocking down one of the least visible but firmly entrenched racial barriers in America.

Immediately after her knockout Easter performance at the Lincoln Memorial, Marian began a whirlwind of command performances, including a performance at the White House before the king and queen of England. Years later, when she finally did step onto the stage at Constitution Hall, Marian radiated confidence and sang a program of songs that seemed to come from a deep wellspring of faith and justice. By the early fifties, she was one of the preeminent woman operatic singers in the world, a diva of the first order who commanded enormous crowds and dazzled critics in hundreds of sold-out performances around the globe.

In 1955, after a long, fruitful career in classical music performance, Marian was invited to perform with the Metropolitan Opera. She had been world famous for almost twenty years, had married a prominent architect, Orpheus "King" Fisher, and started a family of her own. But for the shy young girl who had grown up singing in order to help her mother keep the family together, Marian was overwhelmed at the honor of being the first black woman to sing lead at the Met. For years afterward, she was to dismiss her January 7, 1955, debut at the Metropolitan as having been somewhat subpar: For the first time in her career, the excitement and emotion of the occasion had hindered her performance, Marian believed. "I know I tried too hard," she wrote in her autobiography. "I know I overdid." All the same, the audience was favorable and applauded loudly through several curtain calls. During the legendary 1955 season, Marian sang the role of Ulrica, the tragic heroine in Verdi's *Ballo in Maschera,* at numerous sold-out performances.

For reviewers and opera lovers alike, her debut at the Met was the beginning of a well-deserved period of public celebration of her talents and astounding dignity. Over the next decade, she settled into a life as the grande dame of America's classical music world. When she retired, President Dwight D. Eisenhower asked Marian to accept a post with the American mission to the United Nations, where she served as a cultural ambassador for many years. For the rest of her life Marian Anderson favored select audiences with performances only occasionally, preferring to lead a low-key life as wife and family member.

When she died in her sleep in 1993, the nation mourned the passing of a legend. For other black woman classical singers, including LEON-TYNE PRICE, Jessye Norman, and Kathleen Battle, Marian had paved a way for them to succeed in the demanding, rewarding world of opera. Strengthened by her religious faith, emboldened by her mother's loving support and her determined belief in herself, Marian had shown the world that African-American women indeed deserve a place of honor at the nation's cultural table.

"The chance to be a member of the Metropolitan has been a highlight of my life," Marian wrote in her candid autobiography. "I take greater pride in knowing that it has encouraged other singers of my group to realize that the doors everywhere may open increasingly to those who have prepared themselves well."

13

Ella Baker

1903–1986

Mobilizing the Young

DURING A LONG LIFE of activism and writing, Ella Baker left a valuable legacy for all Americans. Born in Norfolk, Virginia, the granddaughter of slaves, Ella grew up in a loving household where education was revered. Her father, Blake, was a waiter, and her mother was a staunch supporter of the church. In the twenties Ella became the first member in her family to attend college, and she impressed her teachers at Shaw University with her sharp intelligence and dedicated compassion.

After graduating from Shaw in 1927, Ella moved to New York City, where she became a noted journalist. Writing for black-owned newspapers, Ella covered the myriad experiences of black Americans, and her work captured the attention of politicians and community leaders alike. Eventually, Ella became involved in a political reform movement that resulted in President Franklin Delano Roosevelt's New Deal. Thanks in part to Ella's insights, Roosevelt came to realize that jobs and education were the right of all Americans—including overlooked blacks. By the end of the thirties Ella was heavily involved in organizing with the National Association for the Advancement of Colored People. Led by the legendary intellectual, W. E. B. Du Bois, the NAACP was in the forefront of fighting to end discrimination and racial bigotry in America.

During the forties Ella became a field organizer for the NAACP. On behalf of the organization she traveled the backroads of the South, investigating the living conditions of thousands of rural black citizens. What she found was a dire situation in which African Americans worked as exploited laborers and were refused basic rights of American citizens, including voting rights and freedom of speech. Ella worked to encourage black students to become involved in the fight for civil rights. She helped found the Southern Christian Leadership Conference (SCLC) and became devoted to helping young blacks develop leadership skills. As Ella saw it, the future of blacks in America lay in the hands of the young generation, and she became a strong advocate for the education and training of black activists.

During a historic gathering in Raleigh, North Carolina, in 1960, Ella was at the center of a controversy involving the leadership of the civil rights movement. As she saw it, the young, college-educated blacks who had joined the movement deserved to play a prominent role in the fight. More than three hundred students attended the conference, along with Dr. Martin Luther King Jr. An ideological debate erupted over the leadership style of the SCLC. Ella found herself torn between the traditional, church-based power structure of the black freedom movement and the more revolutionary approach favored by the young activists. In an article in a black Southern newspaper following the conference, Ella described some of the points of the roiling debate within the movement: "The Student Leadership Conference had made it crystal clear that current sit-ins and other demonstrations are concerned with something much bigger than a hamburger or even a giant-sized Coke." Ella reminded her readers that "it is important to keep the movement democratic and to avoid struggles for personal leadership."

Eventually, however, Ella reached an impasse with the leadership of

SCLC and decided to join forces with the student-led organization, the Student Nonviolent Coordinating Committee (SNCC). At age fifty-seven, Ella found herself in the vanguard of political activism among young blacks, and her experience and insights were appreciated by them. Said John Lewis, a key SNCC organizer, "She was much older in terms of age, but I think in terms of ideas and philosophy and commitment, she was one of the youngest persons in the movement."

Indeed, Ella's sense of compatibility with young activists grew from her earliest visions. As a schoolgirl growing up in Virginia, Ella had dreamed of someday becoming a missionary. She was drawn to the energy and idealism of the young black activists, and worked consistently to help them form their own definitions of leadership. For years Ella had been concerned that many blacks who were reaching the middle class had become complacent and willing to forget the masses of African Americans who still struggled to make a living. In an article during the fifties, she discussed her concerns about the growing economic divide among black Americans: "The gal who has been able to buy her minks and whose husband is a professional, they live well. You can't insult her, you never go and tell her she's so-and-so for taking, for not identifying. You try to point out where her interest lies in identifying with that other one across the tracks who does not have minks." Ella also worried that the NAACP was becoming too paternalistic and losing sight of its commitment to uplifting the millions of black Americans who struggled daily for basic dignity.

Throughout, Ella remained dedicated to her beliefs and, over the next three decades, even expanded her vision. She traveled to Africa and protested against apartheid and the lasting effects of colonialism. Until her death in 1986 she espoused the belief that all humans must come to terms with their humanity. For her valuable insights and sure guidance, Ella received many important awards during the last years of her life, including commendations from the NAACP, the Urban League, the Southern Christian Leadership Conference, and the Student Nonviolent Coordinating Committee.

She had, among all her speeches and writings, a favorite saying, one that still rings true today: "Strong people don't need strong leaders."

In the annals of modern political and social activism, Ella Baker stands as a formidable example of all the compassion, dedication, and intellectual integrity that black women have contributed to this nation.

14

Josephine Baker

1906–1975

From Jazz Baby to International Style Icon

Few American women of this century have captured the world's attention like Josephine Baker. In an eventful life spanning three major wars, a revolution in style and entertainment, and the onset of the feminist movement, Josephine touched the hearts and souls of millions. A dancer beyond compare, a comedienne, singer, and actress of the first rank, Josephine ultimately moved from the glittering surroundings of a versatile entertainer to the grounded, practical environment of a dedicated humanitarian and social activist. The trajectory of her life provides a stunning example of all that African-American women have contributed to this nation, including art, beauty, and compassion. And more than twenty years after her death in Paris, Josephine's zesty energy and infectious personality remain etched in the pages of modern cultural history.

"Tall, coffee skin, ebony eyes, legs of paradise, a smile to end all smiles," artist Pablo Picasso remarked of Josephine. Indeed, hers was a beauty for the ages, a uniquely accessible combination of openness and mystery. With a limber, well-trained body, Josephine initially stormed the cabaret world in Europe in a series of humorous, primitive dances and routines. By the arrival of the Jazz Age, she would come to symbolize the intersection of brash American style and cool Parisian elegance. In one inspired public-relations stunt, Josephine thrilled European cafe society by calmly walking down the Champs-Elysées in the sleekest of flapper couture, sheathed in a glamorous fur coat, while parading a full-grown leopard on a leash. Her dancing style was one part acrobat, one part vaudeville hoofer, and Josephine enthralled audiences by displaying her beautiful body in skimpy costumes or in the altogether. Some critics argued that her primitive dance routines—often performed with large, dark-skinned men dressed as "African savages"— demeaned black Americans. But Josephine, who hailed from a tough neighborhood in St. Louis, viewed things differently. If black Americans could make light of the stereotyped images that whites held of blacks, Josephine reasoned, then perhaps blacks might thereafter begin defining their own identity and destiny.

Josephine learned early to work hard and speak up for herself. A tireless student of human nature, she resolved early in her career to avoid the trap of obsessing about racial and ethnic differences. And, with contradictory candor, Josephine was also an outspoken critic of racism and gender discrimination long before such public stances became common. "I'm not intimidated by anyone," Josephine said in her first autobiography, *Les Mémoires de Josephine Baker,* published in Paris in 1927. "Everyone is made with two arms, two legs, a stomach, and a head. Just think about that."

By her death in 1975 Josephine had received dozens of national and international awards, including a coveted French medal of honor for espionage work during World War II; she had adopted more than twenty orphans from all over the world and established a nonprofit children's aid foundation inspired by her love of her "Rainbow Tribe." While the American public remembered only the racy dancer, her French fans saw a treasure deserving of a state funeral. But within a decade Americans had rekindled their love for Josephine: Several books and movies of her life hit the market, including an Emmy Award–winning Home Box Office motion picture starring Lynn Whitefield as Josephine.

What is perhaps most striking about Josephine is that she moved determinedly from a gawky young girl struggling for her livelihood and dignity to a supremely confident international star. And few who knew of her difficult beginnings might ever have imagined the path her life would take.

Born on June 3, 1906, in St. Louis, Josephine Baker was the hyperactive and inquisitive daughter of Carrie McDonald and Eddie Carson. Her maternal grandparents were Native American and black, and both had been slaves in South Carolina. By the early nineteen hundreds, Josephine's mother had joined the exodus of Southern blacks to the bustling, industrial Northern cities in what would eventually come to be known as the "Great Migration." Her family lived in a predominantly black ghetto of East St. Louis; Carrie, in her early twenties when Josephine was born, and Eddie Carson were not married. The sprightly young parents were proficient dancers and musicians and often performed in local musical revues in the dancehalls and saloons of black St. Louis. By the time Josephine was a year old, Eddie had left the family for good. Young Josephine had inherited her parents' physical grace and her father's good looks. Unfortunately "Josephine's resemblance to her father was just a distressing reminder to Carrie of the man who left her," according to Josephine's biographer, Phyllis Rose, in *Jazz Cleopatra*. Carrie came to resent her. "In one twist of fate, Josephine lost both her father and her mother's love," Rose wrote.

Carrie soon found a more suitable mate, a foundry worker, Arthur Martin. He and Carrie had three more children and decided to send Josephine to live with her grandmother. The temporary relocation to Grandmother McDonald's house in East St. Louis left a deep scar on Josephine. She couldn't help feeling like her mother didn't want her.

Several months after the birth of her brother Richard, Josephine returned to her mother's home. There she was dismayed to find that her stepfather had been laid off from his steel-making job. The family struggled to make ends meet. They lived in shabby tenements, and Carrie worked virtually around the clock as a laundress, leaving Josephine and the three younger children in the care of Arthur Martin. The entire family slept in one big bed, with the children's heads resting uncomfortably near the feet of the two adults.

Carrie insisted that her children help provide for the family as soon as they were able, and she sent Josephine to work at the age of eight. Josephine got her first exposure to the cold reality of class and racial divisions in America in the home of a wealthy St. Louis white woman. She was required to live in the woman's home and do household chores like preparing food, scrubbing floors, and washing clothes from sunup to sundown. Occasionally, if she woke up late, she was slapped by the white homeowner. Her "room" was in the basement with the family dog. After Josephine received a particularly brutal punishment—her hands were thrust into scalding water because she had used too much soap in the wash—her mother took her away from that home and hired her out to another white family.

Josephine's living and working conditions were much kinder with the new family, and she flourished there. Mrs. Mason, the homemaker who had hired her, was fond of Josephine and gave her clothing and food. She was eventually returned to her mother's care, and once again Josephine felt the sting of rejection. Her mother made her find work wherever she could.

In 1917 disgruntled white laborers in St. Louis began protesting against blacks who were "taking their jobs" in local factories, and an especially bloody civil disturbance ensued. For several days and nights mobs of white men roamed through the black neighborhood in East

St. Louis, burning homes and assaulting African-American families. By the time peace settled in, thirty-nine blacks had been killed, and several hundred had lost their homes to burning and looting. Josephine's mother, during the height of the riot, had spirited her family across the Mississippi River into St. Louis, lugging the few worldly possessions they could carry. It was a harrowing experience.

Josephine developed a means of coping with such dramatic situations in her young life. Like many blacks before her, she learned to mask her unhappiness and insecurity behind a superficial jollity and humor—her famous cross-eyed mugging emerged out of a desperate desire to hide the hurt and pain inside her. It was a skill that would make her one of the most popular comedic personalities of the early twentieth century.

Josephine had a swift introduction to adulthood. Although barely in her teens, she had already demonstrated an uncanny knack for dancing and entertaining. At backyard barbecues and other social events, she had shocked and delighted family members and friends with her mastery of the popular dances of the day. Seemingly without effort, Josephine was able to make her arms and legs perform any dance step, and she began to think she might truly have a special talent. After a fight with her mother, she struck out on her own, finding a job as a waitress in St. Louis at a well-known black social spot called the Chauffer's Club, and her father, Eddie Carson, played in a band at the club right next door. The work was hard, but over time Josephine came to believe that her life might take a different course than that of her mother, who worked unendingly washing other people's clothing and bedlinens.

Popular and outgoing, Josephine soon fell in love with a handsome young man named William Wells. It would lead to the first of five marriages for Josephine, whose unpredictable temperament and free spirit often proved too intimidating for some men. At first, she tried to settle into the life of a homemaker. Josephine quit her job and set about making the room they shared in Grandmother McDonald's house their own. Her life as a housewife was short-lived, however, because William Wells soon left his young wife, saying she expected too much from him.

Again rejected, Josephine nevertheless pressed on. She returned to waiting tables and began paying closer attention to the work of other local musicians and entertainers. By the age of fifteen, Josephine had decided to explore the life of a performer. She joined a well-known St. Louis troupe called the Jones Family Band and was learning the vaudeville ropes. In the early nineteen twenties, a strong network of theaters provided singing, dancing, and lighthearted revues featuring international stars and local buskers alike. In New York, where Manhattan's Broadway offered works by serious playwrights like Eugene O'Neill, Henrik Ibsen, and Thornton Wilder, a great distinction was drawn between these "legitimate" stage productions and bawdier, more freewheeling productions like the Ziegfield Follies and Billy Rose's lavish cavalcades of beautiful women. Further down the theatrical hierarchy were the vaudeville revues, minstrel shows (where performers black and white donned burnt-cork masks to appear as exaggerated caricatures of "Negroes"), and burlesque shows, which were often ribald and not fit for "respectable" women or children.

Black performers were refused the opportunity to play in segregated, whites-only theaters in most parts of the country. In St. Louis, as in most large American cities, a separate, parallel world of vaudeville theaters and performance arenas provided stages for the masses of blacks seeking nightlife and entertainment. Into this world Josephine appeared while still in her early teens.

The Jones Family Band was a modest troupe of hardworking locals who agreed to let Josephine join them after meeting her outside a theater. Spunky, smart, and given to amazing feats of physical agility, Josephine impressed the Jones group, and they made a splash when they premiered at the Booker T. Washington Theater in the heart of the St. Louis black community. Although Josephine danced only a few numbers in their set, she showed obvious signs of being made for the stage. And around the time that Josephine joined the Joneses, the troupe was invited to join a larger, more established traveling band of entertainers, the Dixie Steppers.

When the Dixie Steppers left St. Louis to continue along the black vaudeville circuit, Josephine and the Jones Family Band went with them. Their tour was a seat-of-the-pants affair, and young Josephine was enthusiastic and grateful to be welcomed into a clan that seemed to appreciate her special energy. From the Deep South through the Midwest and Northeast, Josephine saw the world from a new perspective, and she liked what she saw. Onstage, the skinny, loose-limbed girl seemed to blossom.

In Philadelphia, Josephine again fell in love, this time with a young man named William Baker. Although still in her teens, she was sure that this time her marriage would work. Her new husband came from a stable black Philadelphia family, and he worked as a Pullman porter. Josephine stopped working with the Dixie Steppers full-time and moved into her mother-in-law's well-appointed home, enraptured by fantasies of finally living the life of a housewife. Her mother-in-law soon proved to be a match for Josephine's ebullient nature, and things grew tense. Within months, Josephine rejoined the Dixie Steppers, leaving Willie Baker but retaining his name.

By 1921 Josephine had worked her way up from occasional dancer to a member of the Dixie Steppers chorus line. She had created a niche for herself within the troupe, that of the "comic relief" among the bevy of beautiful chorines. When a producer of another traveling black production, *Shuffle Along,* caught Josephine on stage in Philadelphia, he invited her to audition for the show. It was a momentous opportunity, and Josephine nervously agreed to try out. The show, cowritten by popular black entertainers Noble Sissle and Eubie Blake, was rumored to be headed for Broadway. Josephine turned up for the audition and floored the producers with her hilarious and riveting dancing. But at the age of fifteen she was too young to travel with the troupe, and Sissle and Blake declined to give her a part.

Disappointed but undaunted, Josephine resolved to keep trying; when *Shuffle Along* moved on to New York, she followed the company. One night, she lingered around the theater after the show and talked her way into a job as a wardrobe dresser for the actresses and dancers in the show. In a classic backstage development, she became an understudy to one of the dancers, and when that woman became ill, Josephine went on in her place and astounded the director with her funny, polished performance. Within weeks, she had become a vital part of the show's success. "She began to get a reputation of her own, and soon became a box office draw," writes Rose. "People buying tickets asked about the little chorus girl at the end of the line who crossed her eyes." After a fourteen-week run in New York, the producers put the show back on the road, and Josephine was a bona fide member of the company. For the next two years, she toured America with the show, refining her dancing as well as her own image.

Now Josephine's climb to the heights of the world's entertainment community was swift and packed with adventure. She had joined a dynamic group of black composers, musicians, actors, and artists who collectively presaged the Harlem Renaissance. As a protégé of Eubie Blake and Noble Sissle, Josephine rubbed shoulders with established performers like Ethel Waters and jazzman James Reese Europe. By the time a wealthy Chicago socialite decided to mount an all-black revue for a Paris tour, Josephine was a young star in the shimmering universe of black nightclubs and theaters, including the Cotton Club and the Apollo Theater.

On her first trip to Paris in 1924 Josephine instantly fell in love. Only, this time, her new interest was in the cultural enticements of "gay Paree." At last, Josephine felt free and radically creative. In the cafes and salons across the city, a refreshing kind of self-expression ruled the day. For Josephine, Paris was a wide-open playground, a gorgeous city of fanciful sights and sounds and smells. For the French, the nineteen-year-old was an exotic. With her shiny black spit curls, wildly inventive dancing, and impeccable sense of fashion, she created a sensation when she appeared bare-breasted in the all-black *Revue Négre*. Over the next decade, Josephine would shock and engage the entertainment world with her free-spirited celebration of the human body and her outspoken opinions on political issues. She would return to America periodically but considered Paris her home. In dozens of stage productions in Paris and New York (where she danced in the famous *Ziegfield Follies* in 1935), Josephine showed the world that freedom of artistic expression applies to blacks and women performers as much as to any other per-former. Through the early forties, Josephine continued performing in cabarets, nightclubs, and theaters; she also appeared in two motion pic-tures, and was forced to defend herself repeatedly against claims that her work demeaned blacks in America.

Meanwhile, the French government, wishing to capitalize on Josephine's popularity and the fact that she spoke several languages flu-ently, secretly enlisted her to pick up bits of intelligence from the German military men she met at social gatherings and after perfor-mances. Additionally, Josephine threw herself into charity work, donat-ing her time and energy to refugee shelters, helping to feed and clothe those made homeless by the war. During World War II, she joined the Women's Auxiliary of the French Air Force and looked smashing in the crisp, tailored uniform of the regiment. It was a challenging, exhilarating time, and Josephine's work would earn her one of the highest honors the French government can confer: the Legion of Honor.

By the fifties, her fortunes waned, and Josephine was still emotionally drained from the experience of the war years. She had become pregnant by a dashing French officer, but the baby was stillborn. While undergoing treatment, she contracted a serious virus and almost died. Doctors worked feverishly to save Josephine, and she underwent numerous operations. She was devastated to learn that the physicians had had to perform a hysterectomy on her to save her life, and Josephine pined for children she could never have. She had married and divorced twice since her early years as a struggling performer, and Josephine soon decided that she could indeed raise a family of her own. She began adopting orphaned children in France and in places as far apart as Scandinavia and the United States, eventually acquiring a ménage of more than twenty children. She worked constantly in cabarets and concerts to support her large family.

When Josephine brought her triumphant stage act to the United States in 1951, she made headlines by breaking the "color bar" in many nightclubs where black performers played before white-only audiences; in Las Vegas, the black members of her troupe stayed in the hotels where they performed. Accompanied by some members of the NAACP, Josephine traveled around the United States and purposefully drew attention to unfair discrimination laws in dozens of large cities where she appeared. She held press conferences and spoke out vehemently against racist violence that was still taking place in the Deep South and against the barring of blacks from jobs in public transportation in Los Angeles and Oakland, California and other cities. Unrelentingly honest, Josephine used her celebrity to appeal to the nation's conscience. "Her appearances have been marked by perhaps the most outspoken opposition to racial discrimination and segregation ever shown by a Negro artist, except Paul Robeson," the *Philadelphia Inquirer* observed.

Throughout, Josephine delighted audiences in some of the best nightspots in America, including the Stork Club in New York and the Trocadero in Los Angeles. She hobnobbed with notables like gossip king Walter Winchell and author Ernest Hemingway. When Winchell turned on her, accusing her of being a Communist sympathizer because of her firm antiracism, she sued his newspaper chain for $400,000.

Over the next two decades, she continued traveling the world, but her primary residence was a lovely estate in the French countryside, Les Milandes. Although Josephine had married Jo Bouillon, he, too, eventually grew weary of her pace and moved out. Also, Josephine's ever-expanding family of "rainbow" children was driving the couple's expenses higher and higher. Nevertheless, she managed to keep her family together, performing her stage show around the world even after she lost her beloved country estate.

By the mid-sixties, Josephine was revered worldwide. She had been invited to the March in Washington in 1963, and her work during the fifties on behalf of equal rights was duly noted by civil rights activists. Josephine also became fast friends with Princess Grace of Monaco, and joined her to form an important part of the European charity and fundraising community. In 1973 Josephine began suffering from heart problems and could travel less. All the same, she was a cheerful, devoted mother and lived to see her large family happy and safe. After 1963, she never returned to the United States, though she had patched up her difficult relationship with her mother during the forties.

When Josephine died peacefully in France, in 1975, the government buried her with a somber military funeral and full honors. For the thousands of fans who packed the stately Church of the Madeleine for her funeral, words could hardly do justice to the woman who had brought so much vigor and joy to their lives. And around the world, dancers and other artists mourned the passing of a unique spirit, a black woman who had survived an urban ghetto and transformed herself into one of the most exciting performers of this century. In her own inimitable style, with her carefree dancing and dedicated adherence to deep humanitarian beliefs, Josephine showed unequivocally the valuable role that black American women have played in shaping this country.

15

Dorothy West

1907–1998

A Renaissance Woman

DURING A LONG CAREER of writing and social activism, Dorothy West was a prominent member of a legendary artistic community in Harlem. During the twenties and thirties, she moved in heady company. She was a participant in the revolutionary arts movement that broke new ground in the years before World War II, and earlier she was among a loose association of artists, writers, and poets known collectively as the Harlem Renaissance. In 1926 her first published story, "The Typewriter," won second place in a writing contest sponsored by the Urban League's magazine *Opportunity*. In 1932 Dorothy traveled to the Soviet Union to take part in a documentary about racism in America. The controversial project earned Dorothy powerful enemies in the U.S. government at a time when Communism was widely viewed as a threat to democracy. Nonetheless, Dorothy was a confident writer who never shrank from taking an unpopular position.

Born in Boston on June 2, 1907, Dorothy was the precocious daughter of a prominent black family. Since before the Civil War, thousands of black Americans have contributed to the proud historic tradition in Boston. On Beacon Hill and in newer neighborhoods, like Dorchester and Roxbury, families like Dorothy's have long traditions of economic and political activism.

For Dorothy, it seemed only natural that she would spend at least a part of her youth traveling the world. During her years in Europe, she exposed herself to the sophisticated philosophies and political outlooks of a new generation of intellectuals. When she returned to America after a year in Russia, she cofounded the literary and social journal *Challenge,* and later, *New Challenge.* Along with a promising young writer named Richard Wright, Dorothy published intriguing essays and works by many important writers on a range of social and political issues. As the Great Depression wore on, Dorothy found work with the New York City Welfare Department as an investigator, and later was involved with Franklin D. Roosevelt's Works Progress Administration. A writer's project funded by Roosevelt's New Deal administration helped Dorothy and other important writers like ZORA NEALE HURSTON keep their heads above water during difficult times.

In 1940 Dorothy landed a job writing for the *New York Daily News,* making her one of the first African-American women ever to receive a byline in that large and profitable metropolitan daily. In 1947 Dorothy moved to the island of Martha's Vineyard, where a middle-class black community had deep roots in a small village called Oak Bluffs. She became a fixture on the tiny island and won hundreds of devoted readers with her singularly insightful writings in the local newspaper, the *Vineyard Gazette.* Her first novel, *The Living Is Easy,* was published in 1948 and earned significant critical praise. For the next thirty years, Dorothy lived in near obscurity, her role in the Harlem Renaissance all but forgotten by late-twentieth-century readers.

Eventually, Dorothy gained a fresh audience. Some forty years after the publication of her first novel, Dorothy published her second. At the urging of a Vineyard neighbor, Jacqueline Kennedy Onassis, she had taken up writing fiction again. Over the years the two had become friends. At that time, during the eighties, Onassis had become a respected editor at a large New York publishing house, Doubleday. Ever persistent, Onassis spent years persuading Dorothy to write fiction again. Dorothy dedicated the novel to her editor. "Though there was never such a mismatched pair in appearance, we were perfect partners," Dorothy wrote of her friendship with Onassis.

In *The Wedding,* Dorothy shed new light on the lives and loves of the middle-class black residents of an exclusive New England resort town. With a sharp imagination and a fine ear for dialogue, Dorothy created for her readers a vivid world of financial opulence and personal frustration. Her characters were finely drawn portraits of African Americans in an overlooked environment where crime, drugs, teen pregnancy, and violence were *not* the order of the day. All the same, her characters' deep-seated problems were thinly veiled and complicated. In clear detail and with a fine writerly flourish, Dorothy described one of her main characters, Addie Bannister: "Since the day of her birth in Boston, Addie had traveled no farther from home than an island off the Massachusetts coast, a short and uneventful train ride, an even shorter and calmer crossing. In winter, she rarely socialized, almost never stepping outside the old family house in Cambridge, where she swaddled herself in sweaters and bathrobes to rout the penetrating cold that battled the insufficient heat from the old-fashioned, dust-filled floor registers. Surrounded by antiques and antiquation, she hibernated until summer, never visiting her friends in their warmer houses; the hazards of getting about in winter were more than she could cope with, her purse not permitting a taxi or the proper clothes."

In her late eighties Dorothy continued living on the tiny island and writing for the local newspaper. She remained active and always drew the respectful attention of her Martha's Vineyard neighbors when she ventured out for social or business events. In 1994 she published a collection of essays, *The Richer, the Poorer: Stories, Sketches, and Reminiscences.*

In 1998 talk-show host and film producer OPRAH WINFREY mounted a television version of *The Wedding* starring Halle Berry and other prominent black actors and actresses. At long last, Dorothy's important position as the last living member of the Harlem Renaissance became known to audiences worldwide.

16

Katherine Dunham

1909–

Dancing Into History

SOME SIXTY YEARS after she first began studying dance, Katherine Dunham remains a shining light of artistic achievement among African-American women. Like Isadora Duncan and Martha Graham, Katherine Dunham has left an indelible mark on modern dance. Her accomplishments over a half century are even more inspiring considering that few black American women had access to the formal world of theatrical dance during the early twentieth century. As a vocal advocate for human rights around the globe, Katherine is an impressive role model for all artists concerned with social justice. "You dance because you have to," Katherine said during an interview many years ago. "Dance is an essential part of life that has always been with me."

Born June 22, 1909, in Chicago's South Side, Dunham was the cherished second child of her father, Albert Dunham Jr. Her mother died when Katherine was very young, and her father remarried. When her father moved the family to Joliet, Illinois, Katherine began expressing interest in the arts. In public school, she excelled at sports as well as theater and dance studies. In junior college, she determined that dance was something she had to explore. Later, after transferring to the University of Chicago, a large, first-tier college, Katherine became interested in ethnic studies, specifically the cultural roots of dance in Caribbean cultures. She began studying anthropology under Professor Robert Redfield.

Her academic work began to reflect her newfound love of Afro-Caribbean dance, and Katherine became a pioneer in the field of cultural anthropology as it pertains to dance. While still an undergraduate, Katherine cofounded a revolutionary dance group, Ballet Négre. Although she was young and virtually untested on the popular stages of the day, Katherine's academic work also earned her a prestigious fellowship, which she used to travel to the Caribbean. There, during the thirties, she studied first-hand the ancient rituals of dance. During this period, Katherine was also tapped to organize a historic African dance exhibit for the immense Chicago Century of Progress Exposition in 1933. It was a far cry from the Chicago World Exposition of nearly fifty years earlier, in which blacks were barred from participating. After receiving her undergraduate degree from the University of Chicago, Katherine embarked on a long and fruitful career of choreography, dance, and the excavation of hundreds of years of little-understood Afro-Caribbean dance traditions.

Over the next two decades, she experienced a flurry of creativity that coincided with a growing public acceptance of the "exotic" forms of dance practiced by blacks and other indigenous people around the world. With other members of the Ballet Négre (later renamed the Negro Dance Group), Katherine traveled the world, alternately gathering, recording, and performing works culled from tiny villages and primitive cultures.

Soon she founded the Katherine Dunham Dance Company. The next decade was a famously prolific period for Katherine, and included her Broadway debut in 1938 and her work with legendary ballet choreographer, George Ballanchine. Katherine debuted on the London stage in 1948 and danced in numerous Hollywood films, including *Stormy Weather, Cabin in the Sky,* and *Star-Spangled Rhythm,* during the forties. She choreographed the stage version of *Cabin in the Sky* as well as several other groundbreaking dance numbers for stage and screen.

Her experiences in Hollywood convinced her that black Americans deserved a choreographer familiar with the complexities of African-American heritage. Consequently, Katherine set out to explore ways of bringing those complexities to the stage in the form of dance. She became the first black woman to choreograph a major work for the New York Metropolitan Opera, *Aida,* in 1963.

After officially retiring from performing during the sixties, Katherine served as cultural advisor to the government of Senegal, Africa, and, in 1967, founded a revolutionary arts program at the Southern Illinois University. That program today remains one of the most popular arts education opportunities in the nation. As testament to her level of influence in the arts and humanitarian fields, Katherine has been awarded several important honors during her long life, including an Albert Schweitzer Award, a Kennedy Centers Honor, and a Guggenheim Fellowship.

Moreover, Katherine continued writing of her travels and anthropological work and chronicling her experiences with blacks in Jamaica, West Africa, and Haiti. In 1959 she published her autobiography, *A Touch of Innocence.* Residing in East St. Louis, Missouri, Katherine remains dedicated to cultural arts and to the hard work of improving the troubled living conditions in third world nations. In the early nineties, at the age of eighty-two, she stunned the political and activist communities by staging a long hunger strike to emphasize the plight of Haitians struggling under a totalitarian regime. In press conferences in Miami and Port-au-Prince, Katherine brought to the world's attention the poverty and oppression that characterized the lives of Haitians.

As Katherine saw it, the hardships experienced by the Haitian people were not far removed from those of black Americans. Her courageous act helped galvanize Americans to both the plight of Haitians and our nation's underclass. And, in the process, it reminded all Americans of the strength and dedication of the black women who have helped change this nation for the better.

17

Mahalia Jackson

c. 1911–1972

Heavenly Voice of the Civil Rights Era

MAHALIA JACKSON earned the nickname "the Queen of Gospel Song" during a rich life of singing and performing spirituals. As a child in the Deep South, Mahalia grew up in a strict household headed by her father, a Baptist minister. While Mahalia quickly learned to respect the soulful spirituals she heard in church, she also enjoyed the more secular music she heard at the homes of friends—the popular jazz and blues recordings of the twenties and thirties. With the blossoming of the civil rights movement in the late fifties, Mahalia became a vital part of the demonstrations and activism that brought about revolutionary social changes in America. As a valued friend to notable civil rights figures, including Dr. Martin Luther King Jr., Jesse Jackson, Andrew Young, and Medgar Evers, Mahalia lent her heavenly voice and strong sense of justice to the historic movement. Her particular blessing—a strong voice and deep religious faith—required her to contribute to the uplifting of millions of exploited black Americans. In a sad turn of fate, Mahalia first became known to many white Americans through her singing at the funerals of some of the leading civil rights figures of the fifties and sixties, including that of Medgar Evers.

From her base in Chicago, Mahalia could marshal an impressive array of black citizens, politicians, and activists in support of justice and dignity. After the bombing of a Birmingham church in which four little black girls died, there were several frightening showdowns between police and black Birmingham residents. Mahalia vowed to host a concert and rally in the Windy City. In *Parting the Waters: America in the King Years,* journalist Taylor Branch described Mahalia's importance to the civil rights movement: "From Chicago, Mahalia Jackson said people were so worked up over [what had happened in] Birmingham, that she could turn out the entire city to hear King. She vowed to do that in just one week."

Sure enough, within days of the horrific police actions in Birmingham, Mahalia had mounted one of the most poignant rallies of the movement. After a huge gathering at Chicago's Wrigley Field and a whirlwind motorcade ride to the shores of Lake Michigan, Dr. Martin Luther King Jr. arrived at a concert planned by Mahalia. According to Branch, she even put aside a longtime rivalry to show her support for the movement: "In his own speech King was hard-pressed to match the dueling headliners—Mahalia Jackson, queen of gospel, appearing for once with her archrival Dinah Washington, queen of the blues. The three of them held the overflow crowd until two o'clock in the morning, when young Aretha Franklin topped them all with her closing hymn."

Indeed, Mahalia's courageous contribution likely grew out of her own humble beginnings. Born in New Orleans on October 26, 1911, Mahalia grew up in the segregated South during the Jim Crow era. From the eighteen nineties through the nineteen fifties, a "separate but equal" rule required blacks to endure the humiliations of a segregated life. Whether in public parks or department stores or housing, African Americans were forced to accept subpar facilities. Black schoolchildren were expected to study from outdated second-hand textbooks and in buildings that were falling down from lack of upkeep.

The young Mahalia became an important part of her neighborhood church. A powerful singer, she thrilled parishioners and her family members with her renditions of gospel classics like "Precious Lord" and "Nobody Knows the Troubles I've Seen." Yet the stultifying environment of the Jim Crow South (and her father's watchful gaze) made young Mahalia yearn for freedom. At age sixteen, against her family's wishes, she went to Chicago, and eventually found work singing with gospel groups. After several years of struggle, Mahalia saved enough money to open her own business, a beauty parlor. An enterprising young businesswoman with a sparkling personality and strong sense of determination, Mahalia also continued to be an important part of her church. When her financial situation stabilized, she returned to her first true love: singing in church.

At this time, Chicago was widely viewed as a promising mecca to many blacks from the Deep South. In neighborhoods on the South Side and near-West Side, blacks by the thousands made their way each Sunday to churches. And Mahalia's uncanny singing style and strong show of emotion enraptured them. By the mid-thirties she was the pre-eminent gospel singer in Chicago.

Her first recording was released in 1934, and Mahalia became a star in the close-knit community of black religious singers. Ever influenced by her deeply religious upbringing, Mahalia grew famous with her emotional and poignant renditions of gospel standards such as "I Can Put My Trust in Jesus" and "He's Got the Whole World in His Hands." Known for years within the nation's black communities as a virtuoso singer of spirituals, Mahalia drew a sizable white fan-base after her first appearance at Carnegie Hall in New York, in 1950. Thereafter, she became a critically acclaimed international singer and appeared in concerts and festivals in Europe and all around the United States. In 1958 her position as the first lady of gospel song was sealed when she appeared at the tony Newport Jazz Festival in Rhode Island and helped the legendary bandleader Duke Ellington inaugurate his stunning suite "Black, Brown, and Beige."

Between her performances around the globe, Mahalia contributed her unique vocal gifts to the growing civil rights movement. Along with such singers and actors as LENA HORNE, Paul Newman, Marlon Brando, and Sammy Davis Jr., Mahalia entered the fight to end racial discrimination in America. In 1963 she participated in the now legendary March on Washington. Mahalia joined thousands of civil rights activists on the Mall in Washington, where Dr. Martin Luther King Jr., made his historic "I Have a Dream" speech. It was a joyous and triumphant moment for Mahalia, a daughter of the Deep South who had managed to escape the oppression and discrimination of the region in the bleak years before the civil rights movement.

For the years afterward, Mahalia sang for worthy causes. She died in 1972, leaving a void in the elusive place where entertainment meets social activism. Yet thanks to recordings of dozens of her concerts, Mahalia's voice and spirit remain a vital part of our cultural history.

"It's easy to be independent when you've got money," Mahalia said in an interview in the sixties. "But to be independent when you haven't got a thing—that's the Lord's test."

18

Dorothy Height

1912–

Leveling the Playing Field Through Education

THROUGH HER LECTURES and fund-raising for political and social groups, including the great civic organization she nurtured—the National Council of Negro Women—Dorothy Height was still a living example of consistency and commitment well into the nineteen nineties. In the time-honored tradition of passing along experience and knowledge to those who follow, Dorothy has been a valuable role model to hundreds of young black American women. It has been a long but worthwhile journey for the little girl who started her life in the cradle of the Confederacy.

On March 24, 1912, Dorothy Height was born in Richmond, Virginia. Her father and mother moved their thriving family to Rankin, Pennsylvania, when Dorothy was not yet five years old. They wanted their bright daughter to attend public schools that were integrated, and in the abolitionist stronghold of rural Dutch Country, they were able to send Dorothy to well-funded schools. Dorothy excelled at her studies and was graduated from high school with outstanding grades. She decided to apply to colleges outside of the agrarian solitude of small-town Pennsylvania.

Dorothy was accepted at Barnard College, a prestigious women's school in New York with a worldwide reputation for excellence in liberal studies. She was thrilled at the prospect, but it was not to be. A racially discriminatory admissions rule prevented her from attending Barnard. Despite her great grades and test scores, she was not admitted for the fall semester because of a cruel quota system: only two blacks could be granted admission in a semester. It was a prime reason why Dorothy would turn to fighting racial discrimination for years thereafter.

Dorothy was disappointed but undaunted. On the cusp of adulthood, she was determined to get a good education from one of the top-notch universities in the Northeast. She applied to and was accepted at New York University immediately. There she distinguished herself as a dedicated student. Over the next several years, she earned an undergraduate degree and a master's degree before heading out into the world of teaching.

By the late thirties Dorothy had become a familiar face in the civic clubs and educational coalitions in New York. She taught classes at the Brownsville Community Center in Brooklyn, and served on boards and committees for a diverse group of organizations. During a youth award ceremony at the YWCA in Washington, D.C., Dorothy had an opportunity to spend some time with an older black woman she greatly admired—MARY MCLEOD BETHUNE.

Like Bethune, Dorothy had decided to devote her life's work to bettering the educational opportunities and living conditions of masses of disenfranchised African Americans. She was named president of the National Council of Negro Women in 1957 and set about expanding the reach of that significant group. During the nineteen sixties she spearheaded voter registration drives in the Deep South and advocated increased funding for public education in black communities. Thanks to a sturdy, reliable network of more than two hundred local chapters of black women's clubs, Dorothy was able to marshal a formidable army of supporters from all across the United States.

Through her work with the Council for United Civil Rights Leadership and on a welfare committee of the U.S. Department of Health during the fifties and sixties, Dorothy played a vital role in lobbying for passage of new laws and regulations to erase the long years of inequitable treatment of black Americans. Indeed her many years at the forefront of education had given her a realistic view of what was needed to reform conditions for millions of black Americans.

"Racism has affected us so much that we are afraid of each other," Dorothy said in 1986. From her years of working with children, Dorothy had seen the myriad ways racial discrimination in jobs and education had wreaked havoc on black Americans, from low self-esteem to dependency on government agencies to an array of devastating pathologies. She advanced the idea of helping reacquaint black Americans with their proud heritage. Called the Black Family Reunion Celebration, Dorothy's simple but powerful plan was to encourage millions of black Americans to have family reunions more frequently. Through her grassroots connections in universities and in the National Council of Negro Women and the United Nations Department of Information, Dorothy led a renewed charge among blacks nationwide.

Within ten years, an estimated six million blacks had responded by holding family reunions of their own. From the sun-baked expanse of Fresno, California, to the rolling hills of Virginia, thousands of black families gather each year to honor their pasts and plan for productive futures.

Thanks to Dorothy and other black women who have devoted their lives to civic causes and improving educational opportunity, the entire nation came to benefit. Dorothy is a key reason for the growing public awareness of the importance of black women's contribution through United States history.

Indeed, Dorothy Height's long tenure on the frontlines of fighting for equal rights spans two distinct eras in modern American history—the grim, post-Reconstruction separate-but-equal period and the promising dawn of equality, the civil rights movement era. Hers is an impressive life of achievement and a vivid example of how black American women have helped improve this nation.

19

Rosa Parks

1913–

Seeking a Seat, Finding a Place in history

POPLUAR LORE HAS IT that Rosa Parks, an unassuming black seamstress, accidentally struck the spark that ignited the civil rights movement when she refused to give up her seat to a white man on a segregated bus in Montgomery, Alabama, in 1955. Americans need to know that the diminutive, bespectacled woman had demonstrated a tough spine and firm commitment to ending racial segregation long before that. In fact, for all her modesty, Rosa Parks was well suited to the role that catapulted her into history as the first black woman to successfully fight back against legalized segregation in the Deep South—and live to tell the story.

Before the famous incident on the bus, "I worked on numerous cases with the [National Association for the Advancement of Colored People] but we did not get the publicity," Parks said during an interview many years later. "There were cases of flogging, peonage, murder, and rape. We didn't seem to have too many successes. It was more a matter of trying to challenge the powers that be, and to let it be known that we did not wish to continue being second-class citizens," she said. Indeed, a strong desire to right three centuries of racial inequality had burned within Rosa Park's small community long before the nation turned its eyes on the subject in the mid-fifties. For Rosa, everything she had endured before that fateful day in 1955 had convinced her that she had to stand up for what she believed was right. "Back then, we didn't have any civil rights," Rosa recalled years later. "I didn't have any special fear. It was more of a relief to know that I wasn't alone."

Born on February 4, 1913, Rosa Louise McCauley spent her earliest years in Tuskegee, Alabama. Her parents, James and Leona McCauley, were respected citizens of their small town. James was a carpenter, while Leona taught elementary school in the rural, segregated village.

When Rosa was two years old, her mother—then separated from Rosa's father—moved onto her grandparents' farm in Pine Level, Alabama. Rosa first went to school in the same building where her mother taught, an arrangement that meant the young girl had to keep her mind on her studies. "My first teacher was Miss Sally Hill, and I liked her very much," Rosa said in a 1995 interview. "In fact, I liked school when I was very young, in spite of the fact that it was a one-room school for students of all ages, from the very young, to teens, as long as they went to school." Because black children were expected to help their families work in the fields during harvest seasons, the school year was usually short, about five months every year.

When Rosa was preparing to enter junior high school, her mother enrolled her in a private school that had been founded years earlier by liberal white women from the North. Called the Montgomery Industrial School for Girls, it offered a philosophy of pride and self-determination to its mostly poor students. For Rosa's mother, Leona, it was imperative that her daughter be able to "take advantage of the opportunities" provided by the liberal school, "no matter how few they were."

Life in the Deep South during the twenties and thirties was especially trying for blacks. Rosa lived much of her young life in fear. Rosa remembers cowering in her bedroom as the thudding hooves of horses carrying white-robed Ku Klux Klansmen sounded near her bedroom windows. Then the McCauley family would pray for fear that some poor black villager was being lynched. As she grew into adulthood, however, Rosa realized that pervasive fear was harmful to any hope of ever attaining true freedom.

Rosa attended Alabama State Teachers College and fell in love with a young man named Raymond Parks, a barber. After Rosa graduated, the young couple married and moved to Montgomery, Alabama, a bustling city that had become a popular location for upwardly mobile blacks like the Parks. While still mired in a racially segregated system that prevented them from speaking their minds completely or working in lucrative industries, many young African Americans managed to find a sense of community in Montgomery and other mid-sized Southern cities. Rosa and her husband joined the Montgomery branch of the NAACP and became active members. At the Montgomery Voters League and the NAACP Youth Council, Rosa and her husband became familiar faces, volunteering long hours to improve their community.

For the next twenty years, Rosa and Raymond worked tirelessly on campaigns to help better the living conditions of blacks. Much of their work was unheralded at the time, even though they conducted the work at great peril to themselves. During this same period, Rosa also worked as a seamstress and as a maid to help support her family. Such domestic work wasn't exactly challenging for a woman who had graduated from a respected college. Yet few employment choices existed for black women like Rosa in the Deep South.

Throughout these frustrating years, Rosa always remembered her grandparents—who had been slaves—when the going got tough. "Both of them were born before the emancipation, before slavery ended. They suffered a lot as children. They were in slavery, and of course, after slavery life was not much better, but I guess it was some better," Rosa said of her grandparents. Rosa's mother was proud of what her parents had endured, and she instructed Rosa and her brother, Sylvester, to carry themselves well. Rosa says her mother regularly reminded them that "we were human beings, and we should be treated as such."

And so, thanks to a family history that had instilled a healthy sense of confidence in her despite the dire surroundings, Rosa was prepared for what took place on a chilly afternoon in 1955. After a long day at work on December 1, Rosa headed home. As usual she was prepared to sit in the back of the bus, as all black Alabamans were required to do. Legalized segregation meant that many public spaces—including restaurants, washrooms, and department stores—maintained separate facilities for blacks and whites. Under an arcane set of rules established in the late nineteenth century after the "official" end of slavery, blacks lived under a cruel "color bar" that kept them from enjoying the amenities made available to white Americans. It was hardly a "free" lifestyle for residents in what was supposedly a model free and democratic society.

On that cold winter day, Rosa was bone tired. She waited for the bus to take her home, and when it arrived, she found it crowded with African-American passengers. Under the Jim Crow rules, white passengers were allocated seats in the front half of the bus, and the remaining seats were reserved for black passengers. Rosa tells what happened on that fateful evening: "I took a seat that was in back of where the white people were sitting . . . the last seat. A man was next to the window, and I took an aisle seat and there were two women across from me. On about the second or third stop, some white people boarded the bus and there was one [white] man standing.

"And when the driver noticed him standing, he told us to stand up and let him have our seats. He referred to them as 'front seats.' And when the other three [black] people, after some hesitancy, stood up, he wanted to know if I was going to stand up, and I was not. And he [the bus driver] told me he would have me arrested. I told him, 'You may do that,' and of course, he did. He didn't move the bus any further than where we were, and he went out of the bus. Other people got off. . . . didn't any white people get off, but several black people got off."

In a few minutes, two white policemen boarded the city bus. They went to Rosa and asked her if the driver had told her to stand. Rosa was polite but determined. "And then I asked him why did they push us around? And he said . . . 'I don't know, but the law is the law, and you are under arrest.' "

So Rosa finally left the bus and was arrested. The bus driver finished his route and came down to the police station to fill out a complaint. Rosa was found guilty and ordered to pay a ten-dollar fine and four dollars in court costs.

When news of her action hit the papers, a local NAACP official became outraged. He called for black Montgomery residents to boycott the city bus service. For the next 382 days, hardly any blacks used the public transportation system in Montgomery, severely hurting the profits of the bus company. Still, the white power-structure in Montgomery refused to budge, saying it had the right to treat blacks as second-class citizens. The long boycott was a difficult time for Rosa and other members of her community.

Like Rosa, many black Montgomerians did not own cars and depended on the buses to carry them from their tiny villages on the outskirts of the city into the white-owned businesses and homes where they performed menial but much-needed jobs. Only years later did those outside of Montgomery learn that many white women helped the blacks' cause during this strained period. In the finer homes, many of the top society matrons felt dismayed that their maids and cooks found it necessary to honor the boycott. They arranged clandestine car services for many of the black domestic workers. Against their husbands' wishes, these white society matrons drove their black workers to and from their jobs for days on end. And after more than a year of the boycott, Rosa's case reached the United States Supreme Court. Finally, the highest court in the land found the practice of legalized segregation unconstitutional. It marked the unofficial start of the civil rights movement. Rosa, a small-boned, quiet woman, came to be known as the "mother of the civil rights movement."

As far as she's concerned, Rosa did what she had to do. In the years that followed, similar public boycotts and demonstrations in other

Southern towns severely tested the nation. Rosa's treatment resulted in the formation of the Montgomery Improvement Association, a grass-roots organization devoted to ending legalized segregation in Alabama. The group drew the attention of civil rights activists in other parts of the Deep South, and when Dr. Martin Luther King Jr. called for marches and sit-ins in segregated towns, he often invoked the image of the small, strong Rosa Parks.

Her story galvanized the nation outside of the South. Rosa's one act of defiance had brought the attention of civil libertarians worldwide to the plight of blacks in the Deep South. Her quiet strength was useful because Rosa had not screamed or kicked or acted out in resistance: she had merely demanded the same human consideration that anyone who is tired after a long day of work would have demanded. At the time of her arrest, Rosa was forty-three years old and had never before been in trouble with the law.

"I don't remember feeling any anger," Rosa recalled later. "I did feel determined to take this as an opportunity to let it be known that I did not want to be treated in that manner, and that people had endured it for too long."

In 1957 Rosa and her husband moved to Detroit. For the next twenty-three years she worked for Democratic congressman John Conyers. She drew some public attention but mostly lived a life of quiet and hard work. Rosa retired from her civil service job at the age of seventy-five. By then her beloved husband had died, but she had kept up the public service her mother had instilled in her as a child in Alabama. She opened the Rosa and Raymond Park's Institute for Self-Development, a youth self-esteem and jobs program that is still going strong today. The *Detroit News* also sponsors the Rosa Parks Scholarship Fund for promising young journalists. In 1986 she was recognized for all her years of dedicated human rights work when she received the prestigious Ellis Island Medal of Honor.

In *Quiet Strength: The Faith, the Hope, and the Heart of a Woman Who Changed a Nation,* published in 1994, Rosa finally told her own story in her own words. Some reviewers noted that the book was much less dramatic than the version other writers had told for many years, but Rosa took it all in stride.

These days she lives part of the year in Los Angeles and part in Detroit. A bizarre incident in the early nineteen nineties once again drew attention to her. A desperate young man mugged Rosa as she walked home one night, knocking her down and causing her minor injuries. The story outraged Americans, but Rosa said she didn't hold a grudge against the young man. (Police learned who he was and arrested him a few days after the incident.)

Now entering her ninth decade, still strong and quietly determined, Rosa Parks is the embodiment of black women's achievement. Her single act of defiance has a vital place in our American development. With her trademark eyeglasses and carefully braided hair, Rosa Parks continues to inspire millions of Americans of all races and backgrounds. During a 1995 interview she said: "I think it's important to believe in yourself and when you feel like you have the right idea, to stay with it. Of course, it all depends upon the cooperation of the people around you. People were very cooperative in getting off those buses.

"And from that, of course, we went on to other things. . . . There were so many needs for us to continue to work for freedom, because I didn't think that we should have to be treated the way we were, just for the sake of white supremacy," Rosa said. "I want to always be concerned with being positive. . . . And I believe in peace, too, and not violence."

20

Billie Holiday

1915–1959

Beyond the Blues and Into History

FOR TWENTY YEARS Billie Holiday revolutionized the art of jazz singing. As an innovative and thoughtful interpreter of blues and jazz standards, she established a deeply personal performance style that won her millions of fans around the globe.

Billie drew critical and commercial success that continues some forty years after her death. Yet to praise her art without considering the environment that shaped her is to do Billie a grave injustice; as she often remarked, she was able to sing the blues because she had *lived* the blues. And during a remarkably productive period in the thirties and forties, Billie recorded several songs that stand as enduring classics, including "God Bless the Child," "Don't Explain," and "Good Morning, Heartache."

From Louis Armstrong to Artie Shaw to Duke Ellington and Nat "King" Cole, Billie represented the best of contemporary musical expression. "She influenced almost every singer that followed," trumpet player and bandleader Dizzy Gillespie said after Billie's death. To her fans she was "Lady Day," a vision of heartache and emotional honesty, an enigmatic woman with a gardenia behind her ear as she sang of love gone sour and dreams unrealized.

Abandoned by her family at an early age, Billie learned to depend on herself. During her troubled life, she sometimes made errors of judgment that brought her into personal and professional contact with men who did not always have her best interests at heart. In 1956, in the pages of *Lady Sings the Blues,* her ghostwritten autobiography, Billie added to her storied reputation by exaggerating some aspects of her life (her teen years spent running errands for a Baltimore brothel), while skimming over some others (her debilitating heroin addiction).

Nonetheless, her story of her life vividly depicted the many obstacles Billie overcame in her long climb to the top of the modern entertainment world. "You can't get too high for somebody to bring you down," she admitted in her autobiography, a phrase heavy with meaning within the context of her difficult life. But her legend endures, in part, because of the realness of Billie's eventful life: her well-documented ups and downs, her artistic highs and devastating personal lows, continue resonating with people who recognize in Billie the tortured soul of a true artist. Indeed, Billie's life was a mixture of hard luck and uncanny timing, of epic sadness and sweet success. And in the history of twentieth-century musical performance, Billie Holiday produced a body of work which contributes to this nation's status as the leading provider of jazz and blues recordings. "She was unquestionably the most important influence on American popular singing in the past twenty years," Frank Sinatra observed in 1959.

To be sure, few singers since have so effectively touched audiences the way Billie did. For a sad young girl from a broken home, Billie's amazing life is a testament to the resilience of the human spirit—and to the strength and determination of black American women.

Born on April 7, 1915, Billie was actually Eleanora Fagan. Her childhood was filled with uncertainty. Billie's father, a guitarist named Clarence Holiday, abandoned his wife and child shortly after Billie's birth, and her mother never recovered. Growing up at the edge of Baltimore's established black middle-class community, Billie felt early on that she had few advocates. He mother had a nervous breakdown and essentially left Billie alone to raise herself. Desperate for work, Billie turned to a local businesswoman for help. Impressed with the adolescent girl's pluck and sincerity, the madam of a local bawdy house took Billie under her wing. For most of her teen years Billie cleaned rooms, ran errands, and served as a youthful foil for the "working women" there. Years later, Billie noted that it was far from a conventional education but was a valuable experience nonetheless.

Indeed, during those years, Billie developed a love for jazz and blues and spent hours mesmerized by the sounds of Louis Armstrong and BESSIE SMITH that floated from the Victrola at the brothel. In this environment, Billie was forced to grow up fast, even as she struggled against the low-esteem and self-doubt that gripped her. Encouraged by some of the women, Billie eventually shook off her shyness and began singing in local nightclubs.

It was the onset of the Jazz Age, and Billie earned a small cadre of loyal fans in the black nightclubs of segregated Baltimore. With her thin body draped dramatically in borrowed, sophisticated clothing, young Billie discovered she had a good ear for music. She also began thinking seriously about pursuing a career on stage. And when a local musician who had watched her progress suggested she move to New York, Billie felt there was little in Baltimore to keep her from going.

Her father had played guitar with the noted musician Fletcher Henderson, and Billie mustered enough confidence to approach a nightclub owner in Brooklyn. Nervous and intimidated, her early singing style was raw, her voice thin and reedy as she struggled to impress the crowds. Still, Billie's youthful enthusiasm and steady determination endeared her to up-and-coming artists like Lester Young and John Hammonds. "A person without friends might as well be dead," Billie said in 1945, and her loyalty to those who helped her early on became legendary.

By 1931 Billie was a featured singer in a popular Harlem nightclub called Pod's and Jerry's. It was a swell time for singers, performers, and artists of every kind, an era when Harlem positively shimmered with talent. For Billie, the sight of established stars like Duke Ellington, Lionel Hampton, and Louis Armstrong gave her confidence in her growing singing skills. And, in 1933, she made her first recordings. The famous bandleader Benny Goodman asked her to sit in for two "demonstration" recordings, and Billie got her first glimpse of a topflight musical organization. (Ultimately, these two recordings were not successful). But Billie was fast learning her own singing style. In 1935 bandleader and producer Teddy Wilson invited Billie to sing with a new band he was forming, and they began a long association. Slowly but surely, Billie was developing a surefire singing style that was like no other. And philosophically, she was determined to establish her own creative agenda. "You can't copy anybody and end up with anything good," Billie wrote in her autobiography. "If you copy, it means you're working without any real feeling. No two people on earth are alike, and it's got to be that way in music, or it isn't music," she insisted.

Between 1935 and the early nineteen forties, Billie lived the exciting life of a "girl singer," those women performers like Margaret Whiting, Jo Stafford, and Doris Day who "fronted" the big bands. From Benny Goodman to Glenn Miller to Duke Ellington, the big band sound was sweeping the nation. Billie had found a winning combination—a way of integrating a bluesy singing style with the hot sounds of swing. In 1937 she began recording with Lester Young and Buck Clayton, two promising jazz musicians who shared her respect for singers like Bessie Smith and ALBERTA HUNTER. She also joined forces with composers and arrangers such as Count Basie and Artie Shaw and often toured small juke joints in far-flung places like Kansas City and Memphis.

While on a barnstorming tour of the Deep South in the late nineteen thirties, Billie came face to face with racial bigotry. For the first time, Billie feared for her life. The whites in a small rural Southern town had recently lynched a young black man suspected of a crime, and Billie and the other black musicians visiting the village were shocked. Not long after, Billie wrote "Strange Fruit," a song about lynching. Delivered in a melancholy voice, the song is a disturbing ode to black Americans who were hanged by marauding whites. In Billie's version, the "strange fruit" that hung from trees in the Deep South was a blight on the nation.

Back in New York, Billie's following grew. In 1939 she began singing in hip Greenwich Village nightclubs, earning adoration from leading white jazz and blues writers of the day. Although she enjoyed touring—and had become, in fact, a favorite front woman for many bandleaders—Billie had tired of the arduous road trips. Even when her fellow band members were famous, the cities where the band toured were segregated. This meant that polished artists like Lester Young and Louis Armstrong could play only colored nightclubs or were forced to enter and exit white nightclubs through the kitchen. It was a humiliating existence. How, Billie wondered, could an audience applaud performers one minute and jeer at them minutes later out on the street?

Still, Billie resolved to continue singing and recording. As she entered her thirties, her voice developed into a rich, versatile instrument. A string of failed love affairs had brought a new kind of world-weariness to her voice, and Billie was coming to understand the emotions behind many of the words she sang.

By the mid-forties, she had recorded a collection of songs that became classics, including "Strange Fruit," "Lover Man," "Ain't Nobody's Business If I Do,"and "Them There Eyes." Songwriters like Cole Porter, Fats Waller, and Harold Arlen thrilled to hear Billie sing their compositions, for she had matured into a formidable jazz singer. Indeed, as Billie grew more confident of her abilities, she occasionally drew criticism for her exacting recording requirements. "People don't understand the fight it takes to record what you want to record, the way you want to record it," she once remarked. All the same, she had become a star the old-fashioned way—by paying her dues. In 1940 she officially became a solo singer, and she appeared regularly at sold-out performances in top nightspots like Cafe Society and El Morocco.

In 1944 she joined one of the best jazz labels in the country, Decca Records, and had one of the most commercially successful periods of her career. Between then and 1949 she recorded many hits, including "Good Morning Heartache," "Don't Explain," and "Crazy, He Calls Me." In the past, Billie's sound had been supported by a succession of gutbucket blues players—drummers and hornplayers who had learned their craft in smoky dives and rural juke joints. Her early recordings were authentic renditions of downhome standards, and Billie's unschooled interpretations fit perfectly with the raw sound of these blues recordings. At Decca, however, Billie often found herself facing a phalanx of strings, horns, and background singers. In the midst of such lush arrangements, Billie felt somewhat smothered. But as a dedicated professional, she fulfilled her obligations and delivered new versions of many of the songs that had made her famous. Her producers often wanted her to do multiple takes of a given word or phrase. For Billie, so used to live performance and the informal atmosphere of her early recording sessions, the new environment was rather frustrating. "I can't stand to sing the same song the same way two nights in a succession, let alone over two years or ten years," she once said. "If you do, then it ain't music. It's close-order drills or exercise, or yodeling, or something . . . but it's not music."

New opportunities continued to open up for Billie. In 1946 her manager secured her a part in a motion picture, and she ventured to Hollywood. Living on the West Coast for the first time, Billie realized how much she missed the hustle and bustle of New York—not to mention her latest romantic interest, a handsome black nightclub owner.

Billie's part in the film *New Orleans* was that of a maid. She abhorred the role, and over the months she worked on the picture, Billie came to loathe her daily visits to the set. Fortunately, one of her costars was the illustrious Louis Armstrong, whom Billie admired tremendously. Nevertheless, the long, unhappy idle hours in Hollywood wore on Billie. Emotionally fragile, and given to adopting the habits of those around her, Billie began experimenting with drugs. A fellow band member was a longtime user of heroin, and Billie developed a heroin habit of her own.

Over the next decade Billie struggled mightily to overcome her addiction. Her poor taste in men didn't help matters, since she often found her precarious financial situation worsened by lovers who took more from her than they gave. Soon the drug abuse and hard living began to show in her work. Where her singing had developed into a low, sensuous style, she now displayed a slurred, sloppy delivery that alarmed those who knew her well.

Dressed fabulously in long gowns, her smooth, strong face impeccably made up, Lady Day was beginning to show alarming signs of losing control. She continued playing the best nightspots in New York and around the nation, but her luster was fading. Along with the famous flower positioned delicately behind her ear, Billie took to wearing long opera gloves to hide the physical evidence of her heroin addiction. Billie's old friends in the jazz community implored her to clean up her life.

Between 1947 and the early nineteen fifties, Billie was in and out of jails and sanitariums. In one embarrassing episode, she was arrested after a performance, and her bandmates and friends witnessed the awful spectacle of Billie being hustled into a paddy wagon. Her drug-related arrests made headlines, and Billie's performances became a shadow of her former dazzling persona. After years of heavy drinking, ruinous love affairs, run-ins with the law, and struggles with drug abuse, Billie's voice was that of a world-weary woman. Some critics found the change in her voice more effective and applauded her fifties recordings as those of a mature singer whose life experiences added richness to her material.

In 1957 Billie made a legendary television appearance in a broadcast called *Sounds of Jazz*. Accompanied by her old friend Lester Young, she sang "Fine and Mellow" and received riotous applause from the studio audience. Viewed today, the grainy footage shows a woman old before her time, her face lined by all the sorrows and hardships of her life. Shortly thereafter, she recorded again with some of her favorite jazz musicians, Coleman Hawkins, Gerry Mulligan, and Ben Webster.

The 1958 album *Lady in Satin* was a hit, although some listeners couldn't help but notice that Billie's voice seemed to be dimming. In 1959, ill from years of drug abuse and suffering from other ailments, Billie Holiday died in a New York hospital. Ironically, police arrived to charge her with a drug-related offense only hours before she passed away. It was a sad and ignominious end for one of the leading jazz singers of all time.

Today Billie's legend lives on in the form of dozens of compact disc versions of her recordings. In 1972 record producer Berry Gordy succeeded in mounting a lavish tribute to Lady Day. A motion picture version of her autobiography, *Lady Sings the Blues,* was released, and an entirely new audience of fans learned to love Billie and her work. Billie's life story reached a worldwide audience; Diana Ross's fearless performance as Billie earned her an Academy Award nomination for Best Actress, and the sound track sold millions of copies. For the first time, Billie was identified as a pioneering member of the jazz and blues community. It was recognition well earned and a suitable memorial to a woman who had lived the blues she sang.

21

Gwendolyn Brooks

1917–

Poetry in Action

As GWENDOLYN BROOKS describes it, her love of literature and writing developed early. In the critically acclaimed 1996 continuation of her autobiography, *Report From Part Two,* she details her introduction to the world of letters:

> My own Book Story begins with my father's wedding gift to my mother. He gave her a bookcase. Dark. Mahogany. Departmental. It

was (is) rich with desk, drawers, glass, friendly knobs. And it was filled with—The Harvard Classics! I shall never forget visiting it as a little girl—over and over selecting this and that dark green, gold-lettered volume for spellbound study.

Reading Brooks's writing is like sitting down with an old friend, a friend who is well read and interested in the amazing range of possibilities life has to offer. Indeed, in a long life of reading and writing, Gwendolyn Brooks has achieved an enviable balance between personal beliefs and artistic expression. As a young black girl growing up in Chicago, Gwendolyn realized early on that reading provided a means of transportation out of the teeming tenements of the segregated inner city and into the wide adventurous world. Now, some seventy years after Gwendolyn first discovered her love of books, she has shared with the world her unique vision and hopes for a better America. And for her valuable insights and opinions she has been very richly rewarded.

Author of numerous books of poetry and essays, Gwendolyn Brooks is the unofficial godmother of modern poets. Moreover, she is the first African American to win the Pulitzer Prize for poetry and the first black woman to serve as poetry consultant to the Library of Congress. Along with poets like NIKKI GIOVANNI, AUDRE LORDE, and SONIA SANCHEZ, Gwendolyn is a prime example of the positive impact black American women have had on American arts and letters. While her works are usually filtered through the prism of the black experience in the United States, her poems and essays carry important lessons for Americans of every color and income level. "Black literature is literature," Gwen wrote in 1975. "By blacks, *about* blacks, directed *to* blacks. *Essential* black literature is the distillation of black life."

For the generations of devoted poetry fans who admire her, she provides a model of artistic integrity. "She ought to be widely appreciated as one of our most remarkable woman poets," wrote *Ramparts* magazine literary critic James M. Johnson during the nineteen sixties. Indeed, Gwen's relatively low profile over the years astounds some members of the literary community. But for Gwen, seeking the limelight has never been her top priority.

Born on June 7, 1917, in Topeka, Kansas, in her grandmother's home, Gwen was raised in Chicago. She began reading and writing at an early age. Her parents, David Brooks and Keziah Wims Brooks, were pleasantly surprised to see their daughter take to reading effortlessly.

In fact, by the time Gwen had completed elementary school, she displayed a remarkable knack for reciting classic poetry and for writing her own rhymes.

Along with her brother Raymond, Gwen paid close attention to her mother's admonitions. Keziah Brooks wanted her children to have the best opportunities in life, and she insisted that they maintain clean, respectful demeanors at all times. "My mother 'brought up' my . . . brother Raymond and myself in the sunshine of certain rules," Gwen wrote in 1966. "One: we must be clean of body; she scrubbed us vigorously until we children could satisfy her high standards of cleanliness. That was outside! As for inside, long before it was fashionable to consider diet with strict seriousness, she was so inclined. . . . Two, we must be dutiful. Dutifulness has always been her major concept. 'Always do the Right Thing.' "

Her parents encouraged her love of writing and poetry, and Gwen excelled at school. The son of a Tennessee slave, Gwen's father, David, was determined that his children would be sufficiently prepared to meet the rigors of life that they would face. By the time she was thirteen, Gwen had her first poem published in a local newspaper. At an age when many young girls are preoccupied with prom dresses and dating, Gwen concentrated on the craft of writing. Her hard work began to pay off early, when she became a regular contributor to the foremost black newspaper in the nation at that time, the *Chicago Defender.*

Her teachers, impressed by her studious determination, encouraged her to attend college. While attending Wilson Junior College in Chicago, Gwen became a popular student, admired for her friendly nature and serious devotion to literature. By the time she graduated from college in 1937, Gwen's poetry had appeared in two anthologies of contemporary writers. It was an auspicious beginning, and Gwen soon developed the writing style and work habits that would distinguish her work for the rest of her life. Along the way, she also learned that writers could benefit from the kind of education not available in any classroom—the process of soaking up the real world of the streets. "A writer should get as much education as possible," Gwen wrote in 1972, in the first part of her two-part autobiography, *Report From Part One.* "Just going to school is not enough; if it were, all owners of doctorates would be inspired writers."

In 1937 she met and fell in love with Henry Blakely II, a promising young writer and poet she'd met at a NAACP youth gathering. They married in 1939 and had two children, Henry III and Nora.

An astute observer of human nature, Gwen began to focus on the community of black professionals, newly arrived Southerners, and struggling artists in her Chicago neighborhood. It was a world she understood, since she had suffered a few pangs of disappointment in the months after graduating from college. Seeking work, Gwen had been shocked to find that the only jobs available to a young, black, college-educated woman in Chicago in the early forties was that of a maid. Still, she continued to look for jobs that suited her artistic vision, and eventually landed work at a monthly publication called the *Women's National Magazine*. All the while, Gwen quietly wrote deeply personal poems.

In 1943 she won a prestigious new writer award from the Midwestern Writers' Conference. During the next few years, she wrote a collection of poems centering on her fellow Chicagoans, the black men and women struggling to make a living and find their identity in a complicated world. Published in 1945, Gwen's first collection drew immediate praise. *A Street in Bronzeville* explored the lives of ordinary people in Chicago, and displayed Gwen's extraordinary ability to capture the triumphs, disappointments, and joys of modern life. As a young artist, Gwen realized the power of words and images to affect individuals.

While most poets hold sensitive natures finely tuned to the nuances and subtleties of life, Gwen also had the remarkable ability to translate into her own words the issues of concern to others. Like many before her, Gwen learned that the life of a writer is often solitary and mysterious. "So much is involved in the writing of poetry," she said in 1972. "And sometimes, although I don't like suggesting it is a magic process, it seems you really do have to go into a bit of a trance, a self-cast trance, because 'brainwork' seems unable to do it all, to do the whole job. The self-cast trance is possible when you are *importantly* excited about an idea, surmise, or emotion."

Her burgeoning understanding of the difficult poetry-writing process enabled Gwen to pursue her artistic vision. Following the success of *Bronzeville,* Gwen continued writing about what she knew, the people and customs of black Chicago. And while the nation spun into World War II, Gwen was hard at work on her second collection of poems, *Annie Allen,* which featured the thoughts and words of a young black girl grappling with deep philosophical questions of life as well as the mundanities that challenge all young Americans.

With Gwen's ability to capture the speech patterns, slang, and angst of young blacks in the forties, *Annie Allen* became a huge success. It remains one of the most popular poetry collections of this century, taught by literature instructors in classrooms all around the nation some fifty years after its original publication in 1949. Unfazed by quick success, Gwen continued the solitary work of the poet. In 1950 she learned that she had received one of the highest honors any writer could hope for: a Pulitzer Prize. Along with a sizable cash award, the Pulitzer enabled Gwen to continue her special style of socially conscious poetry.

During the next decade she published a novel, *Maud Martha,* and several other poetry collections. As always, her themes concerned real-life situations and the complexities of black life in America. In 1960 she published *The Bean Eaters,* a poetry collection filled with elegant verse and poetic innovation; in 1968 she published a nonfiction work focusing on the months she'd spent at a notorious Chicago apartment complex known as the Mecca. Built in the eighteen nineties, the large, fortresslike structure has become rundown by the time Gwen happened upon it in her early twenties; at the time, she was looking for work, and wound up in the job of assistant to a notorious mystic and numbers runner who lived in the Mecca. The four months that young Gwen worked there left an indelible impression on her, and years later she revived her thoughts and emotions from that period in the form of a sad and funny poetry collection, *In the Mecca.*

In between, she wrote a book of verse for children, *Bronzeville Boys and Girls,* and an ode to Malcolm X, the black revolutionary who was killed in Harlem in 1965, and numerous other poems and monographs.

For much of the turbulent sixties, Gwen presided over a dynamic community of black artists and activists in Chicago. She taught poetry to gang members in Chicago, opening her own home to the troubled teens when public schools had rejected them. Beginning in 1963, Gwen also taught writing at local universities and organized poetry workshops for many disadvantaged children. Like other black women poets who followed her, Gwen always insisted that art could only be improved by incorporating the social issues of the day into the work.

Even as the literary and academic worlds showered her with awards—she received more than fifty honorary doctorates over the years—Gwen has kept her eyes focused on the real world around her and remained true to her personal beliefs and vision. Not surprisingly, she has received some of the most coveted literary and academic awards, including two Guggenheim Fellowships; the Pulitzer Prize; the American Academy of Arts and Letters Literature Award; and the Robert Frost Medal from the American Society of Poets. Gwen also received a key award from the leadership in Illinois: In 1968 she was named poet laureate of the state. The only previous recipient had been the famous writer Carl Sandburg. She was inducted into the National Women's Hall of Fame in 1988 and received a prestigious Senior Fellowship in Literature from the National Endowment of the Arts.

Around Chicago, Gwen's influence was felt in classrooms and in the community. A distinguished chair in her name was dedicated at Chicago State University, and community centers in the predominantly black South Side bear her name. During the late eighties and early nineties, Gwen traveled to many foreign nations, where she lectured and met with other poets. In Europe, Africa, and Asia, Gwen was greeted effusively by her world community of fans. In 1994 she was named the year's Jefferson Lecturer, a coveted humanitarian post in Washington, D.C.

After the death of her husband, Henry, in the mid-nineties, Gwen continued writing. She still relied on the wise words of her mother to help her stay strong as she entered her ninth decade. In *Report From Part Two* Gwen communicated her unique recipe for living life to the fullest. As always, her words held important lessons for any American interested in living a long, richly productive life: "Another healthy habit to form is cheerfulness," Gwen wrote. "Those who are around antagonists will find this characteristic hard to establish, but perseverance and a definite decision to let others have the last word will be well worth the effort."

22

Fannie Lou Hamer

1917–1977

From Sharecropper to Shining Light

THE LIFE OF Fannie Lou Townsend Hamer encompasses a crucial part of twentieth-century American history. Now, some twenty years after her death, Fannie Lou is finally receiving long overdue recognition for her important role in the fight for civil rights in the Deep South of the nineteen fifties and sixties. "I'm sick and tired of being sick and tired," Fannie Lou told an interviewer during the heated days of the civil rights movement. That kind of straightforward expression made Fannie Lou a compelling figure in the tumultuous battle to end racial discrimination in the United States.

In working to end legal segregation in the Jim Crow South for more than a decade, Fannie Lou was beaten, shot at, and jailed. She saw friends murdered and beaten as they fought for their right to live as equals to whites in America. She joined a political movement at a time when doing so meant a death sentence for blacks in Mississippi. And she helped establish a legacy of activism that has carried the most southern of Southern states into the modern era. Her favorite song, which she sang at almost every community gathering she attended, was the gospel standard, "This Little Light of Mine." It became Fannie Lou's signature song, a credo that expressed her special inner fire. "She was a little light—she was actually a very big light—and she shone that light on a lot of the dark places in the American soul," said Kay Mills, author of Fannie Lou's 1993 biography.

Born in Montgomery County, Mississippi, on October 6, 1917, Fannie Lou was the youngest of twenty children born to Lou Ella and Jim Townsend. At a time when many residents of the Deep South, both black and white, lived well below the poverty line, Fannie Lou's family was among the poorest of the poor. After the tragic years of slavery the social institutions of Mississippi rendered blacks second-class citizens. A new feudal arrangement descended on the former slaves. Under the arrangement commonly known as sharecropping, blacks worked land owned by whites, lived in ramshackle housing owned by whites, and were required to buy their food, supplies, seed, fertilizer, and equipment in stores run by whites. In this way thousands of rural southern blacks remained in debt to white landowners for decades after the official end of slavery in America. Life was brutal, hard, and thankless. Only the sanctuaries of family and church provided emotional stability for black southerners trapped in this system.

In Montgomery County and nearby Sunflower County, where Fannie Lou's great-grandparents had been slaves, blacks lived lives without pity, lives that too often ended while they were still young. Liberation from the endlessly backbreaking work, from unsafe working conditions, from the unequal distribution of profits, was a distant dream for a population that had endured generations of hardships and dashed hopes. Few saw reason to believe that their situation would ever improve, in part, because the all-white political leadership was not interested in seeing that happen. The chances that African Americans might elect new political leadership were slim to none, since blacks were intimidated out of exercising their constitutional right to vote by racist whites.

In 1923, at the age of six, Fannie Lou went to work in the cotton fields near her family's home in Montgomery County. Like her relatives before her, Fannie Lou learned that her lot in life would be years of toil, little or no education, and constant fear of the whites who controlled the local political and economic landscape. Fannie Lou managed to attend the run-down local colored public school until the age of twelve, when she dropped out to help her family work the land full-time.

A few years later she married another local sharecropper, Perry "Pap" Hamer, and they set out to start a family. Fannie Lou became pregnant twice, but suffered two miscarriages. She and Pap eventually adopted two neighborhood girls from their rural village, and Fannie Lou remained confident that someday she would be able to conceive. Years later, during the early sixties, Fannie Lou went to a local doctor for a minor ailment, and later learned that she had been given what was known as a "Mississippi appendectomy." While she was under sedation, the doctor had removed her uterus. This practice of involuntarily sterilizing low-income black women was tragically common during that period in the Deep South. In later years, Fannie Lou spoke out strongly on the controversial subject of women's reproductive rights. She became one of the first poor black women in America to take a public stand against abortion and advocate increased funding for women's health care.

But before she embarked on that path, Fannie Lou made her mark as a ferocious fighter in the battle to end racial discrimination in Mississippi. On a steamy August day in 1962, Fannie Lou decided she was fed up with sharecropping. Civil rights activists were pressing for voting rights in neighboring Alabama and in Georgia, and earlier that summer, a group of college students from the Student Nonviolent Coordinating Committee—known as SNCC—had come to Sunflower County, where the Hamer family lived. After listening to the young, enthusiastic student activists, Fannie Lou convinced a few neighbors in her town that they should begin to stand up for themselves. So on that August day she joined seventeen stalwart friends, and they left their tiny Ruleville town and headed by bus for the Montgomery County seat in Indianola. Fannie Lou wanted to exercise her constitutional right to vote, even though she knew that for decades blacks had been intimidated by whites if they so much as mentioned a desire to take part in the democratic process.

Once the group arrived in Indianola, they were greeted coldly by the voter registration staff. Undeterred, Fannie Lou and the other Ruleville travelers demanded that they be registered to vote. At that time, the predominantly white county workers required a "literacy test" of those who sought to become voters filled with arcane legal language and bizarre constitutional references. Few undereducated blacks could hope to pass the test.

Frustrated, the group returned to Ruleville. Fannie Lou then learned that the white landowner who employed her family had kicked them out of their home while she was away. White landowners often used this cruel tactic to punish sharecroppers who displayed "uppity" behavior. Enraged by the landowner's meanness, Fannie Lou determined to keep trying to register to vote. On three separate tries, Fannie Lou was rebuffed. She was turned away on two occasions and, on another, was shot at by an angry white racist.

During the next year, Fannie Lou found support among the growing community of civil rights activists who began streaming into the rural South. By the summer of 1963 she was traveling around the South, taking part in "citizenship education" workshops. It was on one of these trips that Fannie Lou encountered a situation that would test her personal resolve—and her faith in the decency of man. In Winona, Mississippi, Fannie Lou and six other female grassroots organizers were stopped by sheriff's deputies at a bus station. They were arrested for disturbing the peace and taken to a local jail.

Fannie Lou later described what happened:

> Then three white men came into my room. One was a state highway policeman (he had the marking on his sleeve), and they said they were going to make me wish I was dead. They made me lay down on my face and they ordered two Negro prisoners to beat me with a blackjack. That was unbearable. The first prisoner beat me until he was exhausted, then the second Negro began to beat me. I had had polio when I was about six years old, and I have a limp. So I held my hands down and beneath me, trying to protect my weak side. I began to work my feet. My dress pulled up, and I tried to smooth it down. One of the policemen walked over and raised my dress as high as he could. They beat me until my body was hard, 'til I couldn't bend my fingers or get up when they told me to. That's how I got this blood clot in my eye—the sight's nearly gone. And my kidney was injured from the blows they gave me.

Even in a desperately bad time, when physical abuse was common, the beating of Fannie Lou outraged civil rights workers. She had been left alone in the jail cell for hours after the beating, bleeding and badly in need of medical treatment. She was released a few days later, after a young civil rights worker named Andrew Young arrived with bail money. He sent her to Atlanta to meet with Dr. Martin Luther King Jr., and he referred her to the United States Justice Department. Robert Kennedy, then the U.S. attorney general, was so upset by the beating of the women that he personally intervened and filed criminal charges against the law enforcement officers in Winona who had engineered the violence. When the case came to trial in Mississippi some months later, an all-white, all-male jury acquitted the lawmen of all charges.

Once she recovered from her injuries, Fannie Lou threw herself into the civil rights movement, volunteering for work with both SNCC and the Southern Christian Leadership Conference. During the next two years, she would find herself in high-powered company, as middle-class white and black activists from New York, Chicago, and Baltimore continued organizing blacks in the Deep South.

Early in 1964, a presidential election year, a coalition of civil rights groups formed the Mississippi Democratic Freedom party, after failing to gain participation in the regular Democratic party. This grassroots group chose a delegation consisting of poor residents from the state to seek recognition from the national party. At that time, white Democrats were arguing for a slow approach to ending segregation in the Deep South. But for Fannie Lou and the other members of the Mississippi Democratic Freedom party, slow progress was almost as bad as no progress: they sought to challenge the right of the all-white official Mississippi Democratic delegation on the grounds that it did not fairly represent the entire population of the state. Headed by Fannie Lou, the delegation went to the Democratic National Convention in Atlantic City in August and demanded recognition as the official delegation of the Mississippi Democratic party. In the fight over credentials Fannie Lou was chosen to represent the group. She testified before Democratic party leaders. Her testimony, including the vivid description of being beaten and shot at by whites, riveted the convention. But the effect was almost undone by President Lyndon B. Johnson. He deliberately called a press conference that preempted the televising of Fannie Lou's testimony. But network television executives—aware of the dramatic impact of Fannie Lou's heartwrenching story—aired her testimony in its entirety later that evening, so allowing all of America to hear firsthand the horrors of the conflict over civil rights in the Deep South. A year later, securely reelected, President Johnson signed the Voting Rights Act of 1965, which ensured that all blacks of eligible age would be permitted to vote. Once again, Fannie Lou had angered the local white leadership in Mississippi but gained support from sympathetic whites and African Americans living outside of the South.

Fannie Lou continued working to improve the conditions of her Mississippi community. Soon, high-profile activists like singer Harry Belafonte and Andrew Young were looking to her as a guiding force in the tiny villages of Mississippi. She traveled to Africa with a delegation that included Belafonte and met with several presidents and dignitaries there.

During the late sixties and seventies, Fannie Lou continued to work on a multitude of important issues, including educational opportunity, agricultural improvements for blacks, and low-cost housing. Where many of her neighbors gave up on civil rights organizing—after the heady days of the mid-sixties had passed and the Northern workers had left the region—Fannie Lou remained a dedicated activist. Often at local meetings, she would lead the gathering in singing "This Little Light of Mine." Those who knew her believed she was blessed with an especially powerful inner strength. In the mythology of the region, where historic ties to African and Caribbean cultures remained, some even said that Fannie Lou had been granted a mystical, charismatic power by the ancient gods. She never spoke of such matters, but many who saw her rouse a gathering to action believed that Fannie Lou at least marched to a powerful drummer.

In 1971 Fannie Lou ran for the Mississippi Senate and was defeated by a white politician. But she triumphed in bringing much-needed state and federal dollars into a host of social programs for rural blacks in her hometown. By the mid-seventies, recovering from breast cancer and suffering from kidney problems caused by the Winona beating, Fannie Lou was in poor health. She died in 1977, in the same small town where she had lived most of her life.

Many years later, when Fannie Lou's biographer, Kay Mills, visited Sunflower County, she met a man named Willie Simmons—the first black man to be elected to the Mississippi State Senate from that district. Standing up proudly, he told Mills: "I am living Fannie Lou Hamer's dream."

23

Lena Horne

1917–

The Lady, Her Music, and Fifty Years
of Civil Rights Activism

IN MANY WAYS Lena Horne embodies the duality of experience for many black American women in the twentieth century. Born in 1917 at the dawn of the Jazz Age, her life encompasses the early pangs of the women's and civil rights movements and the late-twentieth-century recognition of African-American women as important contributors to our nation's development. With Lena Horne, the daughter of a prominent black family, there has never been any question that African-American women held the power to change the very fabric of the United States.

Outspoken, glamorous, and seemingly possessed of an internal flame that radiated from within, Horne moved gracefully from pampered girlhood in segregated America to an icon of uncomplaining strength, dedicated artistry, and deep integrity. "Because time has been good to me, I treat it with great respect," she said in 1989. And in the late nineties, as she entered her ninth decade, Horne continued to work at her craft and with the numerous family and civic interests that distinguished her life in this half of the century.

As a "down-home girl" who began singing at the urging of her strong-willed, aristocratic grandmother, Lena Horne managed to change the face of American entertainment. Her life is rich with contradictions and tragedy, as well as marked by inspiring triumphs. From the creative vigor of the Harlem Renaissance to the fertile musical ground of the Cotton Club to the bustling soundstages of Hollywood in its Golden Era, Lena Horne has been involved in some of the most fruitful years in modern American cultural history. Her one-woman Broadway show in 1981 earned her a Tony Award and scored knockout box office in theaters all over the country when she later toured with the show. Her friends have included some of the brightest literary, political, and musical lights in this century, including composer Billy Strayhorn, writers Ralph Ellison and James Baldwin, Robert F. Kennedy, and Dr. Martin Luther King Jr. Never a hopeless stargazer, Lena Horne is the first to admit that the going was not always glamorous—and certainly not always easy.

She was born Lena Mary Calhoun Horne in Brooklyn on June 30, 1917. Her mother, Edna Scottron, was a beautiful former debutante. Her father, Ted Horne, was a neighborhood star, a former playboy turned easygoing bureaucrat, the first black employee of the New York State Department of Labor. He separated from Edna Scottron Horne when Lena was not yet three. But during her earliest years, Lena lived with her mother and father in a well-kept Brooklyn neighborhood. The family enjoyed the benefits of the strong network of black civic groups, churches, and businesses that thrived in New York as the nation whirled into the nineteen twenties. Lena made a name for herself early in that community, garnering coverage in the black press in 1919 when she became the youngest member (at the age of two and a half) of the National Association for the Advancement of Colored People.

A photograph of Lena at that time shows a sturdy, confident little girl decked out in a downy white pinafore and neat starched bonnet and clutching a delicate rose. She gazes directly into the camera, her cheeks round, her mouth set in a firm straight line, hinting at the steely beauty she would become. While the photograph showed the beginnings of a formidable presence, it is even more significant when taken in historical context. New York's black communities in the twenties—in Harlem and in Brooklyn—teemed with creative and political activity. Lena's parents were involved in the NAACP at a time when the legendary intellectual W. E. B. Du Bois was its guiding force. The NAACP magazine, the *Crisis,* was selling nearly 100,000 copies each month. The summer of Lena's birth, the NAACP sponsored several "silent protest parades" against lynching, a barbaric tradition in much of the rural South. It is obvious that Lena's later involvement in the marches and demonstrations of the civil rights movement did not happen by accident.

After her father's departure from their Brooklyn brownstone, Lena became one of the few children of divorce in her family's elite circle. As the puritanical codes of the time dictated, no "respectable" family was to endure such a rupture. She later told relatives that she had been "crippled" by her parents' breakup. It was a stigma that would remain with Lena as an adult. Eventually, overwhelmed by the responsibility of raising her child alone, Lena's mother turned over the raising of her only daughter to Cora Calhoun Horne—Teddy Horne's stern, socially prominent mother.

Despite her son's unseemly divorce, Cora Horne kept her head up and instructed Lena to do the same. Ever devoted to civic causes, Lena's grandmother became increasingly involved in community work. In 1921 Cora Horne was a member of the Brooklyn board of directors of the Big Brother and Big Sister Federation. As part of this group, she met with President Warren G. Harding in Washington, D.C. Lena became a regular at her grandmother's civic meetings, and Cora schooled the pretty girl in political activism as well as comportment, dress, and diction. "When I take you to meetings, I want you to listen," Cora would tell young Lena. "When you speak, articulate clearly—don't use slang." Thus was born the clipped phrasing and precise speech of a woman who would come to define the art of popular music performance.

Lena attended a private school, the Ethical Culture School, in the Fort Greene section of Brooklyn. Her at-home time was spent reading or playing dress-up in her grandmother's Victorian-era clothes. Lena first became aware of class differences during these years: An Irish settlement was nearby her grandparents' stately Chauncey Street home, but Lena was cautioned against fraternizing with the children there. Cora thought the Irish children did not "speak well," and she told Lena to avoid them. From time to time, however, Lena did manage to play with immigrant Swedish children whose parents ran a local garage.

Soon Lena was a popular fixture in the black middle-class social scene in Brooklyn, joining such organizations as Jack and Jill, Junior Debs, Links, and the Nonchalants. Cora also took Lena on intercontinental trips, giving the inquisitive young girl exposure to the world beyond Brooklyn.

At this time, it was not unusual for some light-skinned members of this black social class to pass for white. In Cora Horne's circle, some of her friends worked at fine department stores in Manhattan, their customers and employers never realizing these women were Negroes. Seeing so many adults who were ashamed of their race made a strong impression on Lena—she resolved to be proud of who she was.

By the mid-thirties Lena had become a star in that glittering space where New York's entertainment world collides with high society. After appearing in the Junior Theater Guild's *Junior Deb* and *Junior Follies* revue shows in and around Brooklyn, Lena won a job in the chorus line at the famed Cotton Club. Though not yet twenty years old, Lena soon became a standout at a legendary nightclub where New York's cafe society gathered. The death of her beloved grandmother in 1932 led to a deep estrangement between Lena and her mother, Edna, after her mother tried to keep Lena from attending Cora's funeral.

While her family life became more complicated, Lena flourished in the exhilarating atmosphere of the Cotton Club. She got her first big break in a classic fable of backstage theater lore: one night, the leading female singer at the club came down with a sore throat, and Lena was called to fill in for her. She so impressed the show's producers that they began giving her lead work in the popular Cotton Club acts that toured the region at the height of the nightclub's influence. In 1934, in another classic turn, Lena was spotted in the Cotton Club revue by a Broadway producer. She won the part of a "quadroon girl" in a show called *Dance With Your Gods,* a musical drama about voodoo. She won faint praise from the *New York Times*'s notoriously crotchety theater critic of the era, Brooks Atkinson, but decades would pass before she would work on Broadway again.

For the next few years Lena found regular work in big bands, and by the early forties had established a sizable following. In shows at popular venues like Cafe Society and the Apollo Theater, Lena became known as the "Sepia Songstress." Singing a range of music from Tin Pan Alley standards like "Blue Moon" to the modern classic "Stormy Weather" (which was written by Harry Arlen for a Cotton Club show), it was inevitable that Lena would catch the eye of Hollywood. "Let the whole world benefit from your incredible radiance," Duke Ellington told Lena when she first learned of an offer to appear at the hot new Los Angeles nightclub, the Trocadero. It was 1941, and Lena boarded a train in New York and traveled to California for the first time.

For all her impressive list of stage credits, Lena was young and inexperienced in the ways of romantic relationships. By the time she left New York for California, she had given birth to a daughter, Gail, from a brief marriage to Louis Jones. Now a single mother, she needed to work to support herself and her family.

Lena had earned the disapproval of some members of her middle-class family by deciding to go to Hollywood. In black communities in Pittsburgh, Chicago, and New York, the Horne family was well known and generally viewed as the shining model of respectability and economic stability. Lena's father Teddy had resurfaced while she was at the Cotton Club and became a dashing, albeit not entirely reliable, part of her life again. Her mother, Edna, had also become Lena's unofficial chaperone, even after Lena had married, become a mother, and divorced.

Lena's first trip to Hollywood began a long, bittersweet relationship with the movie industry. She appeared in dozens of films, but usually in musical numbers that could be edited out when the films were shown in the segregated South. In these years, Lena became a cynosure of Hollywood's fascination with the exotic. In short films produced for black audiences, she radiated elegance and verve and showed the beginnings of acting skills that deserved nurturing. High-profile films like *Stormy Weather* and *Panama Hattie* won Lena wide recognition. She balked at taking acting roles that would call for her to be an empty-headed maid or a Mammy, and so her screenwork was limited almost exclusively to singing parts.

During this period Lena came to befriend a wide range of important artists and activists, including bandleader Count Basie, director Vincente Minnelli, singer and actor Paul Robeson, dancer KATHERINE

DUNHAM, actress Ava Gardner, and actor Humphrey Bogart. When World War II began, Lena became a fixture on the USO circuit, entertaining black troops at military bases around America. Her political calling led her to join Robeson and other entertainers in a campaign to improve employment practices in California during the early forties.

In 1947 Lena married Hollywood composer Lennie Hayton, a classically trained pianist who was on his way up. Since Hayton was white, the union was controversial. Ultimately, the couple decided that Hollywood was too confining—and too morally hypocritical—to call home. (The couple was also unofficially blacklisted by the infamous House Un-American Activities Committee). For much of the next two decades Lena sang and performed in world-famous nightclubs and theaters around the globe, including sold-out tours that took her to London, New York, Chicago, and Paris.

In the sixties Lena emerged, along with Harry Belafonte and Marlon Brando, as one of the most visible performer-activists in America. She was part of a diverse coalition of performers and artists who met with members of the Democratic party to discuss civil rights protests and the race riots that were gripping the nation. In October 1963 Lena helped organize a star-studded benefit for the Student Nonviolent Coordinating Committee. Held at Carnegie Hall, it featured such luminaries as Frank Sinatra and composers Betty Comden and Adolph Green and Jule Styne, who even wrote a "protest anthem" called "Now!" especially for Lena. It was one of the more glamorous of Lena's efforts to support the civil rights movement. In other, less sensational efforts, she attended dozens of meetings and grassroots functions in small Southern towns and rural villages.

Lena had supported John F. Kennedy as president and after his murder, Lena saw in Robert Kennedy great hope that the years of segregation and Jim Crow laws might finally come to a close. The assassinations of that era, including the killing of Dr. Martin Luther King Jr. and Robert Kennedy in 1968, devastated Lena. Other deaths of close friends and family members soon followed—including Billy Strayhorn and Lennie Hayton, who both died in the early seventies. Lena withdrew from the public eye. Years later, she would call this period of her life one of the darkest she had ever experienced.

In the early eighties, however, Lena was back in top form. Her one-woman show on Broadway became legendary. *Lena Horne: The Lady and Her Music* began as a limited engagement and became the longest-running one-woman show in Broadway history. She won rave reviews and standing ovations nightly. Some overwhelmed critics even compared Lena to performance legends as varied as tenor Enrico Caruso, ballerina Anna Pavlova, dancer Fred Astaire, and diva Maria Callas.

In the years that followed, Lena was "rediscovered" by performers and pop music fans alike. She received a Kennedy Center Honor, ASCAP awards, a Lifetime Achievement Award from the NAACP, and honors from a host of other performing arts organizations. Even after all the political activism and five decades of professional triumphs, Lena was most happy as matriarch to a new generation of the strong-willed Horne clan. To an audience at an NAACP ceremony in the early eighties, Lena spoke most lovingly of her success as a "family blessing." It was a fitting statement from a woman who, like the venerable civil rights organization she had joined at age two, embodied the strength and grace of black American achievement in this century.

24

Ella Fitzgerald

1918–1996

The First Lady of Song

WHEN ELLA FITZGERALD DIED in 1996, America lost a strong link to its cultural past. Moreover, the entertainment community lost one of the pioneering voices in popular music. For millions of black American women who had looked to Ella for spiritual and creative inspiration, the loss was immeasurable.

"I always thank God," Ella told *Jet* magazine in 1988. "I'm here because this is what I love to do. When they say come and sing, that's the medicine." After writing and singing with some of the world's greatest composers, Ella Fitzgerald left a legacy of recordings and performances that will remain a benchmark in classical jazz forever. For a timid girl from a southern town, Ella's legacy is remarkable because her skills surpassed those of uncounted other singers—men and women, black and white—throughout the history of American popular entertainment. "Male or female, the best singer on the planet," legendary jazzman Mel Torme said of her after she died.

Born in Newport News, Virginia, on April 25, 1918, Ella was a shy girl. Her parents were unmarried, and Ella's father died shortly after her birth. In the mid-twenties, her mother moved the family to Yonkers, New York. There Ella grew up in an ethnically diverse neighborhood that included Greek, Irish, Italian, and eastern European immigrants. She attended public school only until the tenth grade. Then, according to her biographers, she fled her mother's home, determined to escape from an abusive stepfather. She lived with friends and relatives in Harlem and supported herself by dancing for change on sidewalks in the busy shopping districts. Ella also supported herself by working as a lookout at a bordello, where she ran errands for prostitutes and watched out for law enforcement officers.

When she was sixteen, Ella was persuaded by some girlfriends to compete in the popular Amateur Night at Harlem's Apollo Theater, which was frequented by dozens of world-famous black entertainers, including composer Duke Ellington and dancer Bill Robinson. One night in 1934 Ella and her friends giddily chose straws to see who would perform in the amateur talent contest. Ella drew the short straw, and her friends pushed her into taking the stage. They had no idea that their shy, slightly overweight friend could sing like an angel. Onstage, her knees knocking together nervously, Ella sang two songs: "Object of My Affection" and "Judy," by popular songwriter Connee Boswell. She won first prize that night, $25. Her friends were thrilled, and Ella began appearing in the amateur night contests regularly, often winning the first prize.

Months later, after her name had become well known in Harlem, an executive at CBS Radio invited Ella to audition. Overcoming her extreme shyness, Ella went to the midtown Manhattan CBS studios and thoroughly impressed the network executives. During this time, the Great Depression kept many Americans tuned to their radios, where the entertainment was inexpensive and the range of offerings—from soap operas to band performances—was wide. Ella was not yet eighteen years old, but she realized that her gift for singing might just provide a decent way to make a living. She signed a contract with CBS Radio, an agreement that she would never fulfill.

Ella's mother died in 1935, and the teenager found herself orphaned. Because she was not yet of legal age, and had no official "guardian" to oversee her interests, the CBS executives did not let Ella perform. She was heartbroken, even more so because city child and welfare officials remanded her to a New York orphanage. Singing was not encouraged in the state home, and Ella was forced to take up "marketable skills" like typing and stenography. Still, she continued to make her way most weekends to the Apollo Theater. And there, one night in 1935, she met a musician from a popular band.

When drummer and bandleader Chick Webb first saw Ella, he made a crude statement about her being "ugly." But Bardu Ali, the Chick Webb band member who had heard Ella onstage at the Apollo, wouldn't let Webb get away without hearing the youngster sing. Chick Webb and his orchestra were playing at the Savoy Ballroom in New York, and Ali convinced the testy bandleader to give the soft-spoken young woman a listen.

Within a matter of weeks, Ella made her first official appearance with the band, in a concert at Yale University. She so impressed Webb—and the wealthy undergraduates—that the bandleader made her his official singer shortly thereafter. Webb also took Ella under his wing in a brotherly manner, paying her expenses out of his own salary when his agent refused to pay her. Webb and his wife also legally adopted Ella, removing her once and for all from the dreary world of the state orphanage. On June 12, 1935, Ella made her first recording with the Chick Webb Band. Soon her recording of "Love and Kisses" hit it big with jazz fans, and Ella was on her way to a productive period of collaborating with Webb.

In 1938, with Al Feldman, a pianist and arranger for the band, she cowrote a song based on a popular children's rhyme. "A-Tisket, A-Tasket" gave the Chick Webb Band its first nationwide hit record. In cities and small towns all over America Ella's voice could be heard drifting from radios. An energetic ode to a young girl's innocence, the song won Ella fans from all walks of life, from other musicians, like Frank Sinatra, and music lovers, white and black, in every corner of the nation.

Chick Webb died unexpectedly in 1939, when Ella was twenty-one. For the next three years she fronted the band, holding it together, touring the jazz clubs and dance halls of America. In 1942, after several of the band members went to fight in World War II, the Chick Webb Band broke up, and Ella was on her own again. But now, she had a loyal community of singers, musicians, and songwriters eager to help her keep singing.

For the next fifteen years, Ella made some of the most astounding recordings in the history of American popular music. In 1946 her manager, Norman Granz, had a brainstorm: Why not have Ella record entire albums of works by well-known popular composers? The first of these—they came to be known as "Ella's Songbooks"—was a recording of the works of Cole Porter. Ella also recorded albums devoted to the works of George Gershwin, Jerome Kern, Johnny Mercer, Irving Berlin, Harold Arlen, and Rodgers and Hart. She had distinguished herself during the thirties and early forties as a phenomenally creative singer (especially her ability to "scat," or sing in a style akin to a musical instrument), and now, with the "Songbooks," Ella became a world-famous classical jazz artist.

By 1955 Granz felt his star client was in a rut. Ella had been recording for Decca Records for almost twenty years, and Granz felt she was being taken for granted. He arranged for her to leave Decca for Verve Records, a label he had founded. At a time when numerous popular black musicians were routinely underpaid by white managers, agents, and record executives, Granz made sure that Ella was paid fairly for her performances and recordings. She began experimenting with her singing, adding calypso numbers and some pop standards. In the late fifties she recorded with Louis Armstrong and Duke Ellington. She won her first Grammy Award, for her *Irving Berlin Songbook,* in 1958. It was the first Grammy ever to be awarded to a black woman musician.

Throughout her creative triumphs, Ella's private life was somewhat bleak. She married twice, but both unions ended in divorce. Her first husband, Benny Kornegay, worked in New York shipyards and didn't much appreciate his wife's chosen work. Her second husband, jazz bassist Ray Brown, enjoyed the financial fruits of her success but wasn't emotionally supportive. But where some other women jazz singers— notably BILLIE HOLLIDAY—seemed to lead troubled lives that mirrored the blues they sang, Ella remained a bright, optimistic trouper.

With prominent fans and friends like Duke Ellington, Frank Sinatra, Dizzy Gillespie, and Lionel Hampton encouraging her, Ella developed a unique singing style that was genuine and spectacularly diverse. From ballads like "They Can't Take That Away From Me" to swinging numbers like "The Lady Is a Tramp" to novelty songs like "Mack the Knife" and "Old McDonald Had a Farm," Ella offered a varied repertoire of songs that was impressive. Ella had a voice that many likened to a clear bell, a keen ear, and perfect pitch. To singers like Sinatra and Mel Torme, she was the epitome of native talent honed by years of dedication to the art of singing.

After developing an improvisational singing style that combined bebop, jazz, and blues, Ella became a favorite on the worldwide concert scene. During the fifties and sixties, she was a staple at the Newport Jazz Festival, the Playboy Jazz Festival, and international music events from Italy to Monterey. "The Italians call me 'Mama Jazz,' " Ella once told an interviewer. "That's okay, as long as they don't call me 'Granny Jazz.' "

In the early seventies, after the deaths of close friends Louis Armstrong and Duke Ellington, Ella decided to slow down a bit. She had been touring almost nonstop for more than thirty years. She began spending more time at her Beverly Hills home and even appeared in commercial endorsements for American Express and Memorex. By the mid-eighties Ella had survived numerous health problems, including failing eyesight and the onset of diabetes. She continued a concert schedule, though, and won a whole new audience of fans by appearing on televised performances such as *Jazz From Lincoln Center* and the Montreux Jazz Festival.

Throughout, she remained a thoughtful, low-key star, a jazz chanteuse without any of the temper tantrums or ego displays that often characterized her contemporaries. During her long, rich career, she carved a path for black woman singers like LENA HORNE, Cassandra Wilson, and Sarah Vaughn. For eighteen consecutive years, she was named outstanding performer of the year by *Downbeat* magazine, the jazz industry bible.

After receiving her first Grammy, in 1958, Ella want on to win a dozen more of the music industry's most coveted award, as well as numerous other high honors from musicians, composers, and educators. She had one son, and raised a niece, but for the most part she lived her life as she wished: writing, recording, and performing songs for an audience that will never forget her soaring notes and perfect phrasing.

When Ella Fitzgerald died in 1996, a host of grateful black women performers turned out to pay their respects to the First Lady of Song. "Ella Fitzgerald made the mark for all female singers, especially black woman singers, in our industry," said Dionne Warwick. Lena Horne, a longtime friend and admirer of Ella's, paid high tribute to the singer: "She is our treasure," Horne said, "We're proud of her. We love her."

25

Ruby Dee

1924–

*Fighting for Equality, From Hollywood
to Washington*

DURING THE GOLDEN AGE of Hollywood, from the nineteen thirties through the fifties, few moviegoers were exposed to the full range of talents of black actors and actresses. Rare was the feature film that explored the complexity of black life in America, and for black women actors like LENA HORNE, HATTIE MCDANIEL and Dorothy Dandridge, opportunities for career growth in the industry were few and far between. Indeed, as the calm conformity of the fifties gave way to the

147

socially turbulent sixties, most black film actresses refused to play the limited, stereotyped parts written for them. Eventually, the public's awakening to the great potential of the nation's African-American actors would bring about a revolution in the movie business.

For the award-winning actress Ruby Dee, the link between social beliefs and artistic integrity has always been strong and inescapable. "When I was young, I dreamt of being a starlet in Hollywood," Ruby Dee recalled during a 1996 interview. "But there comes a time in every African-American [actor's] life when you realize the limitations, that you could play only maids or some little supporting role. Even Lena Horne couldn't get good parts."

For Ruby, her personal battles with the narrow restrictions of the Hollywood community were well worth the effort. Some forty years after she made her acting debut, she stands as a guiding light for many young black actresses. From Angela Bassett to Whitney Houston and Halle Berry, Ruby Dee represents the magnificent contribution black women have made to the nation's modern cinema canon. And after starring in more than a dozen award-winning films over three decades— including LORRAINE HANSBERRY's *Raisin in the Sun* and Spike Lee's *Do the Right Thing*—Ruby Dee certainly embodies the depth of spirit and commitment black women have brought to America's most popular cultural arena—major motion pictures.

Ruby Dee has also lent her unique talent and insights to other artistic venues, including book publishing, the Broadway stage, and commercial and public television. She has exemplified a mixture of creative versatility and political activism that is a benchmark of our democratic right to personal expression. During the sixties, for example, Ruby found time to raise a family, march and organize in the civil rights movement, and appear in several outstanding film and stage productions. Her level of dedication and artistic vision are legendary. "Dee is living proof that family life, artistic accomplishment, and fervent social activism are not incompatible pursuits," wrote Misha Berson, a Seattle theater critic in 1996. Indeed, during the last few years, Ruby has received almost as many honors for her social activism, including an NAACP Image Award, as she has for her stage and film work, including an Emmy Award and an Obie Award.

With her fifty-year marriage to writer, actor, and director Ossie Davis, Ruby is also a model of old-fashioned values. For Ruby Dee it all comes down to a belief in oneself and in the potential for greatness that exists in all of us. From her earliest days as a struggling young actress in New York, Ruby has managed to turn her deepest beliefs into the purest forms of artistic expression.

Born Ruby Ann Wallace on October 27, 1924, in Cleveland, Ohio, Ruby moved with her family to New York when she was very young. Growing up in Harlem during the twenties and thirties, Ruby was exposed to the work of several legendary musicians and writers, including Duke Ellington and ZORA NEALE HURSTON. Collectively, these prolific artists made up the Harlem Renaissance, an era in which blacks produced outstanding works of art and literature that stand today as models of creativity.

Ruby's father worked for the railroads, and her stepmother was a schoolteacher, providing Ruby and her many siblings with a stable, organized home. Initially, Ruby thought she might like to be a writer, and she eagerly read the works of notable black women authors—including DOROTHY WEST and Zora Neale Hurston—as well as classics by William Shakespeare and Jane Austen and Charlotte Brontë. Along the way, Ruby also developed a love of theater and became intrigued with the sights of the many famous black performers who frequented the Harlem neighborhood where she lived.

After graduating from high school in 1945, Ruby enrolled in Hunter College in New York. Not sure of what path her life might take, Ruby was certain of one thing: she knew she had to explore the "acting bug" that seemed to have gripped her. So the small, delicately featured young woman began to spend time with a local theatrical company, the American Negro Theatre (ANT). After graduating from Hunter with a liberal arts degree, Ruby turned her attention to studying acting. It was an exhilarating time in America, with World War II ending in triumph for the United States and the national economy experiencing an enormous postwar boom.

For Ruby, getting up each day and making her way to the Harlem branch of the New York Public Library that housed the theater was like a dream come true. "It's so easy to romanticize now," Ruby recalled in 1996, "but through that group, I saw a different way to be an actor and a different way of what was possible, given the context of racism."

While studying at the American Negro Theatre, Ruby worked with such future stars as Sidney Poitier and Harry Belafonte. The troupe was seen as pioneering, since few theater companies featuring black writers, directors, and actors existed at that time. Indeed, Ruby began writing during this period as well, hoping to become one of the first African-American women to have a play or screenplay produced. She also kept busy in the Harlem community, writing articles for the local black newspaper, the *Amsterdam News,* and attending community events. By the end of the forties, Ruby had become one of the best-known young black actresses in New York. And in terms of her personal life, things had taken a welcome turn as well.

In 1946, Ruby had made her debut on Broadway as a supporting actor in an ANT production of the hit drama *Anna Lucasta.* Starring an all-black cast, the play concerned love and the struggle for identity among African Americans. It was a smash hit, and Ruby was at the crest of a growing wave of black actors and actresses who were earning critical praise from mainstream press and audiences. Although still in her twenties, Ruby was maturing into a thoughtful, dedicated professional. When she auditioned for a role in a play called *Jeb,* a production featuring an all-black cast, she encountered a tall black man with a deep voice who would change her life. Initially, however, she was far from charmed by Ossie Davis.

"When I saw Ossie's picture in the newspaper as the one who got the role [of Jeb] I thought, 'The producers probably went down South and picked this guy out from behind a plow,' " Ruby recalled many years later. But her first impression would prove to be off the mark by a mile. "The truth is, he was an intellectual!" Ruby recalled, chuckling at the memory. "An intellectual, and a very ambitious writer, actor, and director." She soon fell for the promising artist, and they married in 1948. The couple had three children, and, as of this writing, were the grandparents of seven youngsters. Moreover, during their long marriage, Ruby and Ossie have worked together in numerous stage, film, and television productions, including an award-winning Public Broadcasting System educational series in the seventies.

In the late fifties Ruby appeared in the stage and film productions of one of the most celebrated social dramas of the era—Lorraine Hansberry's *Raisin in the Sun.* Focusing on the trials and triumphs of a black Chicago family attempting to move from a poverty-stricken tenement into a white suburban neighborhood, *Raisin* was a smash when it premiered on Broadway at the Ethel Barrymore Theatre in 1959. Many black and white Americans were beginning to question the accepted notions of race, and Hansberry's play brought together the issues of race and class divisions, as well as the complicated subject of male-female relationships, in a moving confluence of circumstances. The motion picture version of the play was also a success, and Ruby's portrayal of the young wife struggling to help her husband deal with anger and rejection won critical raves.

During the early years of their marriage, Ruby and Ossie discovered that they shared a keen interest in the roiling social issues of the day. Together, they joined some of the leading voices in the civil rights movement and helped establish a tight-knit group of celebrities who pledged their time and energy to fighting for civil rights in America, including LENA HORNE, Harry Belafonte, and composer Billy Strayhorn. Ruby and Ossie also befriended such key civil rights figures as Malcolm X, Dr. Martin Luther King Jr., and his wife, Coretta Scott King. Looking back, Ruby says they often managed to find some humor amid all the hardship and difficulty of the civil rights era. "We met Martin [Luther King Jr.] many times at fundraisers at Harry Belafonte's house. He'd be laughing and talking, eating. . . . Martin loved a good party, and he had a devilish streak of humor." For much of the sixties, Ossie and Ruby attended marches and protests in the Deep South and in the Northeast. The couple appeared in dozens of stage and film productions but always managed to answer the call for help when the cause was something they believed in. Consequently, they have been on the front lines of some of the most controversial social movements of this century, including the fight to end racial discrimination in America, the debate over the Vietnam War, and the ongoing fight for equal education and economic opportunities for underrepresented citizens.

In a characteristically honest gesture, Ruby delivered a eulogy at the funeral of Malcolm X in 1965. Her words, soft-spoken and straight from the heart, included the now-legendary description of Malcolm X as "our shining black prince." To be sure, Ruby believed Malcolm was misunderstood and unfairly characterized through much of his life. "Malcolm was a credit to the world," Ruby said during a 1996 interview.

Over four decades Ruby acted in numerous stage and film productions, including a popular 1961 play *Purlie Victorius,* and *The Wedding Band,* for which she received a coveted Obie Award in 1972. Ruby delivered effective performances in two of the most controversial and successful feature films of the eighties, black film director Spike Lee's *Jungle Fever* and *Do the Right Thing.* In working with Lee, Ruby is carrying on her tradition of helping and encouraging younger artists. Audiences in the nineties would come to know her best from her many appearances on Public Broadcasting System programs and numerous network television movies. In 1991 her stunning performance in the network television film *Decoration Day* earned Ruby an Emmy Award for best performance by a supporting actress. Along with the Drama Desk Award for her role in the 1970 play *Boseman and Lena,* and the other acting honors Ruby received over the years, the Emmy Award provided solid proof of her status as a towering figure in the artistic community.

Even as Ruby continued refining and improving her craft, she explored other means of self-expression. Her books included a collection of essays and poems derived from her life and from African folk tales, *My One Good Nerve,* and a collection of humorous poems and essays titled *Take It From the Top.* Along the way, Ruby wrote and directed stage plays, notably *Zora Is My Name,* a 1983 production based on the life and work of Zora Neale Hurston.

In the nineties, Ruby remained an active part of the nation's creative and socially active community, appearing in benefit productions and fund-raising events for a host of worthy causes, including supporting black universities, increased arts education funding, and economic and educational summits. Along with her beloved husband, Ruby was inducted into the NAACP's Hall of Fame in 1989, after having been a member and staunch supporter of such civil rights groups as the Southern Christian Leadership Council, the Congress of Racial Equality, and the Student Nonviolent Coordinating Committee.

In 1998 she appeared in an off-Broadway play based on the folksy autobiographical stories contained in *My One Good Nerve.* After more than forty years in the public eye, Ruby entranced a new generation of fans with her touching monologues and sketches examining the joys, heartache, and triumphs of her life. "You may think it's hard to find humor in things like homelessness and overpopulation and racism. But I manage to do it," Ruby told the *Seattle Times.*

Indeed, Ruby's ability to extract the good from the bad is the hallmark of her philosophy. For the young black performers who follow in her footsteps, Ruby Dee's accomplishments serve as a formidable example of the enlightening, productive work they could someday contribute to America.

26

Shirley Chisholm

1924–

Standard-Bearer for Political Action

SHIRLEY CHISHOLM was the first black American woman elected to represent the people of New York in the U.S. Congress and the first to run as a Democratic candidate for president. For many black American women, especially those who came of age after the tumultuous sixties, Shirley Chisholm remains a superb role model.

From her crisp, rigorous speeches at Democratic conventions and on the floor of the House of Representatives to her fervent dedication to civil and human rights, Shirley's political example carried forward the proud legacy of black leadership in America. And for her double accomplishment of overcoming the racial and gender discrimination that were once rampant in the halls of power, Shirley Chisholm embodied the admirable determination, ethics, and compassion that define the democratic ideal in America.

Like the politically active black American women who came before her—including IDA B. WELLS BARNETT—Shirley forced the nation to reexamine its perception of politics. "Our country needs women's idealism and determination, perhaps more in politics than anywhere else," Shirley wrote in her autobiography, *Unbought and Unbossed*. Indeed, the journey from the humid, picturesque Caribbean island where Shirley spent her early years to her emergence as a political force on Capitol Hill is filled with important lessons about how women and minorities must struggle for equal access in America.

Born November 30, 1924, in Brooklyn, Shirley developed early on a clear sense of her potential. Her parents valued education, and Shirley endeavored to become a good student. Her earliest training would help her overcome several obstacles and disappointments as she eventually moved into the high-powered world of politics. Her mother and father, Ruby and Charles St. Hill, emigrated to America early in the twentieth century, part of a wave of newcomers who arrived seeking economic prosperity and democratic freedoms. The young couple eventually joined hundreds of other Caribbean immigrants in a budding community in Brooklyn. Yet as the economy waned during the late twenties, jobs for immigrants were harder to come by. Feeling that their children might have a more stable home life back on their tiny island, Ruby and Charles sent the three-year-old Shirley and her little sisters to live with her grandmother in Barbados. Shirley spent her early elementary education at the Vauxhall Coeducational School on that lush, sunny island. When she reached the age of seven, her parents sent for her, and Shirley returned to New York. Their economic status had improved enough to make it possible to provide a healthy and safe environment for Shirley.

At first, attending public schools in Brooklyn proved challenging for Shirley. She was demure and spoke English with the soft inflections of her Caribbean grandparents. Although she had been born in New York, Shirley was new to American culture, and administrators placed her in lower-level classes during her first year in Brooklyn schools. But Shirley soon showed herself to be a brilliant and dedicated student, and she excelled. In 1946 she received an undergraduate degree in sociology from Brooklyn College and instantly enrolled in Columbia University.

During this time Shirley met and fell in love with Conrad Chisholm. They married in 1949, the year Shirley received her master's degree from Columbia. She took a job at a day-care center in Brooklyn, a church-run program that served the needs of the working-class community where Shirley lived. Over the next decade Shirley's sharp intellect and deep devotion to the needs of children and parents led her to become more interested in politics. In advocating for health and government policies to improve the living conditions of the poor and working-class families she served, Shirley knew that serious changes had to occur at the political level.

In the late fifties Shirley became a child-care expert for New York City's Welfare Department and got an even closer look at the relationship between politics and the realities of citizens' daily lives. "Health is a human right," Shirley would tell her colleagues in Congress many years later, "not a privilege to be purchased."

Indeed, her run-ins with insensitive bureaucrats convinced Shirley that she had to take a more active role in the political process. In 1964 she ran for a seat in the New York Assembly and was elected; for the next four years, she honed her political skills. She kept true to her beliefs that children, immigrants, and working-class people deserved effective leadership, even if they lacked deep pockets or powerful business connections. And in 1968 she made history by carrying her constituents' concerns straight into the U.S. House of Representatives. For the first time in American history, a black woman had been elected from New York. Shirley had defeated former civil rights activist James Farmer. Her swearing-in was a momentous occasion, and it made headlines around the world when Shirley joined dozens of other freshman representatives on the steps of the Capitol for the opening of the Ninety-first Congress in early 1969.

Early into her first term as a congresswoman, Shirley distinguished herself as a tough negotiator and a supremely dignified politician. She became a vocal critic of many of the formal and informal congressional traditions which offended women: a lack of adequate restrooms for women; male representatives who cursed and made rude jokes in public, sometimes about women, sometimes about blacks or other ethnic minorities; policies and initiatives that were written, debated, and passed with barely a thought for their impact on the lives of American women.

When Shirley was assigned to a low-profile congressional committee, the Committee on Agriculture and to the Rural Development and Forestry Subcommittee, she protested loudly. As a representative from a primarily urban district, how could she possibly serve her constituents while mired in a committee focusing on the needs of rural Americans? Shirley felt she had been sandbagged by the white male congressmen and didn't hesitate to say so. Eventually, she was transferred to the Veterans Affairs Committee and later served on the Education Committee and the Labor Committee, where her knowledge and skills were better put to use.

During the next several years Shirley worked hard to improve conditions not only for her Brooklyn supporters but for all Americans. She joined a congressional consumer committee and cosponsored legislation to require consumer protection and product safety laws. As the Vietnam War raged on, Shirley joined a bipartisan committee seeking to end the military draft and make service in the armed forces voluntary. Shirley also fought to repeal part of an arcane federal security act that required the government to lock up suspected "subversives" in internment camps. Congress voted in September 1971 to do away with that portion of the Internal Security Act.

Shirley also had time to focus on international matters. She felt sympathy for those living in third world countries who suffered from intense forms of oppression. In the early seventies, years before most Americans took up the cause, Shirley began calling for an end to apartheid in South Africa. From the floor of the House Shirley urged her fellow legislators to pressure Britain to stop selling guns to the South African government.

Closer to home, she spoke out against discriminatory hiring practices of American manufacturers. Shirley knew that while the civil rights movement had produced some positive changes for black Americans, the problem of racism continued to dog the nation. "Racism is so universal in this country, so widespread and deep-seated, that it is invisible because it is so normal," she wrote in 1970.

Nonetheless, she also firmly believed in the power of the U.S. Constitution and the will of the people to effect change. Her New York constituents returned her to Congress for six consecutive terms, making Shirley a respected and reliable representative for almost twenty years. During much of the seventies Shirley fought successfully to raise the public's awareness about a host of health, safety, and economic issues, including child care, public education, and equal-employment opportunities. She secured increased funding for early-childhood education programs nationwide, as well as expanded day-care services for middle- and low-income families. In 1971 she cosponsored legislation guaranteeing funding for low-income families, a revolutionary concept designed to limit the slide into poverty for millions of unemployed Americans. With the success of the Adequate Income Act of 1971, Shirley realized she had the potential to impact the lives of millions of Americans sorely in need of an advocate. "What we need is more women in politics," Shirley wrote in 1970. "And not just to stuff envelopes, but to run for office. It is women who can bring empathy, tolerance, insight, patience, and persistence to government."

Her eloquence, diplomacy, intellectual integrity, and sense of personal responsibility eventually helped reshape the American political system. And while her triumphs and achievements stand as a benchmark of how far women and African Americans have advanced in this country, the struggles and obstacles she overcame on her ascent to political prominence still exist in many forms today.

On January 25, 1972, Shirley made history with her announcement that she would run for president. Her declaration set many different forces in motion. While millions of black Americans hailed her courageous step into the national limelight, Shirley received numerous death threats and menacing messages from white racists. But she was lauded by feminist activists like Gloria Steinem for her courage and vision and by white Americans who saw in her a brand of true leadership that was rare in national politics.

Coming as it did during the height of the feminist movement, Shirley's announcement riveted the nation. Yet, in the midst of the maelstrom, Shirley remained calm and determined. She crisscrossed the country in her campaign, and eventually entered the primaries in twelve states. But, in the end, she failed to garner enough votes to earn her the Democratic nomination, and she withdrew from the campaign. All the same, the nation had seen up close a vivid example of the strength, intelligence, and skill of black American womanhood.

During her brief but intense campaign, Shirley's image of uncompromising integrity and solid work ethic changed the outmoded perceptions that many held of black women as lazy or dumb or as holding loose morals. With her prim way of speaking, her thick eyeglasses, straight posture, and dignified bearing, Shirley showed all of America that black women had indeed earned an important place in our political arena. Her run for the presidency, however unsuccessful, had forever changed American electoral politics. Years later, when Geraldine Ferraro, another woman politician from New York, ran for the vice presidency, she cited Shirley as one of her heroines. During her long career in politics, Shirley also received numerous congressional and civic awards, including commendations from the National Association for the Advancement of Colored People, the Urban League, and the Black Women's Political Caucus.

Like BARBARA JORDAN, IDA B. WELLS BARNETT, and other black women political pioneers, Shirley's singular brand of personal strength, religious faith, and keen political skill helped her to add immeasurably to social progress in the United States in the twentieth century. Interviewed in a national newspaper in 1987, Shirley provided a good indication of the personal philosophy that helped her become one of the most important Americans in history: "Defeat should not be a source of discouragement," Shirley said, "but a stimulus to keep plotting."

27

Eartha Kitt

c. 1927–

A Classic Combination of Strength and Beauty

DURING HER LONG and illustrious performing career, Eartha Kitt has earned the praise and admiration of her industry peers, the national political leadership, and millions of fans around the globe. Nominations for several top entertainment awards—including Broadway's Tony, Hollywood's Oscar, and the music industry's Grammy—have been showered upon her.

Precocious, intelligent, and ravishingly beautiful, Eartha Mae Kitt joined an established dance troupe at age sixteen. By her early twenties she had become a principal dancer in the popular KATHERINE DUNHAM dance troupe and had traveled the world. She lived in Paris for many years, turned to solo performing, and won international acclaim with her riveting renditions of many popular standards.

Well into her "golden years," Eartha Kitt remained an active member of America's entertainment community. In the spring of 1998, she returned to the New York stage in a limited run of the classic children's musical *The Wizard of Oz*. Eartha also enjoyed a successful run at the prestigious Cafe Carlyle in New York in 1998, enthralling hundreds of fans and critics alike. Moreover, in television shows and feature films, Eartha Kitt continues to captivate viewers around the world with her distinctive acting style, sultry voice, and phenomenally confident presence.

Yet, Eartha has also endured unimaginable heartbreak and disappointment, including unhappy personal relationships and a bleak period of being ostracized by the United States government. Nonetheless, Eartha Kitt survived, and stands as a formidable embodiment of all the dedication, vision, and wisdom black American women have contributed to America. Throughout her storybook rise from a dirt poor Southern family to the top of the entertainment world, Eartha has always retained an understanding of how precarious good fortune can be. "When I see the homeless," Eartha told a *New York Times* interviewer, "I empathize. I know that there but for the grace of God go I."

Eartha Mae Kitt was born in North, a rural village in South Carolina, on January 26, 1927. Her mother struggled to provide for Eartha and her younger sister by working as an itinerant housekeeper.

Resources were scarce, and young Eartha's earliest memories include merciless hunger and the uncertainty of their existence. Eartha never knew her father, but because she was born with a light complexion, she suspected he might have been a white man. Consequently, Eartha spent many of her young years enduring the taunts and cruel comments of other black children in her rural village who called her "yella." And the most devastating blow of all came when Eartha's mother fell in love with a man who said he didn't want to care for the young girl and left her with her grandmother. "My mother felt a man was more important than her daughter," Eartha told *Ebony* magazine many years later. "I would never have left my child."

Eartha's mother had made a decision that would haunt Eartha for much of her life. She endured the loss of her mother the best way she could, by concentrating on helping her grandmother run her small farm and by avoiding the neighborhood children who so tormented her. It was a solitary period, but one that imbued Eartha with a strong will.

When she was not yet ten years old, a distant aunt in New York wrote to Eartha's grandmother and offered to raise the girl. Eartha was excited and somewhat frightened as she boarded a train bound for the big city. Arriving for the first time in her aunt's Harlem apartment, Eartha was wide-eyed at the electric lights and buzzing sounds of the dense urban environment. And although her relationship with her guardian would turn out to be difficult, Eartha managed to blossom in the artistic black community of Harlem in the thirties and forties. She had escaped the dire fate of black sharecroppers in the Deep South during the Great Depression, and Eartha was determined to make the best of her situation.

Eartha discovered she had a knack for languages. A quick study, she picked up Spanish from the Puerto Rican children who shared her uptown neighborhood and schools. Additionally, Eartha early on displayed an ear for music and studied closely the instructions of her music and choir teachers. Eventually, Eartha's spirited intelligence and uncanny musical ability came to impress one of them. At her teacher's urging, Eartha decided to apply to the exclusive New York High School for the Performing Arts and was thrilled to be accepted—especially since only a limited number of black students were admitted to the prestigious school each year.

Despite her newfound enjoyment in the classroom, Eartha's home life was far from happy. She began to stay away from her aunt's Harlem apartment, sleeping on couches in the homes of friends for weeks at a time. Occasionally, the teenage Eartha would even slip into vacant buildings or sleep on rooftops, so distraught was she with the deteriorating relationship with her guardian. She supported herself through menial jobs like sewing and scrimped and saved so that she could buy tickets to Broadway shows. Eartha was entranced by the elegance and sophistication of the theatre, and she vowed to someday make a name for herself in entertainment.

Eartha eventually drifted away from school. She felt disconnected and was disappointed in herself for blowing an opportunity to graduate from a prestigious high school. But good fortune was preparing to smile on Eartha. While she idly walked down a street in Harlem one day, Eartha was stopped by a dancer from a famous local company. Eartha was keenly aware of the Katherine Dunham Dance Company, especially since she had recently watched the troupe perform in a short film that was sandwiched between two feature movies she had watched while playing hooky from school. At the age of sixteen, Eartha auditioned for a spot in the company, and was accepted. For the next few years, she traveled the globe performing with Katherine Dunham's troupe. She felt she had found a home at last.

Through most of the forties Eartha remained abroad, giving breathtaking performances in South America, the Caribbean, and Europe. Indeed, she showed such an affinity for Paris that she ultimately left the dance troupe and struck out on her own. By the early fifties she had created a sensation on the cabaret scene in Paris. The French adored her saucy personality and throaty, seductive singing voice. Eartha was a lively spitfire, a witty and provocative performer who flirted outrageously with rich playboys and dignitaries and who enthralled audiences and critics alike. The legendary writer, director, and actor Orson Welles was one of Eartha's earliest fans, and he cast her irreverently as Helen of Troy in an experimental production of *Faust*. "I chose you to play this part because you are the most exciting woman in the world," Welles told Eartha. "You represent all women of all ages. You have no place or time," Eartha recalled Welles saying. During her years in Europe, she won over thousands of devoted fans. She also mastered many languages, including French, Italian, and Turkish.

In the fifties Eartha returned to America and appeared in a small but critically acclaimed motion picture directed by Orson Welles. She made a real splash when she appeared on Broadway in a revue called *New Faces of 1952*. Over the next several years, Eartha recorded several hit songs, including "C'est Si Bon," "Santa Baby," and "I Want to Be Evil." In the mid-sixties, she won over a whole new generation of fans—and became one of the first black women to star in a popular sitcom—by playing the role of the sinuous and villainous Catwoman on the ABC television series *Batman*.

Along the way Eartha developed a sharp political sensibility, which garnered headlines. At a social gathering at the White House during the Johnson administration, Eartha outraged some officials by speaking out against the ongoing Vietnam War. For years thereafter she found that few mainstream venues would book her, and she experienced some lean times. By the late seventies, after the public learned that Eartha had been the subject of a controversial government monitoring program, her career resumed. She appeared in numerous television shows and motion pictures, including *The Tonight Show* and the Eddie Murphy film *Boomerang*. She also continued to sing in top-notch cabarets in New York, Paris, San Francisco, and London.

Into her seventies Eartha remained an outspoken believer in her own unique power, a strength that helped her become one of the proudest examples of black women's positive influence in America. "My birth was never recorded," she told an interviewer in the eighties. "I have no birth certificate, therefore I do not exist, and that is why I am a legend."

28

Leontyne Price

1927–

A Voice of Classic Beauty

WITH DIGNITY, A STRONG BEARING, and breathtaking grace, Mary Violet Leontyne Price would triumph over the beliefs of many in the opera world who didn't think black women could sing classical music. But from her earliest days as an eager young music student in the Deep South, Leontyne displayed the inner strength and determination that would fortify her through many professional ups and downs.

In the lush landscape of Laurel, Mississippi, Leontyne grew up steeped in the traditions of her family's heritage. Her parents revered education as a way of improving the conditions of blacks, and Leontyne immersed herself in her studies. She also enthralled parishioners in her father's church with her strong singing voice. Her family and fellow parishioners quickly realized that the young girl had a startling talent, and they all encouraged her to pursue music. Thanks to their loving encouragement and strong religious faith, Leontyne would go on to one of the most sparkling careers in the history of American opera. She would reign as one of the leading divas in the world, winning over audiences and critics alike. A contemporary of MARIAN ANDERSON, Leontyne first had to overcome widely held prejudices against blacks in the nation's classical music community. And, like Anderson, she developed a top-notch singing voice that always defied her skeptics.

Born on February 10, 1927, Leontyne Price spent her earliest years in the bosom of a hardworking, loving family in the rural South. With the onset of the Great Depression few black families found it easy to make ends meet. All the same, Leontyne's parents insisted that their bright daughter remain in public school. Indeed, their vigilance and foresight would prove well-founded.

After graduating from segregated schools in Mississippi, she attended Central State College in Ohio, where she immersed herself in music studies. She wanted to continue her education after graduating, and yet lacked the money to attend a music college. But a friend of the family back in Laurel, Mississippi, had faith in Leontyne's shining talent and lent her the money to go to New York. And there, as a student at Juilliard College of Music, Leontyne began making a name for herself as a serious classical singer. She impressed her instructors at college with her clear soprano and striking stage presence; in 1952 she debuted on Broadway in the Virgil Thomson opera *Four Saints in Three Acts*. After that, she played the part of Bess in a revival of George and Ira Gershwin's opera *Porgy and Bess*. The revival was a smash, and Leontyne stayed with the production for two years, traveling to Europe and around the United States in a triumphant performance. In 1955 she created a national sensation when she appeared in an NBC broadcast of the opera *Tosca,* the first black woman ever to sing opera on national television. In 1957 she appeared in the starring role of *Dialogues of the Carmelites* with the San Francisco Opera Company, and her operatic career took off. Between the late fifties and the late seventies Leontyne sang the female lead in *Madama Butterfly, Aida, Tosca, La Bohème, Il Trovatore,* and *Don Giovanni.* In performances at the Metropolitan Opera, La Scala, and Prince Albert Hall, and other venues, Leontyne earned critical and popular praise like few divas before or since.

With her strong physical features and regal bearing, Leontyne provided a model of excellence in a highly specialized art. Moreover, she won numerous Grammy Awards, NAACP honors, a Kennedy Center honor, and other national artistic citations.

As a living example of the beauty, strength, compassion, and commitment that black American women have contributed to this nation, Leontyne gave voice to the voiceless during her long, fruitful career. It was an honor that she didn't take lightly, for Leontyne continued to recognize the uniquely influential role black Americans have played in forming the cultural landscape of the United States.

"We are positively a unique people," Leontyne told an interviewer during the seventies. "A breathtaking people. Anything we do, we do big! Despite attempts to stereotype us, we are crazy, individual, and uncorral-able people."

29

Maya Angelou

1928–

From Caged Bird to Voice of a Generation

ON A CRISP WINTER DAY in January 1993, Maya Angelou—actress, dancer, teacher, poet—made history. In reciting her touching poem "On the Pulse of Morning" at the request of President Bill Clinton, Maya became the second poet in this century to read verse at a presidential

167

inaugural. Not since 1961, when John F. Kennedy invited Robert Frost to read at his inauguration, had the nation heard the lyrical sounds of poetry ringing in a new administration. And though America had gone through immense changes between the early nineteen sixties and nineties, it was no less reassuring to witness a strong, elegant black woman greet the dawn of a new political era.

For Maya Angelou the occasion marked a great personal triumph. After an eventful life of hardships, spiritual redemption, artistic success, and political controversy, Maya offered the nation a spectacular image of a survivor. Through her poetry, her academic work, and her versatile artistic explorations, Maya remained a perfect embodiment of the great impact black American women have had on this nation. And while some circumstances and situations in her life were harrowing, even devastating, Maya's greatest lesson comes from her belief in forgiveness and personal evolution.

"What I learned to do many years ago was to forgive myself," Maya said in a 1995 interview in the journal *In Context*. "It is very important for every human being to forgive herself or himself, because if you live, you will make mistakes. It is inevitable. Only the angels, the cherubim, and about three rocks don't make mistakes."

With an admirable gift for capturing the mysterious rhythms of language and human interaction, Maya has enthralled millions of readers, theatergoers, and film fans during more than thirty years in the public eye. Her autobiographical books—including the astonishing *I Know Why the Caged Bird Sings*—continue selling hundreds of thousands of copies each year, while recordings of her many poems are popular titles in record stores around the world. For television titan OPRAH WINFREY, Maya was a "spiritual force," a wise and friendly guide whose insights helped Oprah through many personal and professional crises. Among black writers like James Baldwin, TONI MORRISON, and Alex Haley, Maya was a loyal and valuable peer. Indeed, after her debut on the Broadway stage in a revival of Gershwin's *Porgy and Bess,* in 1953, Maya thrilled and enlightened the American public with her dynamic presence and astute outlook. From Africa—where she lived for a time— to England, Asia, and South America, millions of literary fans cherish and revered Maya Angelou, a proud black woman who spoke more than six languages fluently and possessed an uncanny ability to communicate across class, gender, and racial divides.

Her personal journey is inspiring for many reasons, and numerous literary critics and faithful readers have identified the universality of Maya's life story. From a shy, awkward girl who once refused to speak for five years after suffering a devastating sexual trauma, Maya rebounded to become a leading artistic figure in the world community. Characteristically straightforward, Maya always claimed the right to identify and define the meaning of her life on her own terms. "One isn't necessarily born with courage, but one is born with potential," Maya said during a 1988 interview. "And without courage, we cannot practice any other virtue with consistency. We can't be kind, true, merciful, generous, or honest."

Maya's courageous life began in St. Louis, Missouri, on April 4, 1928. Her parents, Bailey Johnson and Vivian Baxter, were struggling to make ends meet in the urban surroundings of bustling St. Louis. They had named their only daughter Marguerite Ann Johnson, but their son nicknamed her Maya. Early on, her parents moved west, settling in California. By the time Maya was four, with her parents' marriage dissolving, she and her older brother, Bailey, were sent to live with their grandmother in rural Arkansas. For the shy, awkward little girl, the new surroundings provided a fascinating mixture of history and promise. In *I Know Why the Caged Bird Sings* she describes learning about life, religion, and human nature at the apron strings of her beloved grandmother, Annie Henderson, whom Maya and Bailey called Momma.

Annie Henderson, a prominent member of the black community in tiny Stamps, Arkansas, owned the only general store that served blacks in the segregated town. Helping her grandmother brought structure and adventure to Maya's days, even if she sometimes feared her grandmother's strict constitution.

To the sensitive young girl, the world of sharecroppers and cottonpickers who shopped at her grandmother's store was strange. For a decade Maya watched as the poor black men and women of Stamps struggled to make ends meet on the paltry sums they earned from white landowners. Annie Henderson was a generous and fair storekeeper, and she often extended credit to customers who desperately needed to feed their families. "No matter how much [cotton] they had picked, it wasn't enough," Maya recalled. "Their wages wouldn't even get them out of debt to my grandmother, not to mention the staggering bill that waited on them at the white commissary downtown." Such dire poverty left a deep mark on Maya's burgeoning sense of justice, and in later years she became a powerful advocate of increasing social services and economic opportunities for rural and low-income families.

During her formative years in Stamps, Maya got her first exposure to class differences and the deeply entrenched racial stereotypes that shaped the lives of blacks and whites in the Deep South. Tall for her age, Maya suffered the taunts and jeers of local children who refused to accept the gangly outsider. She quickly developed a watchful nature as a form of self-defense. Along with her brother, Bailey, Maya attended the local colored church and took part in school activities.

But the bittersweet years with her grandmother in sleepy Stamps ended all too soon. When her father unexpectedly turned up one day, Maya had no way of knowing that her time in Arkansas was, for the time being, drawing to a close. Her father was a big man with an impressive car and hilarious stories about his life in California.

As it turned out, Maya and her brother would spend the next year back in St. Louis with their mother, Vivian Baxter, and their formidable maternal grandmother. It was an abrupt change in lifestyle, but Maya and her brother adjusted as best they could. Their mother's family was socially prominent in the black St. Louis community. Their grandmother was a ward captain and the mother of several strong sons with notoriously short tempers.

More important, in St. Louis, Maya and her brother were reunited with their glamorous mother. She danced and sang in local taverns. It was here that Maya first developed a love of dance and music that would shape her young adult life. And, sadly, it was here that the boyfriend of Maya's mother, "Mr. Freeman," began making sexual advances toward eight-year-old Maya.

Years later, in *I Know Why the Caged Bird Sings*, Maya described her rape in vivid detail. When the book was first published in 1970, many conservative educators and politicians complained that the book was harmful and that Maya was irresponsible for describing what had happened to her. Yet because she was brutally honest in her exploration of innocence lost, the controversy eventually cooled down. The book remains one of the most influential autobiographies ever written. It "liberates the reader into life simply because Maya Angelou confronts her own life with such a moving wonder, such a luminous dignity," said the famous black writer James Baldwin in 1970. "I have no words for this achievement, but I know that not since the days of my childhood, when the people in books were more real than the people one saw every day, have I found myself so moved."

Indeed, the young Maya was forever affected by what happened to her at the hands of Freeman. Although he was eventually arrested and tried for the rape, a lawyer succeeded in getting him out on bail. Weeks later, her mother's ex-boyfriend was found dead behind a St. Louis slaughterhouse, apparently beaten to death. The violence of the events, the rape and the death of Freeman, traumatized Maya. She stopped talking. In her young mind, speaking out (as she had done after the rape) could only cause trouble, so Maya resolved to not speak again.

"I had to stop talking," Maya recalled in *I Know Why the Caged Bird Sings*. "I discovered that to achieve perfect personal silence all I had to do was to attach myself leechlike to sound. I began to listen to everything. I probably hoped that after I had heard all the sounds, really heard them and packed them down, deep in my ears, the world would be quiet around me." For the next several years, she spoke only to Bailey. Maya shared a close bond with her only brother during her earliest years and looked to him for advice and protection. To be sure, Bailey was a friend and trusted confidant, the brave and smart older brother who had stuck by Maya through so many challenging situations.

At first, Maya's muteness was viewed by her family as an odd but understandable response to the trauma she had endured. But over time, her silence came to infuriate her St. Louis family, and eventually Maya and Bailey were sent back to their paternal grandmother in Stamps. There, a wise local woman helped draw Maya out of her self-imposed silence by encouraging her to read classic literature and poetry aloud. "To be . . . invited into the private lives of strangers, and to share their joys and fears, was a chance to exchange the Southern bitter worm-wood for a cup of mead with Beowulf, or a hot cup of tea and milk with Oliver Twist," Maya wrote years later. "When I said aloud, 'It is a far, far better thing I do, than I have ever done . . .' tears of love filled my eyes at my selflessness."

While still an adolescent, Maya learned valuable lessons about self-reliance and the warmth of community during her second period living with her grandmother in Stamps. For a while, she worked in the home of a wealthy white woman, assisting the kitchen staff and doing minor chores. It was an enlightening experience, even if Maya sometimes was made to feel dumb and clumsy by the white matron and her exacting maid. The white woman was unreasonably demanding, and her maid—Maya's boss—seemed content to carry out even her most outrageous requests. For Maya, it was pure drudgery, and she left the job as quickly as possible.

Along the way, Maya soaked in the rich celebrations of life in segregated Arkansas. There was much camaraderie among blacks, and Maya recalls eagerly observing the happiness her relatives expressed when the black heavyweight boxer Joe Louis fought for the world championship. It was the late thirties, decades before the civil rights movement brought the slow but sweeping changes of integration. Blacks across the nation—and especially in the Deep South—greeted with anxiousness and pride each radio broadcast of bouts between Joe Louis, the "Brown Bomber," and his white opponents.

At the general store owned by Maya's grandmother, dozens of local residents gathered to listen to the fights, and when Louis was declared the heavyweight champion of the world, all of black Stamps celebrated. Maya wrote of the pride that blacks felt over Louis's achievement: "Champion of the world. A Black boy. Some Black mother's son. He was the strongest man in the world. People drank Coca-Colas like ambrosia and ate candy bars like Christmas."

Eventually, however, Maya's world would change again. Her beloved grandmother decided that Maya and Bailey, now in their early teens, should return to live with their parents. Finally, the bewildered youngsters reached the mysterious place they had only dreamed about —California. It was hard saying goodbye to their beloved Momma, but Maya and her brother were instantly enchanted by their new life with their own mother, a high-spirited woman. She worked in restaurants and bars in Oakland, and ran a profitable weekly card game. Effervescent and easygoing, Vivian Baxter loved her two children, and worked hard to support them.

Maya was enjoying her new life and began, for the first time, feeling confident in herself. As World War II broke out, she was attending her first integrated school, Washington High in San Francisco's fog-shrouded Richmond District. When a smart and generous English teacher recognized Maya's talent for reading and speaking, she recommended the blossoming young girl for a scholarship to a local theatre arts program. There, Maya at last came out of her shell, learning to dance, act, and sing in a special school for young adults: she was showing signs of the stately, dignified woman she would ultimately become.

All the same, when Maya's charming father asked her to spend summer vacation with him and his new girlfriend in Southern California, Maya eagerly packed her bags. During the weeks she spent with her adventuresome father—who took her to a Mexican cantina for a festive evening of drinking and dancing—Maya discovered the enriching world of other ethnic groups, the spicy fragrances and lyrical language of Latin America. When she had a falling out with her father's girlfriend, Maya ran away from her father's home and lived for the next month with a merry band of teenagers in a junkyard. It was an eye-opening experience. Maya felt for the first time that she had found a group of peers who did not judge her by her looks or by her possessions. She reveled in the independence of the little community and took pride in being able to provide for herself by working menial jobs. After a month on her own, she phoned her mother and asked her to send a plane ticket so that Maya could return to her.

At age fifteen, she felt newly liberated. She returned to her mother in San Francisco with a worldly outlook. "I reasoned that I had given up some youth for knowledge, but my gain was more valuable than my loss," Maya said. Therein lay the roots of Maya's guiding philosophy—the willingness to continue learning as much as possible and the ability to forgive oneself and others for shortcomings. Over the next three decades, Maya's life was a swirl of activity and growth. She took a job as a streetcar conductor in San Francisco, becoming the first black woman to hold such a job. She graduated from high school and became pregnant after a brief tryst with a neighborhood teen. Her mother, Vivian, helped her decipher the mysteries of parenting, and Maya adored her son, Guy Johnson.

As the post–World War II economic boom brought prosperity and good times to much of America, Maya found plenty of outlets for her growing creativity. She became a popular dancer in a famous North Beach nightclub in San Francisco and continued improving her acting and performing skills. She won a coveted role in a revival of *Porgy and Bess* and thrilled to the sights and sounds of foreign lands when the opera toured the world. On her travels, Maya met a dashing military man named Tosh Angelou, and they married.

For several years, Maya lived in exotic cities in Egypt and Africa and edited a political magazine. Returning to America in the sixties, Maya studied dance with such luminaries as Martha Graham and Pearl Primus and appeared in numerous plays and revues. By the end of the decade her political sensibility had sharpened, and Maya threw herself into the civil rights movement. She had also begun writing plays and poems, and some of her works became popular additions to regional theatre groups in New York and California.

When Dr. Martin Luther King Jr. asked Maya to head the northern office of the Southern Christian Leadership Conference (SCLC), she agreed. And when King was assassinated in 1968, Maya joined thousands of Americans in mourning his loss. When *I Know Why the Caged Bird Sings* was published in 1970, Maya's frank story of her youth set off a cascade of publicity. Over the next decade she produced an impressive array of poetry and nonfiction, and starred in several critically acclaimed plays. She was amazingly prolific, earning nominations for a National Book Award and the Pulitzer Prize for her poetry and autobiographical writing. She wrote a screenplay called *Georgia, Georgia* and became the first black American woman to see her own script transferred onto the big screen. She played a featured role in the landmark television series of Alex Haley's prize-winning novel *Roots*.

Over the years, Maya continued traveling and lecturing around the world, especially in Africa, where she spent many months among the people of Ghana. Open-minded and generous, Maya had a knack for enveloping the customs and rituals of those around her, and she became an important cultural ambassador to many nations. In return, several presidents, including Jimmy Carter, Gerald Ford, and Bill Clinton, turned to Maya to serve on various humanitarian and artistic commissions. Maya was awarded honorary degrees and received dozens of commendations, including being named 1975 Woman of the Year by *Ladies' Home Journal*.

Throughout a remarkable life of tragedy and success, Maya remained a grounded and realistic individual. Her early trauma, and the guilt which dogged her for years thereafter, enabled Maya to grow into an astonishingly sensitive and astute woman. In the eighties she accepted a professorship at Wake Forest University in North Carolina and embarked on a new life as the preeminent teacher of writing, folklore, and poetry in America. For millions of young television viewers in the nineties, Maya was probably best known as the woman Oprah Winfrey called her friend and advisor.

With more than two dozen award-winning books to her credit— including *I Know Why the Caged Bird Sings, All God's Children Need Traveling Shoes,* and *Gather Together in My Name*—Maya Angelou stood as a literary icon of formidable influence and wisdom. Undeniably, her keen eye for the complexities of life and her remarkable talent for capturing the rhythms and mysteries of the human experience will provide meaningful lessons for generations of readers to come. Her role in shaping America's understanding of women, people of color, and the shared humanity of all world citizens was undeniable.

As always, Maya best summed up the guiding principle that made her one of the most revered women in the United States: "I have forgiven myself," she said in a 1985 interview. "I'll make change. Once that forgiveness has taken place you can console yourself with the knowledge that a diamond is the result of extreme pressure. . . . Pressure can change you into something quite precious, quite wonderful, quite beautiful and extremely hard."

30

Lorraine Hansberry

1930–1965

Voicing Truth in Three Acts

DURING HER TRAGICALLY SHORT LIFE Lorraine Hansberry produced a small body of work that remains a benchmark of excellence in contemporary theatre. In *A Raisin in the Sun,* her first published play, Lorraine successfully dramatized important social issues in a piquant family setting that engaged and enlightened critics and the public alike when it opened on Broadway in 1959. At age twenty-nine, after a charmed and

challenging youth in Chicago's middle-class black community, she had
reached a pinnacle of artistic success. By the time she reached her early
thirties, Lorraine was poised for greatness, a smart, successful, hardworking black woman playwright.

Beautiful and outspoken, Lorraine was determined to bring her
impressive artistic gift to bear on the pressing issues of the day—racial
inequality and gender and class divisions. As the daughter of a prominent Chicago businessman, Lorraine had lived a fairly comfortable life,
albeit one that was informed by the poverty and lack of opportunity
that many thousands of other black Chicagoans faced. Lorraine's parents
might have sent her to a private school, but they wanted her to know the
reality of life for most African Americans in Chicago in the thirties and
forties. The twelve years that Lorraine spent in poorly funded, primarily
black public schools forever shaped her political outlook.

When she died unexpectedly in her early thirties, just as her second
play was opening, the community of artists who had come to love and
respect her was overwhelmed by its sense of loss. "Sweet Lorraine,"
the writer James Baldwin remarked softly upon learning of her death,
and millions of fans around the nation identified with his sadness. She
had done the unthinkable in her short life, on and off the public stage:
She had married a white man in the days before the civil rights movement began breaking down the prejudice against interracial relationships; and she had written for a pioneering literary journal founded by
one of the world's greatest performers and controversial political
activists, Paul Robeson. Lorraine had managed, in an amazingly short
time, to speak truth in the face of injustice.

Along the way she had produced a gem of a play. Indeed, decades
after its debut at the Ethel Barrymore Theatre in New York, *A Raisin in
the Sun,* still effectively conveys the poignancy, absurdity, and emotional
conundrum of race relations in America. It presaged the roiling activism
and public demonstrations that came to pass with the civil rights era,
and laid bare the heart of black Americans' despair over racial discrimination. Lorraine Hansberry had a knack for stating the truth as
she knew it.

Born on May 19, 1930, Lorraine Hansberry was the cherished
daughter of Carl and Nan Hansberry. In their world, African Americans
were a vital part of the nation's fabric, and Carl Hansberry saw himself
as a productive part of Chicago's economic engine. A former political
candidate, the owner of a successful real estate management business,

Hansberry saw no reason why his family should not share in one important aspect of the American Dream: a nice life in a nice house in a nice neighborhood. So while Lorraine was in the primary grades in Chicago's predominantly black public schools, Carl Hansberry sued a white landowner and the city of Chicago, charging that the unstated, "separate-but-equal" housing politics were exclusionary and unfair. And shortly after Lorraine's tenth birthday, following a 1940 Supreme Court decision in Hansberry's favor, the family moved into an all-white suburb.

Lorraine was thrust into a new world. On the good side, her inquisitive nature had plenty of new questions to ponder: Why were human beings cruel to each other? How could blacks and whites hate each other if they did not even know each other? On the downside, Lorraine found herself in a sea of unfriendly faces, and the sensitive young girl endured taunts and threats from many of the white children in her new neighborhood.

Nonetheless, Carl and Nan Hansberry saw early indications of Lorraine's sharp intellect and strongly encouraged her to excel in school. It sometimes made for awkward social moments, but Lorraine continued attending the underfunded schools in a black neighborhood while she struggled to adjust to living in a predominantly white neighborhood. These early years of living what W. E. B. Du Bois called the "duality" of the black experience, the process of learning to move between the black and white worlds, shaped Lorraine into a sublimely confident individual.

Wisely, her parents believed that Lorraine had to learn to appreciate the world in which many blacks lived and to empathize with those who had not managed to achieve the American Dream. Moreover, Lorraine's parents were popular members of the thriving black middle class in Chicago. Their stately home became a gathering spot for visiting black intellectuals and entertainers, including Langston Hughes and Du Bois.

For a time, young Lorraine directed her burgeoning creativity into drawing and graphics, and she dreamed of attending the prestigious Art Institute of Chicago after graduating from high school. (She accomplished this, but ultimately transferred to the University of Wisconsin at Madison.) Throughout, Lorraine was an astute observer of human relationships.

Like thousands of other aspiring writers and artists, Lorraine viewed

New York in the early fifties as a creative mecca. Helped along by her parents' connections and her own growing list of artistic friends, Lorraine settled in Manhattan at the beginning of the black arts movement. In Harlem and Greenwich Village, young writers and actors like James Baldwin, NIKKI GIOVANNI, Harry Belafonte, and RUBY DEE were developing a unique brand of artistic activism.

Lorraine immediately landed a writing and editing job at *Freedom,* the magazine founded by Paul Robeson. She flung herself wholeheartedly into the stimulating environment. Her keen editing skills and flair for writing earned her the respect of the black intellectual community. Lorraine soaked in the intriguing flavors of her new surroundings, frequenting poetry readings, art galleries, and other cultural events in the vanguard of artistic expression. While the troubling specter of racism remained a fact of life, Lorraine had at last found an environment in which race relations seemed comfortable. And when she met a handsome young writer on a picket line at a local university—black athletes were excluded from its teams—it hardly mattered to Lorraine that he was white and Jewish. In a matter of weeks, Lorraine and Robert Nemiroff became virtually inseparable.

Lorraine's parents had believed strongly in integration and raised Lorraine to see the potential for goodness in everyone, regardless of their color. All the same, Lorraine startled them by marrying Nemiroff, and her decision caused a temporary rift in her family. Yet she loved Nemiroff, a friendly, thoughtful writer who shared her sense of humanity and appreciation of art and culture. And when his work began to pick up, Lorraine turned her attention full-time to writing something that had been on her mind for many years: the story of her parents' fight to move into an all-white Chicago neighborhood.

The result was a masterpiece of dramatic social commentary. In *A Raisin in the Sun,* the story of the Younger family is a study in modern relationships as well as a pointed depiction of the lingering impact of slavery and racism in America. She took the title from a Langston Hughes poem, "Harlem," about hopes dashed, that asks what happens to a dream deferred, and Lorraine chose it for its lyricism and poignant sadness. To this day the play remains one of the most popular modern dramas, a favorite of regional theatre groups and high school and university drama departments. Over the years many notable actors, among them Sidney Poitier, Danny Glover, Louis Gossett Jr., Ossie Davis, and

Ruby Dee, have starred in productions of *A Raisin in the Sun*. Considering the finely tuned action of the piece, it's no wonder.

Through the eyes of Mama, a widowed family matriarch; Walter, her son, an ambitious young black man; Ruth, his wife, a frustrated, well-meaning homemaker; and Beneatha, the daughter who is striving for her college degree while undergoing a racial identity crisis, Lorraine built a story of love, disappointment, and spiritual redemption. Her plot involves an honest, hardworking black family seeking to better its station in life. But in Chicago in the early forties, most blacks had no opportunity to earn more than a subsistence income.

For Walter Younger, anger and resentment have coiled within him so tight that he turns to drink. His job as a chauffeur pays little and his efforts to find more gainful employment are repeatedly thwarted by racial discrimination. For Lena, the family matriarch still mourning the death of her husband, all she wants is for her children to become productive, respectable adults. When the family comes into a financial windfall in the form of insurance money, a contretemps develops over how to spend the money. For Mama, a home in the suburbs, away from the dirt and grime of their inner-city tenement, is unquestionably the solution; for Walter, owning a local bar is his vision of securing the family's future.

One fateful night Walter, fed up with his family's refusal to recognize his dream, explodes: "Man say to his woman, 'I got me a dream.' His woman say, 'Eat your eggs.' I say, 'I got to take hold of this here world, baby!' And the woman say, 'Eat your eggs and go to work!' The man say, 'I got to change my life, I'm choking to death, baby!' And all his woman say is, 'Your eggs is getting cold!' "

Lorraine's exploration of the mother-son construct, the husband-wife dilemma, and the tense relationships of blacks and whites is unpredictable and familiar all at once.

While Lorraine didn't think of herself as a prodigy, her first play was widely considered a flawless achievement. When the promising young director Lloyd Richards agreed to direct it, Lorraine was flattered and anxious. As the play went into readings, Lorraine struggled with tying together all the important points she hoped to make: that men and women must work harder at understanding each other, and that black Americans must continue finding the moral high ground in the midst of seemingly insurmountable opposition.

On the night of March 11, 1959, the play opened at the Ethel Barrymore Theatre on Broadway. By the onset of spring, Lorraine had emerged as a bona fide star of the theatre, a young black playwright with an innovative, astoundingly successful play to her credit.

Hailed by critics as an impressive debut and a thoughtful treatment of race relations in America, *A Raisin in the Sun* went on to win the coveted New York Drama Critics Circle Award for best dramatic play of 1959. Moreover, the play drew thousands of black Americans to the Barrymore, a venue that did not often offer mainstream productions with themes of direct concern to African-American theatergoers. When the prestigious New York Drama Critics Circle Awards were announced, Lorraine's name and image were broadcast worldwide. At age twenty-nine, she had successfully bridged her two worlds, finding a remarkable union between her political and social beliefs and her artistic vision.

It was an exhilarating time, and Lorraine relished the praise even as she dug into her next project. *The Sign in Sidney Brustein's Window,* Lorraine's second play, focused on the life of a "Jewish intellectual in Greenwich Village," as she described it. While she worked, Lorraine kept her eyes on the developing social movements of the day. At that time, the Deep South was a cauldron of racial unrest. Like other Americans, Lorraine watched in horror as televised images of hundreds of blacks being beaten by white racists hit the airwaves. As Lorraine saw it, the issue of racial oppression, whether in the form of housing discrimination or all-out violence, was vividly captured by the scenes of blacks in cities like Greensboro, North Carolina, being assaulted for trying to integrate public spaces.

Ever outspoken, Lorraine became a popular visiting lecturer at colleges and drama clubs around New York. She frequently denounced the inhumanities that were rending the nation's communities. As an amateur historian, Lorraine drew parallels between the social upheaval of America in the sixties and the ancient struggle for equality, a history that must be considered in order to better understand modern conditions.

In early 1964, during a now-famous speech at a Town Hall Forum in New York, Lorraine declared: "Negro protest and revolt is not new. It is as old as the slave trade. Negroes came here fighting back. They mutinied on the high seas; they organized hundreds of insurrections which were ruthlessly and predictably put down; they indulged in sabotage, mutilation, murder, and flight" in the quest for freedom.

By the early sixties, Lorraine was undergoing a period of personal growth, and her relationship with Nemiroff had become strained. They divorced amicably, and Lorraine continued writing, completing several short stories and plays between 1961 and 1964. By the end of 1964, as her second play was about to enter previews, Lorraine began experiencing severe headaches. She had for years been a night owl, and enjoyed smoking cigarettes and the occasional cocktail while out on the town. When she began having fainting spells in the winter of 1964, she wrote it off to stress. Her closest friends insisted she see a doctor. Their worst fears were confirmed.

On January 12, 1965, Lorraine Hansberry died from a brain tumor. *The Sign in Sydney Brustein's Window* opened that same night, and the entire theater district seemed to register sadness over her death.

Months earlier, Lorraine had written a thoughtful assessment of her most beloved work, *A Raisin in the Sun,* pinpointing with amazing clarity what she viewed as the play's shortcomings. Her self-criticism was admirably objective and succinct. "A central character, as such, is lacking from 'Raisin,'" Lorraine wrote. "I should be delighted to pretend that it was inventiveness, as some suggest for me. But it is also craft inadequacy and creative indecision. The result is that neither Walter nor Mama Younger loom large enough to . . . command the play. I consider it an enormous dramatic fault, if no one else does."

All the same, Lorraine's seminal work still stands as a shining example of how black women have shaped the nation's understanding of the intricacies of personal relationships. After her death, a flurry of publication of Lorraine's other works ensued. Although *The Sign in Sidney Brustein's Window* did not fare well on Broadway, other works met critical acclaim upon their posthumous publication, including the unfinished play *Les Blancs;* a short story, "The Drinking Gourd"; and her autobiography, *To Be Young, Gifted and Black.*

In perhaps the greatest tribute of all, Lorraine's screenplay for the motion picture version of *A Raisin in the Sun* was roundly hailed as one of the best film adaptations of a stage play to appear on the screen in decades. For modern black women writers like Julie Dash and Ntozoke Shange, Lorraine Hansberry cleared a path for their vision, even as she set a towering standard of theatrical excellence.

31

Odetta

1930–

Strumming the Sounds of Freedom

FOR MORE THAN A DECADE in the nineteen fifties and sixties, Odetta Holmes reigned as a vital addition to the world of popular folk music. Her stirring versions of many blues and folk standards, including "John Henry" and "If I Had a Hammer," served as part of the artistic back-drop of the social movements of the era.

With a deep, resonant voice and hearty respect for folk tales and myths handed down by generations of black women, Odetta took to the stage by herself for the first time in a Los Angeles nightspot, the Turnabout Club, in 1949. At first the crowd was shocked to see a confident-looking young black woman command the stage. But by the end of her first few solo outings on the growing pop and rock scene, Odetta had become a star.

Drawing on the tradition established by blues and gospel singers like the "Empress of the Blues," BESSIE SMITH, and the Deep South guitarist Leadbelly, Odetta became a shining example of black women's significant contribution to the nation's popular culture. "Folk music straightened my spine, and kinked up my hair," Odetta told an interviewer in 1970, referring to the heritage she discovered by becoming a folksinger. "It has given me a sense of us as a people."

Born in Birmingham, Alabama, on December 31, 1930, Odetta Holmes was the studious and good-natured child of Reuben and Flora Holmes. Seeking work, her family moved to the sunny environment of Los Angeles during the thirties, and Odetta was drawn to performing arts while still in high school. She participated in most of the school's theatrical events and showed an affinity for the music lessons she took. She excelled in the choir and became a star singer by the time she was a sophomore.

For a time she thought she might like to become a classical singer, but that changed after she accompanied some friends to a local coffeehouse where some up-and-coming musicians were performing. While still an undergraduate at Los Angeles City College, Odetta took to showing up at the nightclubs and coffeehouses around Los Angeles. Usually accompanying herself on guitar, she pioneered an intriguing style of folksinging. Combining the popular, spare performing style of the day with age-old blues and gospel music traits, Odetta riveted audiences by spinning mesmerizing tales of personal relationships, racial injustice, and folk myths. Because of her ties to the Deep South, she had a rich understanding and appreciation of the strong blues and gospel strains that characterized much of traditional American folk music.

Consequently, Odetta succeeded in earning a devoted following. By the early sixties, as the folk music scene expanded worldwide, she had become a sensation, appearing on stages from Canada to England to New York and Washington, D.C. And wherever she traveled, she carried along her most valued possession: an old, wooden acoustic guitar she had nicknamed Baby. Playing with a unique strumming style that could sound like thunder, rain, a train, or the wind through the trees, Odetta enthralled audiences with her stunning folk renditions. In describing her trademark and hard-to-copy playing style, Odetta told a reporter from *Frets* magazine that she enjoyed varying her rhythmic repertoire: "I'll play the same few chords, but by varying my strumming, by harmonizing notes within a chord and picking some other notes, I'll achieve the sounds of fullness. I love the opposite forces I can create by singing a smooth melody line and hearing my rhythm playing churning away beneath it. I love those dramatics in music."

Odetta twice played special concerts at Carnegie Hall, and was invited to a command performance at the White House in 1963. She also appeared on network television programs, including a guest spot on a Harry Belafonte variety show.

She also became a tireless researcher of indigenous forms of music and frequented the Library of Congress to draw on the extensive musical archive there. She performed with such popular music luminaries as Count Basie, Bob Dylan, and Peter, Paul, and Mary, and was the proud recipient of numerous music industry awards, including the coveted Grammy. Her renditions of Negro spirituals such as "Ain't No Grave Can Hold Me Down" and "Hold On" remain the definitive modern recordings of a unique American art form.

Often garbed in beautiful African robes and headdresses, Odetta cut a dignified figure on stage. She made several television and concert appearances with performers like Joan Baez and Harry Belafonte over the years, but Odetta usually preferred to take the stage alone. The freedom to improvise was always an important part of her stage success.

In 1989 Odetta reemerged at the top of the popular music scene by taking part in a series of socially conscious fund-raisers called the Voice of Change series. As always, Odetta enraptured her fans with her strong, distinctive strumming and clear singing voice. "She strung together blues and spirituals, many of them unfamiliar," said a *New York Times* reviewer. "Over the steady rhythm of her guitar and her tapping foot, she sent her voice to its clear heights and its nasal depths, bringing out the field holler roots of her music."

Once again, a new generation of music lovers had discovered the soul-stirring benefits of that rich legacy of blues, gospel, and folk music. Thanks to Odetta, the voice of the past promises to be a part of America's future.

32

Toni Morrison

1931–

International Icon, American Literary Legend

WHEN CHLOE ANTHONY WOFFORD was born in Lorain, Ohio, in 1931, few Americans ever thought of black women as serious writers. Now, after an amazing writing career that has captured the subtleties, triumphs, and tragedies of black American life, Toni Morrison is the preeminent example of literary success in the twentieth century. Author and editor of several books, Toni Morrison enjoys both critical and popular success, a rarity for almost any writer in the competitive world of letters. But Toni Morrison is far from being just "any" writer. While some critics find her writing obscure and oblique, they also recognize her knack for shedding new light on the human heart—and on what she calls "the nature of oppression."

Toni Morrison, perhaps more than any other American writer—black or white, male or female—has made it safe for American readers to look within themselves and ask the difficult questions about what it means to be human. Her novel about the lingering impact of slavery, *Beloved,* won the Pulitzer Prize for fiction writing in 1987. That would have been a crowning achievement in any writer's career, but for Toni Morrison, more world-class honors would lie ahead. In 1993 she became the first black American woman to receive the prestigious Nobel Prize in Literature.

The Stockholm awards ceremony was a glittering event that drew worldwide attention to her. Dressed in a stately gown and with her thick, graying hair pulled back majestically, Toni Morrison stood as a powerful testament to all that black women have achieved in America. It was a touching visual image, and one that Toni says she never could have imagined when she was growing up in a small Midwestern city. Back then, during the Great Depression, African Americans were still struggling with the legacy of slavery, still working in low-rung, menial jobs—the backbreaking jobs that contributed to the nation's development but were hardly conducive to artistic creativity.

Located on the shore of Lake Erie, Lorain, Ohio, in the nineteen thirties was a quiet town with a blue-collar population of both blacks and whites. The child who would become Toni Morrison lived in a modest neighborhood with her mother and father and four siblings. Theirs was a proud family. But their existence was typical for African Americans who resided in Northern cities: Many blacks from the Deep South had arrived in the North seeking equal opportunities only to find that these cities were in fact still stained with segregation. No official color bars existed, but jobs for African Americans were low-paying and scarce, and the power structure of most towns was generally unsympathetic to nonwhite residents.

Chloe Anthony Wofford was the second of four children born to George and Ramah Wofford. (Years later, she shortened her middle name to Toni, and stopped using Chloe altogether because people found it difficult to pronounce.) During a 1998 interview with CBS television's *60 Minutes,* Morrison recalled her father as a stern but complicated man. A shipyard worker, he had moved to Ohio from the Deep South to escape the strangling grip of white supremacy. He worked numerous jobs to support his family during the twenties and thirties and bought a home in a racially mixed section of Lorain. George Wofford had witnessed harsh discrimination by whites during his Southern childhood, and he held strong prejudices. "He believed that he was absolutely morally superior to white people," Toni told 60 Minutes interviewer Ed Bradley in 1998. "He didn't like white people, because of all that he had been through. I mean, he wouldn't even let them into the house!" Toni recalled during the interview. "If a white insurance man or something came to the front door, he wouldn't let [him] in." Young Toni respected her father's wishes, but eventually she came to live her life in a completely different way. She understood that the conditions that had defined her father's life should not necessarily define her life.

Toni led a happy, relatively uneventful childhood. Her mother was active in the local church and shared with her children stories and folk legends that had been passed down to her by her mother and grandmother. These early stories would reappear in much of Toni's later work.

The Wofford family was determined to hold on to their racial heritage, but when Toni attended elementary school, she was shocked to learn that she was the only black child in her class. She studied hard and soon became a whiz at reading. Her earliest literary influences were writers like Fyodor Dostoyevski, Leo Tolstoy, and Jane Austen: Toni immersed herself in their works. She developed friendships among the white children at her school. Years later, she said that she never felt the sting of discrimination—at least until she grew old enough to begin dating. In 1949 she graduated with honors from Lorain High School.

When Toni applied to Howard University in Washington, D.C.—one of the most successful and prominent black colleges in America—she was confident she'd be accepted. Sure enough, she received a letter of acceptance. But the school was somewhat expensive, and Toni despaired that she might not be able to afford it, but her mother told Toni she would help pay to send her to the university. "She worked nights for years in order to pay for my education," Toni said years later. In a somber voice Toni recalled her mother's sacrifice for her: "She worked as an attendant in a ladies' washroom, from the early evening 'til midnight every night—for tips. And every cent she made, she sent to me."

Toni said she felt honored to be able to repay her mother later and make sure that her mother's last years were comfortable.

But before the literary success came many years of hard work. As an undergraduate at Howard, Toni distinguished herself with quiet dedication to her studies. She majored in English and took courses in the classics. Toni loved the arts (including dance and theatre), and joined the university's dramatic club, the Howard University Players.

While working with the theatre group, Toni traveled to the Deep South for performances. She had never before gone there, but she knew very well the stories of Southern life that her parents had shared with her during her childhood. Still, Toni was appalled to see the living conditions of Southern blacks. Poor, undereducated, and often exploited by cruel white landowners, the rural African Americans left an ineradicable impression on the young Toni. In the early fifties blacks in the Deep South seemed trapped in a time warp, a throwback to antebellum slavery.

Toni graduated from Howard University in 1953 with a degree in English. She wasn't sure what she wanted to do with her life, but she was certain that she wanted to continue learning. So she moved north again, this time to a cold corner of upstate New York. At Cornell University, in Ithaca, Toni spent two quiet years earning a master of arts degree. Her thesis focused on suicide in the works of William Faulkner and Virginia Woolf.

In 1955 she accepted a teaching post at Texas Southern University. After moving to the flat, arid Southwest, she suddenly found herself living in a world that was familiar and foreign all at once. At Howard—the school of choice for many successful middle-class black families—black heritage and culture was hardly acknowledged. But the scene was different at TSU. At this historically black college in the heart of Texas cattle country, a strong sense of African-American pride was evident. The TSU students sponsored a black history week, and the curriculum offered a range of studies emphasizing African-American contributions to this nation. It was an eye-opening experience for Toni, especially in an era when the civil rights movement was still in its infancy. Toni spent two years at TSU, then accepted a faculty position at her alma mater, Howard University.

At Howard Toni found herself in the midst of a burgeoning black arts movement. As a prominent black academic community, the university drew many individuals who would later become active in the civil rights movement and the more radical black movements of the ensuing years. With young students like Andrew Young, Stokely Carmichael, and a determined young writer named LeRoi Jones, Toni unwittingly played a vital part in formulating the philosophies of the movement. By teaching writing and literature to these young turks, Toni nurtured some of the greatest young minds of the era. One of her students, Claude Brown, later went on to write the classic book *Manchild in the Promised Land*. Unbeknownst to Toni at the time, she was learning some of the most effective traits of an editor: encouraging budding talent while insisting on a high level of literary integrity.

In 1958 Toni married Harold Morrison, a Jamaica-born architect. They had two children, Harold Ford and Slade Keven, but the marriage was ill-fated. In later years, Toni declined to talk about her marriage, beyond indicating that it had been "difficult." During this period, she joined a small writer's group and relished the time spent with other people who appreciated literature. For one of their meetings, Toni wrote a short story, a poignant look at a little girl she'd known back in Lorain. As Toni described it in her fictionalized version, the little black girl prayed to God to send her a pair of blue eyes. Toni's writers group applauded the little story, but she set it aside thereafter.

It was during this period that Toni's marriage began to come apart. She divorced Morrison in 1964 but kept his name. She moved to Syracuse, New York, and took a job editing textbooks for a major publishing house. It was a solitary but fulfilling life, with Toni going to work during the day, leaving her two young sons in the care of a housekeeper.

By the mid-sixties, Toni had taken to writing nearly every day, usually in the evening after the boys had gone to sleep. She resurrected the story of the little black girl who had prayed for blue eyes, filled in her narrative with remembrances of her childhood in Lorain, and soon found that her characters seemed to come to life. By the end of the decade, Toni had accepted an editing job at Random House in New York. She became a senior editor, a position few women had attained, let alone an African-American woman. For the next several years, she continued to work on other writer's manuscripts, but she began thinking more seriously about her own writing.

Over the next few years she edited books by prominent black public figures, including Angela Davis and the heavyweight boxing champion Muhammad Ali. All the while, Toni was working up the courage to submit some of her own writings to publishers. In 1970 her dedication paid off. Her first novel, *The Bluest Eye,* was published to much critical acclaim. Her story of the sad little girl who so wanted to be white touched many readers.

Success did not immediately cause Toni to quit her editing job, though. More than anyone, she knew that writing was difficult, committed work, and that one book alone did not make a career. She also continued teaching, taking an associate professorship at the State University of New York at Albany. As a writer, she was interested in exploring the complications and nuances of being black in America. Her second novel, *Sula,* also well received, focused on the complex relationship between two black women. It struck a chord with thousands of readers, black and white. The book was nominated for a National Book Award for fiction.

For the next several years Toni continued writing and editing and teaching. In the late seventies she accepted a visiting professorship at Yale University and began work on her third novel. *Song of Solomon* was a fascinating examination of the troubling impact of racism on residents of a small town. Filled with startling images of mysticism and religious commitment, *Song of Solomon* was her first attempt at writing male characters. The book won the National Book Critics Circle Award as well as the American Academy and Institute of Arts and Letters Award. President Jimmy Carter, a native Southerner and great fan of American literature, appointed Toni to the National Council of Arts.

By the early eighties, Toni had become a prominent writer. Her novels didn't always earn as much money as more sensational books, yet millions of readers were drawn to her unique forms of literary expression. In 1981 she published the novel *Tar Baby,* her first look at relationships between blacks and whites. Where previously Toni had concentrated almost exclusively on the ways in which black Americans view whites, she expanded her repertoire with *Tar Baby.* It included the vantage point of a white protagonist. The book was hailed by critics, and Toni landed on the cover of *Newsweek.*

The next decade was filled with work and personal fulfillment for Toni. At last she felt confident enough of her writing skills to begin thinking of herself as a "real writer." In 1983 she quite her editing job at Random House. A year later, she accepted a full professorship at the State University of New York at Albany and once again moved to the quiet region of upstate New York. There she wrote her first play, a fictionalized version of the life of Emmet Till, a young black man who was lynched by Southern whites in 1955. Till had been accused of whistling at a white woman. His tragic death remains a benchmark for many black American activists and politicians. For Toni, her interest in the "nature of oppression" made the Till story a natural way of combining her love of history, race relations, and theatre. The play opened at the Marketplace Theatre in Albany in 1986 but did not enjoy a long run elsewhere. Still, Toni continued writing.

Her next novel, *Beloved,* was a heartfelt look at the legacy of slavery in one Southern black family. Years earlier, Toni had come across a short historical document describing the life of a slave named Margaret Garner. In 1851 Garner had run away from her slavemaster in Kentucky and fled to Ohio. Some time later, when her Kentucky slavemaster finally tracked her down, Garner attempted to kill her children, saying she'd rather see them dead than brought up as slaves. It was a gripping, frightening story, and one that stunned readers when Toni turned her marvelous imagination and writing skills to fictionalizing the account. Filled with folklore, ghostly images, and horrific stories of recrimination and personal loss, *Beloved* became an instant bestseller and catapulted Toni into the upper reaches of the literary world.

Beloved became Toni's most successful book commercially. In 1988 it received the Pulitzer Prize for fiction. It did not receive a National Book Award; in fact, it was not even nominated. In an unprecedented step more than forty well-known black writers signed a letter of protest and sent it to the *New York Times.* As they saw it, Toni deserved a National Book Award, and the slight when she failed to gain even a nomination was monumental. The letter from the black writers was headlined a "testament of thanks" [to Toni], but many in the publishing world recognized the unified voice as one of legitimate protest.

Toni pressed on with her work. In 1992 she published *Jazz,* a melancholy look at blacks in Harlem during the twenties. Reviews were mixed, but Toni's fans bought *Jazz* in droves. That same year she published *Playing in the Dark: Whiteness and the Literary Imagination,* a nonfiction collection examining race relations in literature. During these years, Toni enjoyed the kind of public and professional reverence most writers can only dream about. Along with teaching (she accepted the position of Robert F. Goheen Professor in the Council of Humanities at

Princeton University in 1987), Toni edited a controversial collection of essays exploring the infamous hearings of the Senate Judiciary Committee on the conflict between Supreme Court nominee Clarence Thomas and Anita Hill, *Race-ing Justice, En-Gendering Power.* In 1996 she also edited a similar collection, *Birth of a Nation'hood,* an examination of black American perspectives on the O. J. Simpson murder trial.

But Toni's crowning moment came in 1993, when she learned she had been chosen to receive the Nobel Prize in Literature. Citing her commitment to writing, human relations, and classic literature, the Nobel committee bestowed upon Toni one of the international community's highest honors. She had become the first native-born African-American writer to receive the award and the first black woman in history to carry the title Nobel Laureate. Throughout, Toni maintained a dignified composure, encouraging promising young writers and keeping her eye on America's love-hate relationship with blacks.

In 1998 she published *Paradise,* a mythical look at an Oklahoma town influenced by powerful and mysterious women. While touring the nation in support of the book, Toni spoke often about her belief that the human spirit knows no race, class, or color. She told a reporter from the *Boston Globe:* "Each of our lives is about finding a way to deserve to be here. The only thing I can do, and have done, and will do, is somehow incorporate into the world that horror you feel when something awful happens, and to redistribute the moral problem so other people can have this connection to another's pain. That's what art does."

Indeed, Toni was inspirational to numerous other writers, especially to other black women—including MAYA ANGELOU and ALICE WALKER. Like uncounted other Americans, these women attribute their healthy self-images, in part, to the model provided by Toni.

33

Audre Lorde

1934–1992

Celebrating the Personal and the Political

DURING HER ALL-TOO-SHORT LIFE, Audre Lorde wore many hats: poet, civil rights activist, feminist, and gay rights leader. For the daughter of West Indian immigrants who came of age before the civil rights and women's rights movements, Audre's accomplishments are made all the more remarkable because she pioneered a new kind of artistic expression, that which integrates the personal with the political. She worked her way up in the literary world at a time when few publishers or readers took seriously the work of black women writers. She advocated for women's studies programs at universities long before the notion of "political correctness" entered the nation's consciousness. She saw the value in those Americans who exist on the margins of our society and honored them with her poetry, energy, and sensitivity.

By the time of her death from cancer in November 1992, Audre Lorde had served as the poet laureate of New York State, received numerous academic and literary awards, and enthralled millions of readers with her vivid essays and poems focusing on the plight of minorities and the underclass. For modern black women poets like SONIA SANCHEZ and NIKKI GIOVANNI and Sapphire, Audre Lorde provided a sterling role model. For the many students she impacted during a long teaching career, Audre's life and work provided a solid foundation for young artists struggling to find their identity.

"Audre Lorde has been a pioneer in making available her voice as a teacher, a survivor, an activist, and a crusader against bigotry," said black filmmaker Ada Gay Griffin following Audre's death. Like uncounted other budding artists, Griffin viewed Audre as a supremely inspirational figure—as well as an accessible individual who was always willing to lend an ear. Hers was a remarkable life of letters and personal commitment, one that was nurtured in a segregated Northern enclave of black creativity—Harlem of the thirties and forties.

Audre Geraldine Lorde was born in New York City on February 18, 1934. Her parents had immigrated to the United States from the Caribbean and joined a thriving West Indian community in Harlem. From childhood, Audre took her education seriously. Like many immigrants, the Lorde family viewed education as a key to unlocking the world's potential. And while still in junior high school, Audre began turning her reading and writing skills toward personal expression. Poetry provided a private but satisfying outlet for her insecurities. During the early forties, African-American girls faced few options for their lives—marriage, clerical work, teaching, or nursing. Audre sensed she wanted to take a different direction, but was unsure as to how to make that happen. Quiet, sensitive, and composed, she spent much of her time alone, with writing her solace.

"I was in high school and I was a mess," she recalled in an interview many years later. "I was 'introverted,' 'hypersensitive,' I was too 'intense'—all of those words that other people used for little black girls who were just trying to live." While a student at Hunter High School, Audre was thrilled to learn that one of her poems had been chosen for publication by a young woman's magazine, *Seventeen*. An academic advisor had discouraged her from even sending the poem to the magazine, declaring it to be a "bad sonnet." The magazine did publish the piece, and Audre's tender sense of identity was fortified. She moved on, enrolling in Hunter College and undertaking a rigorous schedule of liberal arts courses. She graduated in 1959 and immediately enrolled in the library science program at Columbia University.

Like millions of other young women of the era, Audre was torn between her instincts, which led her to explore writing, literature, and an open-minded way of thinking, and the conventions of the day, which dictated that "respectable" young women either worked in service-oriented jobs, or married, stayed at home, and raised children. After completing the master's program in library science at Columbia in 1961, Audre married a promising young attorney, Edwin Rollins. For the next several years, Audre lived up to the conventional expectations of the times. She took a job as a librarian and gave birth to two children. All the while, though, she continued writing on her own. In 1968 the swirl of political activism began to intrigue Audre.

Her first book of poetry, *The First Cities,* was published in 1968, and Audre became a serious voice for the controversial questions about personal relationships, democracy, and artistic integrity. Later that year, she accepted a position at a small university in the Deep South—Tougaloo College in Mississippi—to serve as poet in residence. It was a unique opportunity for Audre to experience life on the front lines of the civil rights movement. Although some of her advisors didn't understand her willingness to place herself in the Deep South at a time when blacks and sympathetic whites were being beaten and killed, Audre had to go. It would prove one of the most eye-opening experiences of her life. "It changed my life," Audre recalled years later. "I had a chance to work with young black poets in what was essentially a crisis situation. White townspeople were shooting up the edges of Tougaloo at night. Many of the students had been arrested. I realized I could take my art in the realest way, and make it do what I wanted. I began bringing together my poetry and my deepest-held convictions."

Two years later Audre published her second poetry collection, *Cables to Rage,* which described her anger at the many social injustices of the day. The collection, which was well received, also contained hints of a change in Audre's personal life: She was beginning to admit her lesbianism. In the early seventies sexuality issues were extremely controversial, and particularly so in the African-American community. Encouraged by her academic peers and close circle of friends, Audre refused to hide or be ashamed of her burgeoning feelings. In 1970 she divorced Ed Rollins and continued writing.

Over the next few years Audre enjoyed a period of phenomenal creativity. She received a grant from the National Endowment for the Arts and published several other poetry collections and essays, including *The New York Head Shop and Museum* and *From a Land Where Other People Live,* which was nominated for a National Book Award in 1973. Throughout, Audre continued studying and learning, developing a keen interest in domestic politics as well as the international policies that affected the lives of residents in the Caribbean islands of her ancestors.

In 1976, for the first time, a major publishing house printed a collection of Audre's previous works. *Coal* marked Audre's introduction into the mainstream of book publishing and earned favorable reviews in prominent publications, including the *New York Times.* Audre began lecturing and speaking to arts and women's groups around the nation. She cofounded a small publishing house for women of color called Kitchen Table—Women of Color Press and published her seventh book of poetry, *The Black Unicorn,* in 1978. A personal treatise, the collection revealed Audre's deep attachments to West Indian culture and further articulated her desire to see Americans attain political, racial, and sexual liberation. Arriving during the height of the women's rights movement, Audre's work was hailed as mature, sensitive, and well suited to the turmoil of the times.

In 1978 she was diagnosed with cancer, a scary turn of events that leads many people to begin slowing down with their work. Not Audre. "Her life took on a kind of immediacy that most people's lives never develop," Audre's son, Jonathan, recalled years later. "The setting of priorities and the carrying out of important tasks assumed a much greater significance in her life." Indeed, in 1979, Audre was one of the first speakers at a national march for gay and lesbian liberation, held in Washington, D.C. She continued traveling for many months at a time, journeying to Africa, the West Indies, and other countries, where she worked to forge alliances among women's groups. Along the way, she found time to venture to Berlin, where she received treatment for the cancer that threatened to overtake her body.

In 1980 Audre returned to Hunter College, where she taught English and rapidly became one of the most popular professors on campus. Melinda Goodman, a poet and former student, recalled, "Audre put an excitement and intensity into her classes that made us feel like whatever we were discussing was the most fascinating topic in the world." Thanks to Audre's devotion to incorporating current events into one's art, several budding talents found nurture in her courses at Hunter. To be sure, for young black poets like Donald Woods, who is gay, Audre provided affirmation that his point of view had value. Whereas many young blacks—especially those whose lifestyles fell outside the boundaries of conventional, conservative expectations—often felt alone and ashamed of their differences, Audre reassured them that they had a place at the table of artistic and political life in America. "There are plenty of us who think of Audre as a mother," said Jewell Gomez, a former student of Audre's at Hunter College.

For the next several years Audre continued writing and lecturing. In the early eighties she published *The Cancer Journals,* a startlingly personal collection of essays detailing her battle with cancer. Many of the essays also took on the medical profession, which Audre criticized as being wholly insensitive to the needs of women and minority patients. An autobiographical novel, *Zami: A New Spelling of My Name,* was published to critical acclaim in 1982. In 1988 she published another deeply personal collection of poems and essays, *A Burst of Light,* and rejoiced a year later when she learned that the collection had earned her the coveted National Book Award for poetry.

By the end of the decade Audre had relocated to St. Croix in the Virgin Islands, a small, verdant island that nourished her sense of artistry and well-being. In 1984 she cofounded a woman's advocacy organization for South Africans called Sisterhood in Support of Sisters.

Deeply concerned with the living and spiritual conditions of women in impoverished circumstances, Audre took on a new name during this period, Gambia Adisa. She published several works under the pseudonym Rey Domini. Toward the end of her life, a young generation of poets and artists discovered Audre's work. Although she spent the last seven years of her life living and writing in St. Croix, Audre continued to provide inspiration to those who sought her out. Even while she struggled to overcome the devastating effects of the cancer, she managed to work to improve the lives of others: she founded a domestic violence prevention group for indigenous women, the St. Croix Women's Coalition.

In 1991 Audre learned that she had received one of America's most prestigious literary prizes—the Walt Whitman Citation of Merit. The award was extraspecial because it carried with it the distinction of making its recipient the poet laureate of New York State. When Audre passed away at her island home in 1992, more than five thousand members of her community of fans, artists, friends, and family members mourned. Her words and spirit were memorialized in a simple yet touching gathering at New York's Cathedral of St. John the Divine. Located in Manhattan, the church was an appropriate place to remember the life of the shy young girl from Harlem.

"Audre was a model of someone who knew how to let good things into her life," said Melinda Goodman. "She gave the same kind of attention to the woman selling mangoes outside the supermarket in St. Croix as she gave to her friends, family, and professional associates," Goodman recalled. "She taught, through her example, the necessity of getting up and keeping going—of mourning our losses and valuing the beauty and power of each of us, the ones who carry on."

34

Sonia Sanchez

1934–

Nurturing the Spirit With Poetry

AS A YOUNG WRITER in Harlem during the nineteen fifties, Sonia Sanchez got a firsthand glimpse of activism and art in action. By the mid-sixties, she was publishing highly personal poems in such prominent journals as the *Liberator, Negro Digest,* and the *Journal of Black Poetry.* Always in the vanguard of social activism, Sonia was a key member of the well-known black arts movement, an informal collective of writers, painters, poets, and political activists including Stokely Carmichael, NIKKI GIO-VANNI, and LeRoi Jones (Amiri Baraka). For many years, she was a revered teacher at universities in America and a staunch supporter of political and social causes. In the time-honored tradition of women like MARIAN ANDERSON, GWENDOLYN BROOKS, and AUDRE LORDE, Sonia has always endeavored to find a workable balance between her artistic expression and her hopes for an improved America.

"Her poems are raps, good ones, aimed like guns at whatever obstacles she detects standing in the way of black progress," critic William Pitt Root wrote in the journal *Poetry* of Sonia's moving work. "Her praises are as generous as her criticisms are severe, both coming from loyalties that are fierce, invulnerable, and knowing. Whether she's addressing her praises to Gwendolyn Brooks or to the late Malcolm X, to her husband or to a stranger's child, always they emerge from and feed back into the shared experiences of being black."

In her first book, *Homecoming*, published in 1969 to critical acclaim, Sonia explored the lingering effects of slavery in America and the "culture of oppression" that writers like TONI MORRISON were also beginning to examine. Using a new kind of realistic writing, Sonia plumbed the street slang and neighborhood vernacular of black America that was too often dismissed by "serious" writing critics.

Her body of work contains a binding thread, a singularly important message found in most of her poems and essays: the presence of our shared humanity and the proud heritage of accomplishment and achievement which black Americans must draw upon to overcome centuries of discrimination and oppression. Some of her most touching and effective poetry concerns difficult issues such as violence and poverty in the black community, and Sonia has been unflinchingly critical of self-destructive behavior among all Americans. As she sees it, her portrayals of black American life are genuine and unvarnished by conventional literary modes. Indeed, the early years of the woman who would become Sonia Sanchez were filled with solitary pursuits and plenty of time for self-reflection.

Born Wilsonia Driver on September 9, 1934, in Birmingham, Alabama, Sonia spent her early years in the home of her grandmother. Her mother, Lena Driver, had died when Sonia was very young, and her father, Wilson L. Driver, thought it would be best if Sonia and her sister lived with his mother, at least until he could become financially secure enough to raise his daughters. These early years spent in the Deep South amid the rich cadences and speech patterns of rural blacks would leave their mark on her.

In the late forties, Sonia's father sent for Sonia and her sister. In an abrupt change in lifestyle, she found herself living amid the busy energy and big city environment of Harlem. It was a lively, exciting period, and artists of every kind filled the legendary black neighborhood with the sights and sounds of their work. Sonia kept her mind on her studies and took to writing to help sort out the confusion and loneliness she felt. Living in small, untidy quarters, she realized that keeping journals and diaries of her thoughts and impressions helped her to cope. Years later, during an interview, Sonia recalled herself during those early days in Harlem as a "very shy child, a very introspective child, one who stuttered."

Sonia was an inquisitive, studious young woman by the time she was accepted at Hunter College in New York, where she studied political science and received an undergraduate degree in 1955. Encouraged by a new, experimental creative atmosphere sweeping the nation after World War II, Sonia then enrolled in a graduate program at New York University. While studying poetry with the well-known writer Louise Bogan, Sonia came to discover her genuine talent for poetry and prose. Her newfound personal awareness also coincided with the emergence of a new kind of political and artistic expression.

In 1968 Sonia married a writer and activist named Etheridge Knight, with whom she had three children over the next several years. After their marriage ended, she married Albert Sanchez, whose name she adopted for her writings.

Beginning in the late sixties, Sonia found herself in the middle of the growing black arts movement. In coffeehouses and classrooms and on street corners, black writers pioneered a forceful kind of literary expression. Along with Nikki Giovanni and a handful of other young idealistic artists, Sonia founded a poets cooperative called the Broadside Quartet. They shared resources, wrote and performed plays and poetry, and broke new ground in the process.

Sonia also traveled to Cuba, the West Indies, Europe, and China to give readings of her works. Audiences found her speaking voice mellifluous and profound, and Sonia soon became skilled at public readings. She believed that the sounds of spoken language could be musical and supremely effective in communicating artistic expression, and Sonia helped pioneer the popular current genre known as "slam poetry." Over the next two decades, she recorded several albums of her work, wrote numerous collections of poetry and essays, and continued mining the overlooked territory of the black American experience.

During the nineteen eighties, Sonia's personal poetry began to explore the "neoslavery" of the modern black experience. In works like *Homegirls and Handgrenades,* Sonia has chronicled relationships between blacks and whites, men and women, and women with each other.

Meanwhile, she taught at important institutes of higher education, including Amherst College, the University of Pittsburgh, Spelman College, and the City College of New York. In a long and innovative writing career, she won several prestigious awards for her insightful poetry and essays, including a PEN Writing Award, a grant from the American Academy of Arts and Letters, and an American Book Award.

Perhaps most important, Sonia continued the tradition of teaching others, so that she would continue to learn, as well as leave a legacy. As a valued member of the Poetry Society of America, the NAACP, and the Academy of American Poets, Sonia kept her finger on the pulse of the ever-changing artistic and social scene in the United States. She received an honorary doctorate from Baruch College and served on the Pennsylvania Council on the Arts. As the Laura Carnell Professor of English and Women's Studies at Temple University in Philadelphia at the time of this writing, Sonia was in a position to be both a vital role model and teaching guide for thousands of students and readers.

Like so many other African-American women educators and artists before her, Sonia vowed to carry on the tradition of uplifting the disfranchised. "Selflessness," Sonia once wrote, "is key for conveying the need to end greed and oppression" around the world.

An astute observer of life, Sonia continued in the late nineties to write about the black experience in America and of her hopes for the nation's future. A dedicated believer in personal growth, she urged all Americans to maintain a tolerant, humanistic outlook.

35

Barbara Jordan

1936–1996

Standing Tall, Speaking Truth

ANYONE WHO EVER HEARD Barbara Jordan deliver a speech remembered the sound of her voice: deep and resounding with authority. Hers was a voice that could rattle windowpanes and conventional wisdoms. After her birth in Texas during the tough years of the Great Depression, Barbara Jordan rose from the very bottom of America's socioeconomic ladder to the heights of the nation's political power structure. Her life might be charted by the astounding number of firsts she achieved—first black woman to join a prestigious Texas debating team; first black woman to work for a powerful white Texas judge; first black woman to be named "Governor for a Day" in a longstanding Texas ceremonial tradition; first black woman elected to the Texas Senate; first black woman to be keynote speaker of a Democratic National Convention. And her most significant first was undeniably the most compelling: In 1972 Barbara Jordan became the first black woman elected to the United States House of Representatives from Texas since the Reconstruction era.

For black American women who followed her political lead, Barbara Jordan represented a towering example of personal bravery and professional integrity, a woman, a jurist, and a legislator beyond compare. "For one thing, [Barbara] understood that she was black, and she was more than black," said Eleanor Holmes Norton, congressional delegate for the District of Columbia, after Barbara Jordan's death. "She understood that she was a universal figure, that when Barbara Jordan talked, America listened. It was important to her that black America listened, but she clearly was a woman who had, and knew she had, influence beyond her own racial group."

Barbara Charline Jordan was born on February 21, 1936, in Houston, Texas. Like many blacks in the wide, flat Southwestern expanse, the Jordan family was cash-poor but rich in spirit. Her father, Benjamin Jordan, was a Baptist minister and a strict disciplinarian who forbade his daughters to attend parties and other frivolous social events. Along with her mother, Arlyne, and two older sisters, Barbara was a familiar presence in Houston's racially segregated Fifth Ward. Up and down Lyons Avenue where the Jordan family lived, Barbara and her sisters were widely regarded as smart, good-natured, and exceptionally devoted to their educational studies. Years later, Barbara recalled her early days with unsentimental clarity: "We were poor, but so was everyone else around us. We were never hungry, and we always had a place to stay."

By the early fifties Barbara was an academic star. She impressed her teachers with her focus and determination in the classroom. She graduated with honors from Phillis Wheatley High School (where she had been a leader of the oratorical society) and immediately enrolled in Texas Southern University, a historically black university. At this time the South was just showing the beginnings of the nascent civil rights movement. But for Barbara, ensconced in the political science and government department at TSU for four undergraduate years, attaining a sound education seemed the wisest way to prepare for the larger struggles that lay ahead. She spent countless hours studying the U.S. Constitution, the Declaration of Independence, and popular political movements.

At Texas Southern Barbara's blossoming oratorical skills made her a popular and vital member of the university's debating team. Not many black colleges had such debating teams, and the few that existed rarely competed against teams from white universities. But by the time Barbara graduated from TSU, her team not only competed against several all-white debate clubs, it came out on top. On the debating team, she worked hard to develop a clear tone of voice and distinctive speaker's presence. Her experience on the team also provided her with valuable critical thinking and speaking skills that added to her effectiveness in later years.

Barbara graduated at the top of her class in 1956, a formidable young woman, one unafraid to speak her mind and well equipped with the oratorical skills to do so. Inspired by Edith Sampson, a distinguished black attorney who had served at the United Nations and who spoke to Barbara's class at Phillis Wheatley High School, Barbara had long known she was going to become an attorney. She traveled north to attend law school. At Boston University she embarked upon a path that was virtually unheard of for black women at the time: constitutional law. Barbara found her years there somewhat difficult, since her education at all-black schools had not prepared her well for the rigors of competition in a New England university. Nonetheless, she persevered and earned her degree in 1959.

After graduating from law school, Barbara promptly passed both the Texas and the Massachusetts bar and returned to Houston to practice law. At first she practiced law from her parent's Lyons Avenue home, using a dining-room table as her desk. She then served as an administrative assistant to Harris County judge Bill Elliot and became interested in local politics. After volunteering to work in elections for the Harris County Democratic party, Barbara decided to run for office. In 1962 she mounted a campaign for the Texas House of Representatives and was defeated. Ever optimistic, Barbara was encouraged by the small number of votes she did receive, and she ran again for the same seat in 1964. She lost again but held on to her resolve.

Two years later, in 1966, Barbara ran again, this time for the Texas Senate, and she won. By becoming the first black woman elected to the Texas Senate since 1883, she gained the support of such national figures as Lyndon B. Johnson and members of the Kennedy family. Her political star was on the rise, but Barbara disdained pretentions of glamour. "What the people want is very simple," Barbara said many years later. "They want an America as good as its promise."

To that end, Barbara became a staunch defender of the nation's constitutional principles. In 1972, when she was elected to the U.S. House of Representatives from a newly drawn Texas congressional district, she entered the history books not only as the first black woman to attain such a lofty position, but also as a distinguished interpreter of legal issues in America.

In 1972 Barbara and a promising young candidate from Georgia named Andrew Young became the first black southerners in the U.S. Congress since the Reconstruction era. Over the next few years, Barbara's face and voice became familiar to millions of Americans outside of Texas. To be sure, her keen legal mind and devotion to the law made her a force to be reckoned with on Capitol Hill. Nevertheless, it took a national leadership crisis of historic proportions to bring Barbara an entirely new level of recognition: As a member of the House Judiciary Committee, Barbara played a key role in the famous hearings on articles for the impeachment of President Richard M. Nixon.

During that somber period of government, Barbara remained a fierce defender of the U.S. Constitution, a legal expert emboldened by the earliest principles of American democracy. During hearings broadcast to the entire nation, she told fellow congressmen investigating President Nixon's conduct in office that the Constitution required elected representatives to stay the course: "My faith in the Constitution is whole," Barbara intoned, her brow furrowed in concentration, her voice heavy with meaning. "It is complete. It is total. I am not going to sit here and be an idle spectator to the diminution, the subversion, the destruction of the Constitution." Her impassioned oratory on that hot summer day in 1974 forever placed her among Washington's elite.

Along with her work on the Judiciary Committee, Barbara also served her Texas constituents by sitting on the House Committee on

Government Operations and the Steering and Policy Committee of the House Democratic Caucus. By 1976 Barbara was among the best-known elected officials in the nation. She was awarded honorary degrees by several prestigious universities and was often referred to as one of the greatest American orators of all time. She was reelected to the U.S. House of Representatives and became a bona fide hero to townsfolk back in Houston. Late that year, Barbara reached unimagined heights in the nation's political arena: She delivered the keynote address at the Democratic National Convention. Held in New York on July 12, 1976, the convention was especially tense because the nation was still reeling from Nixon's resignation two years earlier. President Gerald Ford was running on the Republican ticket, and the Democratic party was hoping to recapture the White House following the period of tremendous turmoil. When Barbara took the podium at the convention, a hush fell over the normally boisterous crowd.

After a brief opening statement describing the proud tradition of Democratic conventions, Barbara got right to the point: "But there is something different about tonight," she said, her voice deep and true, her bearing tall and regal as she addressed the nation.

> There is something special about tonight. What is different? What is special? I, Barbara Jordan, am a keynote speaker. . . . And I feel that, notwithstanding the past, that my presence here is one additional bit of evidence that the American Dream need not forever be deferred.

To wild applause, Barbara continued her speech, outlining the deep significance of a true democracy. Her knowledge of the Constitution and the Declaration of Independence stood her in good stead as she described for delegates and the American public the paramount moral incentive that drives this nation—even in immense crisis:

> Many fear the future. Many are distrustful of their leaders, and believe that their voices are never heard. Many seek only to satisfy their private work wants. To satisfy private interests. . . . If that happens, who then will speak for America? Who then will speak for the common good? . . . For all it's uncertainty, we cannot flee the future. We must become new puritans. . . . We must address and master the future together. It can be done if we restore the belief that we share a sense of national community, that we share a common national endeavor. It can be done.

Barbara's plea to stay true to the "common good" resonated with the American public. After that spellbinding speech, she became even more in demand in political and academic arenas. Undoubtedly, she might have used her newfound popularity to feather her own political nest or to join a corporate world desperate for a high-profile, educated, well-connected black woman. Instead, in 1977, Barbara announced that she would be returning to Texas from Washington. Unbeknownst to many except her closest friends and family members, Barbara had been diagnosed with a muscle disorder. During the next few years, her body—once tall, strong and dignified—would slowly betray her. But Barbara's mind remained razor sharp. She became one of the most sought after professors at the University of Texas at Austin. She continued working in politics, serving as a consultant and advisor to numerous regional and national elected officials.

Her love of constitutional law also remained undiminished. Barbara became the first black woman appointed to one of the most prestigious academic posts in America: The Lyndon Baines Johnson Centennial Chair in Public Policy at the University of Texas. Through most of the eighties she continued teaching and lecturing in her home state, turning out hundreds of legal papers and political essays and captivating new generations of political and legal students.

Few Americans outside of Texas realized that Barbara now required the aid of a wheelchair and that her body was in the final stages of a debilitating muscle disease. In 1992 she made one of her final national public appearances. Perhaps in an effort to rekindle the enthusiasm Barbara had sparked during the seventies, the Democratic leadership asked her to deliver the keynote address at its national convention. On July 13, 1992, Barbara again faced a national audience and political community that was very much in need of inspiration.

Though her body was now bowed, her formerly imposing frame seated in a wheelchair, Barbara's voice was still strong. She urged the Democrats to "seize this moment." And when a young Arkansas candidate named Bill Clinton took the podium later at that convention, Barbara Jordan had extended an important challenge to him and to the nation. After describing what she saw as a strong need for economic reform, she spoke about other, more elusive matters facing Americans at the end of the twentieth century:

We are one, we Americans, and we reject any intruder who seeks to divide us by race or class. We honor cultural identity. However, separatism is not allowed. Separatism is not the American way. And we should not permit ideas like political correctness to become some fad that could reverse our hard-won achievements in civil and human rights. Xenophobia has no place in the Democratic Party. We seek to unite people, not to divide them. And we reject both white racism and black racism. This party will not tolerate bigotry under any guise. America's strength is rooted in its diversity.

It was a remarkable speech, especially considering that for most of her political career, Barbara had let the basic principles of the U.S. Constitution speak for her in racial matters. Her speech to the 1992 Democratic National Convention riveted the nation, and Bill Clinton undoubtedly benefited from her cool, reasoned appeal. In 1993 Clinton officially recognized his debt to Barbara by appointing her chair of the U.S. Commission on Immigration Reform. In 1994 she received the Presidential Medal of Freedom, in recognition of her three decades of defending human rights in America.

When Barbara Jordan died on January 17, 1996, thousands of grieving Texans surged onto the campus at Austin where she had taught. In Washington, D.C., politicians commandeered the podiums in the House and Senate chambers for hours-long tributes to Barbara. For popular Texas newspaper columnist Molly Ivins, Barbara's life exemplified dignity and professional dedication in the face of racial and gender discrimination and an array of other odds. "She was a woman of magisterial dignity, and she wore that dignity like an armor because she needed to," Ivins said after Barbara's death. "When she first came to the Texas Senate, one Senator used to call her 'that old nigga-mammy washer-woman'; and then there were others who treated her with that sort of courtly condescension that such 'gentlemen' reserve for the 'little lady.' Jordan overcame all of that by sheer strength of personality, by ability, by force of her intelligence. And, of course, by her superb voice, the rhetoric. We always said that if Hollywood ever needed somebody to play the voice of God Almighty, they ought to get Barbara Jordan."

Jordan's death reminded President Clinton that America was indeed beholden to its black American women. Speaking at her funeral in Houston, the president paid tribute to Barbara's proud legacy of political activism and to her personal commitment to democracy: "Barbara

Jordan's life was a monument to the three great threads that run con-stantly throughout the fabric of American history—our love of liberty, our belief in progress, our search for common ground. Wherever she could, and whenever she stood to speak, she jolted that nation's atten-tion with her artful and articulate defense of the Constitution, the American Dream, and the common heritage and destiny we share, whether we like it or not."

"If she were an athlete," recalled California Democratic representa-tive Barbara Boxer, "she would have been a world-class hurdler because she spent her whole life leaping over barriers with grace and dexterity."

36

June Jordan

1936–

The Power of Poetry

AS A POET, ESSAYIST, ACTIVIST, AND EDUCATOR, June Jordan speaks to the very soul of black American women. She also represents a modern example of the positive impact African-American women have made on this nation. With her astute observations about life, love, and personal responsibility, June has helped readers better understand the common human experience. The author of a dozen books, including some children's books, June is a skilled chronicler of the complex, rich, and inspirational lives of many overlooked Americans. "And for ourselves, the intrinsic 'Purpose' is to reach, and to remember, and to declare our commitment to all the living, without deceit, and without fear, and without reservation," June said in a 1971 interview with the prize-winning author, ALICE WALKER. "We do what we can. And by doing it, we help ourselves [be more] trusting. . . ."

Born July 9, 1936, in New York, June came of age in a remarkably creative atmosphere. During the thirties and forties, some of the nation's stellar artistic talents had settled in Harlem and Brooklyn within predominantly black enclaves. Musicians like Cab Calloway, Duke Ellington, and BILLIE HOLIDAY made a strong impression on the city's black youth, and June was no exception. Writers like Countee Cullen, Langston Hughes, and DOROTHY WEST cut striking figures on the city's cultural landscape, and collectively they shed much-needed light on the misunderstood lives of blacks in America.

By the time she graduated from high school, June had determined that she would take full advantage of educational opportunity. At the time, African-American women were all but invisible to much of society. Most black American women still shouldered the legacy of centuries of slavery as domestic workers, and they had few ways to achieve the American Dream. For June, however, a strong family and the tenor of the times were in her favor: She applied and was accepted at one of the best colleges in the nation—Barnard, the alma mater of the successful writer ZORA NEALE HURSTON. A dedicated student, June concentrated on her literature studies, and eventually realized her own love of poetry and the classics. When she graduated from Barnard in 1957, she enrolled in another world-class college to continue her education: the University of Chicago.

Like the bustling communities of Harlem and Brooklyn, Chicago fostered some of the greatest black artists of this century. Pulitzer Prize–winning poet GWENDOLYN BROOKS hailed from Chicago, as did playwright LORRAINE HANSBERRY. For June, Chicago was an exciting new world, and she threw herself into the dynamic community of black artists and intellectuals. While there, June became intrigued by the absence of women and blacks on the faculty. Indeed, few women or ethnic minorities held tenured positions at the nation's top colleges. At last, June had found an area where she might be able to combine her artistic vision with her growing political awareness. She began lecturing in Chicago and turned to her writing as a form of personal expression and academic exercise.

In 1964 the civil rights movement was at its height. Public demonstrations against bigotry and racial discrimination in the cities of the Deep South earned daily headlines around the nation. In several large cities—among them New York, Chicago, and Detroit—deadly riots had taken place. For young, idealistic blacks like June, the years of accumulated slights and repressed frustrations had brought them to a breaking point. As June saw it, great potential existed for righting many injustices through peaceful, nonviolent means. And as she reasoned, educational parity might just hold the key. "After the murder of Dr. [Martin Luther] King [Jr.], I stopped using the words 'revolution,' and 'revolutionary,' " June said in a 1997 essay. "I thought they were tired."

Depressed by the waste and destruction of the assassinations and ensuing race riots, June decided that working inside the academic world could provide a useful and productive means of addressing many of the conditions which led to so much turmoil in the black community. She began writing personal, heartfelt poems and essays about her beliefs. June also began advocating for increasing the number of women and minorities hired by major American universities.

In the course of her own research, she discovered the life and work of another great black American woman—FANNIE LOU HAMER. As a poor sharecropper in the Deep South, Fannie Lou had put her life on the line to fight for equal rights. During the sixties, in the heart of the Delta, Fannie Lou had led hundreds of exploited blacks in an attempt to win the right to vote. Her life was a revelation to young June, and she decided to bring Fannie Lou's story back to the nation's consciousness.

"Revolutionary trust is something I discovered first in the heart of Fannie Lou Hamer," June wrote in 1997. Enthralled by the drama and commitment of Fannie Lou's legendary struggle against white supremacists, June decided to write a book about her life. At the same time, June was beginning to earn notice as a gifted writer and teacher. Her first book of poetry, *Who Look at Me,* was published in 1969.

More than twenty years before a nationwide debate over the value of "Black English" gripped the nation, June was exploring the phenomenon of young African Americans who used a controversial form of slang to communicate. June's poetry collection sparked a heated ideological debate over the use of Black English, and she defended the practice as a necessary part of some black Americans' personal evolution. All the same, June continued to focus on the subjects nearest to her heart and her beliefs. And when she approached a New York editor about the possibility of writing books for children and young adults, her professional writing career was underway.

In 1972 June published her biography of Fannie Lou Hamer. Aimed at students, the book filled a void in the curriculum of most public education institutions. Better than anyone, June realized that millions of young blacks were often being educated without very much attention to all the contributions African Americans have made to this nation.

Over the next decade June wrote several critically acclaimed collections, including *Some Changes* and *Things That I Do in the Dark*. In addition to teaching at colleges and arguing for the addition of multicultural studies at the nation's universities, June also explored journalistic writing. In local publications and national magazines like the *Nation,* June delivered the thoughtful arguments for increasing the rights of women and minorities. She began receiving favorable attention from the nation's artistic community and was awarded several top honors which enabled her to continue writing, including a Rockefeller Foundation grant and a fellowship from the National Endowment for the Arts.

During the eighties June continued her vocal advocacy for women and ethnic studies programs at the nation's universities and wrote about her struggle to bring progress to this area. Several essay collections—including *Civil Wars, Moving Towards Home,* and *On Call*—described with poignant imagery and accessible language June's humanitarian philosophies.

By the end of the decade June had begun to explore another artistic forum which seemed perfect for her particular interests—playwriting. A longtime admirer of black musicians and composers, June decided to try her hand at writing for the stage. Inspired by black women playwrights like LORRAINE HANSBERRY and the contemporary work of Ntozake Shange, June wrote the book for two plays dealing with race and gender, *The Issue* and *Bang Bang Uber Alles*. Both plays received favorable reviews but failed to catch on with audiences. In 1994 June wrote the libretto for *I Was Looking at the Ceiling and Then I Saw the Sky,* a modern American opera in two acts. This show fared slightly better and had a respectable run in California, New York, and Europe.

Nevertheless, June was still dedicated to finding new ways of sharing her hope for a more united America. In the early nineties she accepted a teaching position at one of the nation's most prominent institutions of higher education—the University of California at Berkeley. Over the next few years she helped establish a leading poetry school at Berkeley and became a revered professor of African-American studies there. For her work in the vanguard of ethnic studies and poetry, she was honored with awards from the National Association of Black Journalists, the Massachusetts Council for the Arts, and the New York Foundation for the Arts. Never afraid of political controversy, June also published essays examining America's role in the war between Israel and Palestine and lectured extensively on gender relations and human sexuality.

For her students she provided a living example of how the individual can make a positive impact on the world. In a 1997 essay published in the *Nation*, June described her hopes for her students, whom she recognized as holding the future of our shared national experience: "In their own time, UC Berkeley's revolutionary student poets have learned the necessity of trust because they attempt to say exactly what hurts or delights them. They reach for words that create rather than attenuate community. They witness what happens when anybody tells the truth and, therefore, they try to protect and expand the safe space that telling the truth requires."

For generations of readers who will benefit from her legacy, June Jordan indeed embodied the value and compassion, the "safe space," that black American women have contributed to the United States.

37

Betty Shabazz

1936–1997

Keeping Faith Amid Tragedy

ASIDE FROM HER MARRIAGE to one of the nation's true revolutionaries, Malcolm X, Betty Shabazz was an inspirational parent and educator. After her husband was assassinated in Harlem, in 1965, Betty struggled to raise her six daughters virtually alone. She attended college in New Jersey, earning an undergraduate degree, and then received a doctorate in education at the University of Massachusetts at Amherst, in

1976. Thereafter, she joined the faculty of Medgar Evers College in Brooklyn and was named director of the office of institutional advancement in the nineteen eighties, the position she held until her untimely death in 1997.

In June 1997, after a fire started by Betty's adolescent grandson had ended her life, a host of notable American scholars, activists, and political figures spoke movingly of Betty Shabazz's deep compassion and strong dedication to fighting injustice and inequality. "Betty Shabazz has not been given the amount of credit she deserves in shaping America's Civil Rights Movement," said Myrlie Evers-Williams, widow of Medgar Evers and then chairwoman of the National Association for the Advancement of Colored People. Coretta Scott King, widow of slain civil rights leader Dr. Martin Luther King Jr. preferred to remember Betty for her long years of dedicated work in the academic arena and on behalf of social causes. Scott described Betty as "a wonderful, caring person," an intelligent, motivated woman who had "carried forward her husband's legacy."

Indeed, Betty lived an extraordinary life. Hers is a remarkable story of inner strength in the face of enormously daunting odds. It is a modern testament to the resourcefulness, independence, strong will, and keen intelligence of the black women of this nation. To be sure, Betty Shabazz was the first to point out that she continued to learn and grow throughout the knocks, triumphs, disappointments, and milestones of her years. For the millions of black American women who admired Betty, it was those very challenges which helped shape the formidable person she became.

"I am not for women having typical female roles," Betty said during a speech in the eighties. "I had to do everything. I was the head of the household. When my husband lived, that was the role I played. When he was assassinated, I had to do everything. If I didn't make the money and bring the food in and pay the mortgage and pay the car note and pay the school bill, we didn't eat, we didn't sleep, and we didn't have a house."

Betty Sanders was born in Detroit on May 28, 1936. Her adoptive parents owned a local store, and Betty spent her early years in a protective family environment. After graduating from public school, Betty ventured to the Deep South for the first time. Previously, her life had been a routine cycle of school, church, Bible studies, work at her parents' shop, and sedate social activities in her Detroit neighborhood. But when Betty traveled to Alabama to study elementary education at the Tuskegee Institute, she experienced a harsh awakening. Racism in many forms permeated the small Southern village surrounding the historically black university, and Betty was saddened and confused by the disparate treatment of blacks.

After she transferred to a nursing program at Brooklyn College in New York, Betty first encountered the handsome young man who would change her life. As she described their meeting years later, Betty did not have much of an inkling that the man formerly known as Malcolm Little would become a guiding force for millions of black Americans. A friend had taken Betty, then a junior at Brooklyn College, to a local Islamic temple to hear a fiery young speaker named Malcolm X.

"I looked over and saw this man . . . sort of galloping to the podium," Betty said, recalling Malcolm's rangy presence and energetic gait. A few months later, Betty joined the Nation of Islam. At that time, the organization was little known outside of black communities across America. Founded in Detroit in the early thirties, the Nation of Islam preached self-determination and educational commitment for American blacks. Its leader, Elijah Muhammad, also spoke of separatism and of hatred for white Americans. The group was controversial, and not just among white Americans. Many blacks felt the Nation's rhetoric was inflammatory and detrimental to the integrationist cause being promoted by many Christian, middle-class black leaders.

All the same, Betty fell for Malcolm X and joined the Nation. After a swift courtship, Malcolm phoned Betty one day while out of town and proposed marriage. They made a striking pair: Malcolm was tall, composed, and brilliantly turned out in crisp suits; Betty was equally dapper, quietly powerful, and blessed with a radiant smile and thick, glossy black hair. Moreover, the couple exhibited a love and respect for each other that was palpable. Within the first few years of their marriage, Betty gave birth to four lively, inquisitive girls.

Betty worked hard to keep her young family together. Since Malcolm was a key leader within the Nation of Islam, Betty often found herself alone with her growing family while her husband traveled to temples around America. Nonetheless, she was dedicated to the fight for justice and equality for black Americans. She worked within the Nation of Islam as a health advocate, drawing on nursing training she had received while studying at Tuskegee Institute in Alabama and at Brooklyn College.

Over the next several years, Betty sometimes traveled in the United States with her husband as he organized regional temples of the Nation of Islam. She was a strong, silent presence throughout the turbulent years when Malcolm began to move away from the Nation of Islam. In 1964 Malcolm officially severed his ties to the Nation of Islam, and the couple traveled to Saudi Arabia for their first visit to Mecca. Their return to the United States began a frightening period for Malcolm and Betty, because their separation from the Nation was not amicable. For several tense months Betty and her children became the targets of bombings and harassment from some Nation members who were unhappy with Malcolm's decision to leave the group.

A year later, in February 1965, Betty and her four daughters were in the audience at Harlem's Audubon Ballroom when three gunmen fired at Malcolm X as he addressed the crowd. Betty, who was pregnant with twins, thrust her daughters onto the floor and shielded their bodies with her own as the bullets flew. Rising amid the smoke and chaos minutes later, she moved to the stage to find the bullet-riddled body of her husband. It was a horrific development, one that would thrust Betty into a difficult new role as sole provider for her large family.

Over the next two decades, Betty joined with the wives of other slain civil rights leaders, Coretta Scott King, and Myrlie Evers-Williams, to continue the work begun by their husbands in the fifties and sixties. For Betty, raising the public's awareness to the plight of children and the underclass was her first priority.

Helped by a small handful of friends who watched her struggle to feed her six daughters, Betty pursued the education she had abandoned when she married. By working in the day and attending school at night, she received an undergraduate degree from a small New Jersey college before attending the University of Massachusetts at Amherst, where she received a Ph.D. in education.

Betty seized the reins of her life and began a new, exciting direction for her future. In the early eighties she accepted a post at Medgar Evers College in New York City, and embarked on a productive career as a primary fund-raiser and administrator for the school. Throughout her years at the college, she wrote dozens of papers and articles focusing on education and health issues. Her work, as well as her commitment to raising her daughters in a safe environment, won accolades from many organizations, including the NAACP, the Urban League, and *Essence* magazine.

When one of her daughters, Qubilah, developed a drug problem in the early nineties, Betty agreed to help raise Qubilah's son, Malcolm. In the summer of 1997, according to police officials in the town where Betty lived, Mt. Vernon, New York, young Malcolm set a fire at the home he shared with his grandmother. Betty received severe burns over most of her body and remained in critical condition for more than twenty days. When she died in a New York hospital on June 23, 1997, her daughters were at her bedside. It was the end of an admirable life, but not the end of Betty Shabazz's legacy.

38

Johnnetta Cole

1936–

Furthering Academic Opportunity

FOLLOWING IN THE FOOTSTEPS of pioneering black women educators like MARY MCLEOD BETHUNE and BARBARA JORDAN, Johnnetta Cole, former president of Spelman College in Atlanta, set a new standard for educators around the nation. For more than one hundred years prominent black women like MARIAN WRIGHT EDELMAN and ALICE WALKER have pledged their support and allegiance to Spelman College, the premier college for black women in America. Indeed, Edelman, founder of the Children's Defense Fund, helped raise the profile of the sleepy Southern college to new heights as trustee of the university for ten years during the eighties. And when Johnnetta Cole became the first black woman president of the university, she continued improving educational opportunities for thousands of young black women.

"I would hope that Spelman students will not only graduate to become great surgeons or corporate executives," Johnnetta said in a 1987 interview, "but that they will also be among the core of folk who are seeking solutions to such issues as homelessness in America." To be sure, institutions like Spelman and Bethune-Cookman College, in Florida, have a long, proud history of training black women to step into important social and political roles.

During her tenure at Spelman, Johnnetta saw the direct connection between the fiscal health of the college and the prospects of the thousands of young women who study there. She oversaw a fund-raising campaign that secured more than $35 million for the upkeep and improvement of the college. In 1992 officers of the Leila Wallace Reader's Digest Endowment Fund announced a record contribution to Spelman College, an immense sum of money that would allow the university to offer scholarships to needy girls from around the nation, as well as facilitate several long-awaited capital improvements. For Johnnetta, the gift provided a way for black American women to play a vital role in the development of the United States. In announcing the gift, Johnnetta said the university would use the money to launch a $29 million scholarship program as well as a curriculum development program. Furthermore, during her years as president Johnnetta sought the support of Spelman alumnae and an impressive list of public figures, including actor and comedian Bill Cosby, who value the legacy of historically black universities.

Undoubtedly, Johnnetta's early exposure to the importance of higher education helped shape her determination and drive. She was the daughter of college graduates. She was born in Jacksonville, Florida, on October 19, 1936, at a time when many blacks viewed education as the only surefire way of improving their future. Johnnetta's parents were dedicated to the education of their family and to their community. For John Cole and Mary Betsch Cole, it was never a question whether their daughter would pursue a top-notch education. John Cole had graduated from Knoxville College in Tennessee before embarking on a successful career in insurance. Her mother, Mary Frances Lewis, had graduated from another well-known historically black college, the small but respected Wilberforce University, and for several years had taught and served as an administrator there. Moreover, Mary Frances came from a socially prominent black family in the Deep South: her grandfather, Abraham Lincoln Lewis, had founded one of the most successful black-owned insurance companies of the era, the Afro-American Life Insurance Company.

While growing up in the South, Johnnetta first began thinking about her heritage. Considering the example of her grandfather's hard work and perseverance, Johnnetta became fascinated with the anthropological aspects of the black experience in America. During the nineteen forties, as segregation required blacks to form and maintain their own business, religious, and social organizations, a strong sense of self-sufficiency and determination prevailed. Despite lynchings, discrimination, segregation, and a lack of political power, a solid middle-class community had developed in many Southern black communities. As a young student, Johnnetta endeavored to explore the history of personal strength that had enabled blacks to succeed despite overwhelmingly negative odds. As for her grandfather's success, Johnnetta traced it to his African roots. She said: "And so these men came together, and in a way which, years later as an anthropologist, I would understand to be the tradition of the Su Su of West Africa, they began a society that grew into the Afro-American Life Insurance Company."

Johnnetta immersed herself in her education. She graduated early from segregated public schools in Florida. Enrolling at Fisk University in Tennessee—another prominent historically black university—Johnnetta found an educational specialty that suited her inquisitive nature and interest in black history. A prodigy, she had entered college early through a special program for overachievers. She considered becoming a doctor, yet her curiosity about ethnography and black culture kept calling. She transferred to Oberlin College in Ohio, an institution with a long history of abolitionist involvement. While there, she decided to major in anthropology. After receiving her undergraduate degree from Oberlin, she ventured to Illinois.

At Northwestern University, in Evanston, she sought a graduate degree in anthropology. She studied with anthropologist Melville J. Herskovits. After earning a master's degree, Johnnetta then began doctoral work at Northwestern and soon met the man who would become her husband, Robert Cole. Together, the promising young couple traveled to Africa, where both conducted field research for their advanced degrees.

In 1967 Johnnetta Cole received a doctorate in anthropology from Northwestern University. During this period, many campuses around the nation were experiencing a student revolution. The civil rights movement was reaching its zenith, and the anti–Vietnam war movement was bringing unrest to campuses. At schools like San Francisco State University and the University of California at Berkeley, many black and Latino students were beginning to demonstrate for the inclusion of ethnic studies programs. For Johnnetta, this burgeoning social movement provided new opportunities. She accepted an associate professorship in anthropology at Washington State University in the Pacific Northwest; she was also named director of a new program at the small college, the Black Studies Department. The political upheavals had caused many college administrators to begin taking seriously the field of black studies, and Johnnetta was supremely qualified to establish ethnic studies as a serious academic discipline. The position provided a unique opportunity for Johnnetta to combine her chosen field of study with a deep personal interest in the black American experience.

Three years later, she accepted a similar post at the University of Massachusetts, where she remained for several years. By the early eighties, Johnnetta had become one of the most respected scholars in the nation. Indeed, during her thirteen years at the University of Massachusetts, Johnnetta would bring a rigorous scholarship to the field of black studies. She explored the unexplored universes of black American women, writing several important papers, including examinations of militancy among African-American women and the depiction of blacks in popular culture. In 1983 Johnnetta joined the staff at Hunter College in New York City, where she remained until 1987 as a visiting professor of anthropology.

And in the spring of 1987, she was named president of Spelman College. It was a triumphant event, both for Johnnetta, a daughter of the South, and for the college, where no black woman had ever served as chief.

Before her retirement from Spelman in 1996 to write and reflect on her productive life, Johnnetta spoke of the spirit of pride and determination and compassion she hoped to encourage among her young charges. Coming from a woman who certainly has left a remarkable legacy of her own, Johnnetta's words ring with truth, dignity, and hope for all Americans: "There is a saying that solutions to problems are often found by people who can see out of more than one eye. And it is black women who are able to see out of their blackness, out of their womanness, often out of their poverty and sometimes out of their privilege," Johnnetta observed. "So I believe it is going to be black women who will find the answers to many of the problems we face today."

39

Mary Frances Berry

1938–

Fighting for Compassion in Government

As ONE OF THE FIRST black American women to climb to the top of the
U.S. government bureaucracy, Mary Frances Berry has been a forceful
voice for increased funding for child care and families in the latter part
of the twentieth century. "Men assume that if they don't take care of
their kids, someone will," Mary said in an interview in *Ms.* magazine.
"While women assume that if they don't take care of their kids, nobody
will." With cool common sense, a keen intelligence, and a legendary

capacity for encouraging compromise, Mary has been a formidable presence on the national political scene for more than twenty years. And her accomplishments are all the more amazing considering her hardscrabble beginnings in the Deep South.

Mary has earned numerous advanced academic degrees and served in a number of important government positions during the past three decades. From 1977 to 1980 she served as assistant secretary for education in the U.S. Department of Health, Education, and Welfare (now Health and Human Services), where she oversaw an annual budget of $13 billion. In 1993 she was named chairperson of the U.S. Commission on Civil Rights. Overall, her hands-on involvement in setting policy and advocating for justice has had an impressive positive impact on the lives of millions of Americans.

Born on February 17, 1938, in Nashville, Tennessee, Mary was the second of three children. Her parents, George and Frances Berry, struggled to provide for their family. Because work was scarce, Mary and her siblings were placed in an orphanage for several years. It was a dire time, and Mary learned to become self-sufficient in the midst of uncertainty. During the years before the civil rights movement, life for young African-American girls in the Deep South was fraught with peril and pitfalls. All the same, after being reunited with her mother, Mary began to show a flair for her educational studies. Encouraged by a friendly teacher, Minerva Hawkins, Mary began to realize that education might just provide her and her family a way out of the grinding poverty they experienced. Hawkins was stern and demanding, for she saw in Mary the early spark of a remarkable intelligence.

"You, Mary Frances! You're smart, you can think, you can do all the things I would have done if it had been possible for me," Mary recalls Hawkins telling her while she was a sophomore in high school. "You have a responsibility to use your mind, and to go as far as it will take you." Two years later, young Mary made Hawkins and her entire family extremely proud by graduating from Pearl High School at the top of her class. From there, the possibilities were endless.

She enrolled at Fisk University, a historically black university in Tennessee, focusing on history, chemistry, and philosophy. After transferring to Howard University—the nation's preeminent black university—she received an undergraduate degree in 1961. Mary decided to press on with her education and eventually earned a graduate degree in history from Howard. All the while, she worked nights in local hospitals to help pay her tuition.

During this period, Mary realized that she had a deep interest in black history. She decided to continue her education and applied to the University of Michigan in Ann Arbor. While there, she expanded her academic interests to include constitutional history.

In 1965, thanks to her sterling academic record and dedication to historic detail, she was awarded the Civil War Roundtable Fellowship Award, becoming one of the first black American women in history to win the coveted academic honor. After receiving her doctorate from the University of Michigan, Mary embarked on a teaching career. At Central Michigan University, she took a post as assistant professor of history and, with characteristic determination and skill, also managed to study. By 1970 she had received a law degree and accepted a full professorship at the University of Maryland. Throughout the long solitary years of study, Mary kept in mind some words her mother had once said: "Be overeducated. If somebody else has a master's degree, you get a Ph.D.," Mary recalled to *Ms.* magazine. "If somebody has that, then you get a law degree, too."

Indeed, Mary had risen to the top of the academic teaching community while still a young woman. She was named acting director of the Afro-American Studies Department at the University of Maryland, making her one of the first black women in the nation to head up a relatively new kind of academic field of study. A few years later Mary was promoted to the office of university provost, where she served for two years. As provost, she oversaw the university's Division of Behavioral and Social Sciences, making her the highest-ranking African-American woman at the University of Maryland.

In 1976 Mary scored another historic "first" when she accepted an exciting offer from the University of Colorado. She was named chancellor of the college's newest campus, in Boulder, and became the first black woman in American history to serve in the top post of a major university. Her tenure there was short-lived, however, as President Jimmy Carter sought Mary out to work in his administration. In 1977 she was named assistant secretary of Health, Education, and Welfare, becoming the top educational officer in the nation. During her tenure she fought to increase funding for families and public education and was a vocal advocate for social programs that promoted job training. It was a triumphant moment for a woman who had come to value education as one of life's most important challenges.

In 1980 Mary again answered the government's call. President Carter appointed her to the U.S. Commission on Civil Rights, an organization devoted to monitoring the nation's antidiscrimination laws. At this agency Mary took part in a massive affirmative action study that was groundbreaking in its call for equal opportunity and access for women and minorities in America.

Mary's incredible track record was stalled, however, during Ronald Reagan's presidency. Although she was registered as an independent voter, Reagan took issue with Mary's work at the Commission on Civil Rights and attempted to fire her. Along with another top woman administrator, Mary successfully sued the Reagan administration and won the right to keep her job. All the same, it was a bitter period in Mary's life, and she soon went back to the academic arena.

She returned to her alma mater, Howard University, where she spent several years as a professor of history and law. In 1987 Mary accepted the Geraldine R. Segal Professorship of American Social Thought and Professor of History at the University of Pennsylvania. She also began to write books, turning to her expertise in history and government studies to produce thoughtful tomes on blacks in American history and women in politics. She also became active in social causes, publishing many papers on apartheid in South Africa and racial discrimination in America.

Throughout her long career, Mary has received more than twenty honorary doctoral degrees and several public service and academic awards; she was named one of *Ms.* magazine's Women of the Year in 1986 and also received honors from the NAACP and the Southern Christian Leadership Conference.

In the late nineties she was a prime example of the strength, dedication, and intelligence that black American women have contributed to this nation's success. As a valued member of the University of Pennsylvania faculty, Mary's insights and observations provided her students with concise guidance and instruction.

"Civil rights opened the windows," Mary said during an interview in the eighties. "When you open the windows, it does not mean that everybody will get through. There are people of my generation who did not get through. We must create our own opportunities."

40

Marian Wright Edelman

1939–

Advocate for Children, Advisor to Presidents

MARIAN WRIGHT EDELMAN represents the determined spirit of black American women in this century. Her list of accomplishments is long and includes work as a student activist and civil rights movement organizer as well as a stint as director of the Mississippi branch of the National Association for the Advancement of Colored People's Legal Defense Fund. As founder and president of the Children's Defense Fund,

Marian wielded a significant level of influence among national legislators and policy makers. She also retained a deep connection to the issues and concerns of millions of black Americans struggling with the complexities of modern life.

She was born in Bennettsville, South Carolina, on June 6, 1939. Her parents, Arthur and Maggie Leola Wright, named her after the legendary black classical singer, MARIAN ANDERSON. The year that Marian Wright entered the world, her namesake performed a landmark concert on the steps of the Lincoln Memorial in Washington, D.C. Indeed, Marian Wright has lived up to the quiet strength of the famous opera singer.

Marian excelled in school despite the poor quality of education available to blacks in the Deep South and went on to attend Spelman College, the preeminent black university for women in Georgia. Marian was later admitted to Yale Law School, graduating in 1963 with a law degree.

At this time, the civil rights movement was creating massive social upheaval in the Deep South, and Marian was anxious to lend a hand to the fight for racial equality. Armed with a top-notch education and a strong sense of herself and of her potential, Marian eventually became the first black American woman admitted to the Mississippi Bar Association.

As the civil rights movement gathered steam, Marian increasingly found herself in important company. In the mid-sixties she accompanied U.S. Attorney General Robert F. Kennedy to Mississippi in a landmark tour of rural living conditions among African Americans. Additionally, she worked with Dr. Martin Luther King Jr. to organize a Poor People's March on Washington, D.C., which took place shortly after King's 1968 assassination.

During this period, frustrated by the lack of resources being dedicated to civil rights concerns, Marian went to work for the Washington Research Project, a public-interest law firm. In 1973 she founded the Children's Defense Fund, a nonprofit, privately funded youth advocacy group. Through its work with local and national agencies and its revolutionary focus on the conditions of children around the nation, the Children's Defense Fund grew into a formidable advocate for underprivileged children in America.

Along the way, Marian met and married an idealistic lawyer named

Peter Edelman, and together they had three children. She continued to work in the academic arena. She oversaw a much-needed fund-raising drive while chairwoman of the Spelman College board of trustees in the years between 1976 and 1987. An impressive speaker, Marian became well known nationwide for delivering some of the most poignant calls for compassion and social responsibility in the second half of the twentieth century.

Indeed, during an important address to the State of the World Forum in the mid-nineties, Marian laid out some of the questions she believed all Americans had to attempt to answer as the nation was about to enter the new millennium: "A thousand years from now, will civilization remain and humankind survive?" she asked rhetorically. "Will America's dream be alive, be remembered, and be worth remembering? Will the United States be a blip or a beacon of history? Can our founding principal that 'all men are created equal and are endowed by their Creator with certain inalienable rights' withstand the tests of time, the tempests of politics, and become deed and not just creed for *every* child? Is America's dream big enough for every fifth child who is poor, every sixth child who is black, every seventh child who is Hispanic, and every eighth child who is mentally or physically challenged? Is our world's dream big enough for all of the children God has sent as our messengers of hope?"

A close and respected advisor to President Bill Clinton and First Lady Hillary Clinton, Marian experienced a disappointing encounter with them over the subject of a welfare reform bill. The bill was widely viewed as problematic to millions of undereducated Americans who struggle to find jobs and affordable housing. Marian disagreed with President Clinton's decision to sign the act, and her close friendship with the First Lady suffered a temporary rift. Nonetheless, Marian's work at the CDF continued to produce compelling arguments that all Americans must pay closer attention to the plight of our nation's children. First Lady Hillary Clinton told a television interviewer in May 1998 that she continued to regard Marian Wright Edelman as a trusted and valued friend.

In its annual reports the CDF emphasized the tenuous living conditions and inadequate educational opportunities facing millions of children each day: "If a child is not white, or white but not middle class, does not speak English, is poor, needs special help with seeing, hearing, walking, reading, learning, adjusting, growing up, is pregnant or married at age fifteen, is not smart enough, or is too smart, then in too many places, school officials decided school is not the place for that child," lamented one early CDF report.

Marian, along with her husband, a law professor at Georgetown University, remained dedicated to advocating for increased funding for early child-development programs through her work at the Children's Defense Fund. Over the years, she received several important awards and fellowships for her work, including the Albert Schweitzer Humanitarian Prize and a MacArthur Foundation Fellowship.

As Marian told the rapt audience at the State of the World Forum in 1994 she believed in the great potential in everyone. "Children don't vote, but adults who do must stand up for them," Marian said during the memorable speech. "While personal responsibility, moral example, and private charity are crucial, so are jobs, decent wages, child care, health care, clean air, water, and public safety that government must ensure, in collaboration with employers. All the soup kitchens and homeless shelters in the world cannot substitute for community and economic development which provide jobs with decent wages and dignity."

41

Tina Turner

1939–

Soul Survivor

IN THE MID-EIGHTIES the world once again fell in love with Tina Turner. A veteran soul singer and a dedicated performer, Tina had blazed a trail through the tumultuous pop music world at a time when women were often seen merely as window dressing for male performers. With the global success of her 1984 album, *Private Dancer,* Tina found a way of combining her twenty years of singing and performing soul songs with a hard-edged rock-and-roll sound. The results were spectacular, and Tina received several long-overdue music industry commendations, including Grammy Awards and MTV Awards for her hit song, "What's Love Got to Do With It?"

Moreover, Tina at last had emerged from under the thumb of her ex-husband, Ike Turner, the man who had taken her from a small southern village to the top of the pop music world during the fifties and sixties. Her comeback was especially poignant because, during her long career, Ike had become abusive and controlling, and Tina nearly lost sight of herself. "I was just a country girl, you see," Tina wrote in her bestselling 1986 autobiography, *I, Tina.*

Even so, hers was always a uniquely charismatic personality. Further, Tina Turner weathered the disappointments and tragedies of her life like a soldier. Some forty years after she first gained fame as a member of Ike Turner's legendary soul band, she was still a consummate professional and exciting popular entertainer. Like OPRAH WINFREY—a die-hard Tina fan who aired several shows featuring the singer's 1997 Wildest Dreams world tour—millions of fans around the globe revered Tina. In the annals of American entertainment history, few individuals have captured the spirit of perseverance, commitment to songcraft, and personal growth like Tina Turner.

When Hollywood decided to make a motion picture of Tina's life story, the drama, triumph, and heartache of her life reached a worldwide audience. The 1993 movie, starring Angela Bassett, earned an Academy Award nomination. The top-grossing film could only touch upon the true depth of experience in Tina's life, but for fans of popular culture—and of stories involving strong women overcoming terrible obstacles—the film remains a modern classic.

When one considers the early years of the woman who would become Tina Turner, it's not hard to imagine that she was imbued with a rare kind of inner strength from the very beginning. Born in a rural village near Nut Bush, Tennessee, on November 26, 1939, Anna Mae Bullock was the daughter of a well-known family. Her lineage included Cherokee Indians, and young Anna Mae carried the wide cheekbones and thick dark hair of her grandparents. Life in Nut Bush during the forties was filled with routine details, and Anna Mae had an enjoyable if uneventful childhood. Like many black children growing up in the Deep South before the civil rights movement ended legalized segregation, her days were spent in school, Bible classes, and church. Like other great blues and gospel singers—ARETHA FRANKLIN and BESSIE SMITH come to mind—young Anna Mae first explored singing while in the youth choir of her church. At the Spring Hill Baptist Church in Nut Bush, Anna Mae astonished parishioners and fellow choir members with her remarkably strong voice.

Her father, Floyd Richard Bullock, managed a local farm, and her mother, Zelma, was a neighborhood spitfire who always spoke her mind. Tina and an older sister, Alline, grew up in a comfortable household. Her father kept a plot of land near their house and raised vegetables, chickens, and pigs which kept the family's pantry full year-round. As Tina recalled years later, they didn't think of themselves as poor: "Daddy's garden must have covered an acre: cabbages, onions, tomatoes and turnips, sweet potatoes, watermelons—we planted it all."

Anna Mae wasn't especially close to her parents, but they took good care of her. When World War II broke out, her parents decided to move to Knoxville to work in the growing industries there, while Anna Mae and her sister were sent to live with their grandmother near Nut Bush. While there, Anna Mae was taken to Pentecostal churches, where the evangelical fervor of the services enthralled her. After several months, Anna Mae and her sister were sent for by their parents in Knoxville.

The reunion with their parents was short-lived, however, as Richard and Zelma were experiencing marital discord. In 1950 Zelma left her husband and daughters and moved to St. Louis to live with an aunt. Her departure was a devastating blow to Anna Mae, who suddenly realized how much she loved her mother. "I wanted her to come back for us, for Alline and me," Tina recalled. A few years later the girls' father also left them and moved to Detroit. He left Anna Mae and her sister with an older cousin. It was an unhappy arrangement, but Anna Mae made the best of it. This did not last, and Anna Mae went to live with her grandmothers, first one, then the other.

She attended a local high school and became a cheerleader for the championship basketball team. During the mid-fifties young Anna Mae also discovered popular music. Swing and big bands like Duke Ellington's and Count Basie's could be heard over the radio, and Anna Mae fell in love with the exciting rhythms and tunes of a new kind of music. She also developed a taste for country and western music, since the Tennessee music scene was largely defined by those rural genres.

After high school, Anna Mae and her sister moved to St. Louis to join Zelma Bullock. The river city was a big change for them, a town with tall buildings, a bustling industrial community, and a thriving black district. Young Anna Mae idolized her older sister and began tagging along when Alline went into East St. Louis nightclubs on weekends. It was at the Club D'Lisa that Anna Mae first set eyes on Ike Turner. At that time he was the leader of a popular band called the Kings of Rhythm. The club scene was energetic and rough around the edges, and Zelma Bullock didn't exactly approve of her youngest daughter's infatuation with the much-older bandleader. Yet when Ike convinced Zelma that he would make Anna Mae a star, she relented.

Over the next few years, Anna Mae would turn her strong voice and dynamic personality into the primary draw for Turner's band. Along the way, as the group purchased a bus and began barnstorming through black nightclubs nationwide, Ike Turner decided to make Anna Mae the "front woman" of his band. After they released their first hit record, "A Fool in Love," in the late fifties, Turner decided to make a couple of important changes in their lives: he changed Anna Mae's first name to Tina (he thought it sounded exotic), and he persuaded the young singer to marry him. They already had a child together by this time, and despite some reservations, Tina agreed to the marriage. "We were two totally different people, and I knew it couldn't work out," she wrote in her autobiography. Adding to her discomfort was the fact that Ike continued to be romantically involved with other women. "I was hurt and I was scared, but I couldn't think about turning back," Tina wrote of their marriage.

Indeed, Ike Turner came to depend on Tina to such a degree that he increasingly resented her growing importance in the band. Turner, eight years older than Tina, had been struggling for years to make it big. And when he realized his greatest success rested with the pretty young girl he had "discovered," it brought an explosive love-hate element to their relationship. Consequently, while their fame grew, and Tina became the iconic soul singer of the sixties, the couple's relationship was riven with sadness and anger.

Between 1964 and 1974, the Ike and Tina Turner Revue was one of the hottest bands in the world, recording top-ten hits like "Proud Mary" and touring in the United States and London with the Rolling Stones and other popular bands. Tina was a whirlwind of singing power and dancing energy. Along with her backup singers and dancers, the "Ikettes," Tina developed a kinetic performing style that remains mesmerizing when viewed today on videotapes or in rock documentaries.

Despite the critical and commercial success, Tina was in despair. Often, Ike would become physically abusive toward her. On several occasions, Tina was bruised and battered in fights with Ike, and her friends urged her to leave him. But she lacked the self-esteem to make a break and felt guilty because she knew that Ike depended on her. Today, of course, women in abusive relationships can usually find supportive social services from agencies designed to help women trapped in perilous circumstances. But for Tina Turner in the early seventies, it seemed there was no way out. "That was a shameful period for me," Tina wrote in her autobiography.

Then a knowing friend intervened. The friend introduced Tina to Buddhism, and the singer began to find her inner strength through meditation. In Dallas, after a particularly brutal fight with Ike, Tina found the courage to leave. With only thirty-six cents and a gasoline credit card in her purse, Tina made her escape.

The next ten years were filled with hardship and uncertainty. After she moved with her three children out of Ike's home, she realized how bleak her situation really was. She had a sterling reputation but no ready means of supporting herself. Tina began the long slow climb back to the top of the music charts. She toured supper clubs and state fairs, her energy and unique performing style thrilling fans across the nation. Then, following a show at the Fairmont Hotel in San Francisco, Tina met Roger Davis, a rock-and-roll manager who said he could put her back at the top of her field. He redirected her from soul to rock and roll. After several months of working with a crackerjack band, they recorded the album that would rocket Tina back to the top of the charts—*Private Dancer*—in 1984. It was a triumph for Tina, and she mounted a sold-out concert tour that brought her seasoned performing style to fans around the world.

In 1985 Tina won three Grammy Awards. She experienced the renewed admiration of her performing peers and the support of a new generation of record buyers. Since then, Tina has recorded several other top-selling albums and found new personal happiness through Buddhism and a close relationship with a German man.

In 1997 she had another top-twenty single, "Wildest Dreams," and once again set the world on fire with a live concert tour that thrilled millions of fans. Her story, with all its hardship and disappointment, is inspirational because Tina Turner never gave up on herself. For millions of music fans worldwide, she is the epitome of the strength, dedication, and intelligence that black women have contributed to America's artistic realm. Moreover, she continued to believe in her own self-improvement:

"Most of my earthly dreams have come true," Tina concluded in her autobiography. "I'm glad I never stopped pursuing them. But I always knew that singing and dancing weren't the fulfillment of my destiny. I always seemed drawn to spirituality, but I was smart enough to realize that I shouldn't confuse performing and spiritual teaching."

42

Charlayne Hunter-Gault

1942–

Breaking Down Barriers

CHARLAYNE HUNTER made history when she became one of the first African Americans to attend the University of Georgia. In 1962 the civil rights movement was in full swing, and Charlayne, a freshman who risked her own safety to attend the university after graduating from high school with top grades, learned firsthand about the horror and injustices of the Jim Crow "separate but equal" policies that had marred the Deep South for decades.

Since then, Charlayne has gone on to contribute her unique insights and valuable journalistic training to the betterment of the United States in essays and articles for a host of prestigious publications—including the *New York Times* and the *New Yorker*. Charlayne has traveled the world uncovering important stories of social development and political concerns for millions of readers. Moreover, as a contributing reporter to the Public Broadcasting System's *MacNeil/Lehrer Report* (later renamed *The News Hour with Jim Lehrer*), Charlayne was a highly visible example of all the determination and expertise African-American women have contributed to twentieth-century journalism.

Hers was a hard, slow climb up the media ladder. Charlayne has always drawn on the values and principles of integrity she learned as a bright child of the Deep South. "When I was offered my first job in television," Charlayne recalled in 1988, in an address to the University of Georgia graduating class, "the news director laid out for me all the qualities I had that he felt would make me a good television journalist . . . and then he added, 'Of course, you have a kind of lazy way of talking, but we can fix that.' As some of you may have noticed, that really didn't get fixed. I never allowed it. And I am now working for a program where that kind of difference is seen as a positive, a genuine reflection of the diversity of the nation and the world we attempt to report [on]."

Born on February 27, 1942, in the tiny village of Due West, South Carolina, Charlayne was the first daughter in a proud family. Her father, Charles Hunter, was a Methodist chaplain in the U.S. Army. Her mother, Althea, was a beautiful and warm Southerner with high expectations for her daughter. Growing up in the Deep South in the war years, Charlayne spent her earliest days in comfortable surroundings with her mother and grandmother. The Hunter family was a respected part of black communities in Georgia, Florida, and South Carolina, and Charlayne enjoyed spending summers with relatives in other far-flung Southern villages. Occasionally, young Charlayne would board a train with her grandmother and have many adventures visiting relatives in New York. Her first encounter with Harlem during the late forties left a vivid impression on Charlayne, and she determined to return to the bustling city someday.

Indeed, with Charlayne's father accompanying black regiments into the European engagements in World War II, the tall, inquisitive young girl grew to rely on her large extended family and neighborhood playmates. During her first fifteen years, Charlayne moved to many different cities with her mother and father, as he was assigned to various stations in service to the U.S. Army. A thoughtful, intelligent child, she managed to keep her mind on her classwork despite being uprooted many times during the years of her primary school education. In cities like Atlanta, Georgia; San Bernadino, California; and Anchorage, Alaska, Charlayne suffered the wrenching experience of making new friends and then leaving them abruptly when her father was assigned to a new post. Throughout her family's many travels, Charlayne took heart in knowing that her parents would always consider the verdant expanses of the South as home.

By the time Charlayne graduated from high school, she was a shining example of academic achievement and teenage wholesomeness. Popular with students and teachers, Charlayne was the homecoming queen at her Georgia high school as well as a valued member of the National Honor Society. A sharp student of English, history, and writing, Charlayne also developed a healthy awareness of the social concerns of the day.

Although she knew that no blacks had ever been admitted to one of the South's most revered institutions of higher learning, Charlayne eventually set her sights on attending the University of Georgia in Athens. Since adolescence she had wanted to be a journalist, and the University of Georgia had a journalism school. "I never knew until years later just how deeply worried the adults were over the prospect of us going to the University of Georgia," Charlayne wrote, referring to herself and another outstanding black student, Hamilton Holmes.

Together, the two eager young graduates of Turner High School in Atlanta eventually integrated the prestigious if racially discriminatory university. Her first days on the campus were difficult, and Charlayne rarely left her dormitory for fear of being physically assaulted by white students. Indeed, school administrators temporarily suspended Charlayne during her first few weeks on campus, saying they did so for her own safety. Photographs of Charlayne leaving the school under police escort were broadcast around the nation, and thousands of Americans, black and white, wrote to the National Association for the Advancement of Colored People expressing their support for Charlayne and Hamilton Holmes. Eventually, thanks to lawyers at the Legal Defense Fund, Charlayne was able to return to the campus.

The rest of her years at the University of Georgia were strained and challenging. Charlayne was subjected to all manner of abusive and demeaning treatment from her intolerant white classmates, but she was fortified by her family's love and support, as well as by the encouragement of many blacks who wrote to her during her years of undergraduate study. She turned these difficult years into an advantage, earning a journalism degree in 1963 that enabled her to achieve a successful career in the American media.

As a young journalist, Charlayne wrote for the *New Yorker, New York Times,* and *Saturday Review,* specializing in urban affairs. In 1978 she joined the *MacNeil/Lehrer Report,* a Washington-based nightly news program. In 1997, after almost twenty years with the program, Charlayne left her full-time position to live in South Africa, where her husband, Ron Gault, had been reassigned by his securities brokerage company. As of this writing she was working as a contributing reporter to the television news program, as well as National Public Radio, and filed reports from her home base in Johannesburg.

After overcoming the stings and disappointments of life in the Deep South before the arrival of the civil rights movement, Charlayne emerged as an especially articulate reporter who focused on the triumphs and struggles, the heartaches and joys, of the world's underrepresented peoples. She received many awards during her long journalistic career, including being named Journalist of the Year by the National Association of Black Journalists in 1986. Overall, Charlayne's life and career have provided an excellent example of the depth of knowledge, commitment, compassion, and dedication of African-American women in the last half of the twentieth century.

For the generations of black women journalists who will follow her, Charlayne's lifetime example of integrity and consistency carries the ring of practical and enlightened wisdom: "I was brought up knowing that you don't let anybody get you down," Charlayne said during an interview in the nineteen eighties. "And you don't let anybody get the best of you."

43

Aretha Franklin

1942–

The Queen of Soul

ARETHA FRANKLIN enraptured the American music world and fans around the globe with her powerful, gospel-influenced singing style. "Lady Soul," or the "Queen of Soul," has recorded numerous number-one hit songs and dozens of rhythm and blues, pop, and gospel albums that have sold millions of copies worldwide. And her modest demeanor and down-to-earth sensibility have commanded the respect and admiration of her music industry peers for more than forty years. She is the last of a dying breed—although Aretha is reluctant to hear her lifetime of hard work and artistic dedication described in such lofty terms: "I'm too young to be a legend," Aretha told an interviewer in 1988. As far as she was concerned, "I'm still the lady next door. That keeps my feet on the ground."

A deeply religious early childhood helped prepare Aretha for success. Her father, C. L. Franklin, was a prominent minister in the black community in Detroit, and Aretha learned to sing by listening to the choir in church each week. Indeed, Aretha remained true to herself through personal disappointments and professional missteps, including failed romantic relationships and an early recording contract with an unimaginative major label that nearly stopped her pop music career in its tracks. All the same, she has reigned as the very soul of personal perseverance and artistic integrity.

According to Peter Guralnick, author of *Sweet Soul Music,* which examines blues-inspired singers during the second half of this century, Aretha is a chief purveyor of the unique musical sound that distinguishes American popular music from that of any other nation in the world. "I remember seeing her on David Frost's TV talk show," Guralnick writes. Aretha was making an extremely rare television appearance accompanied by her father. Watching the broadcast, Guralnick was mesmerized by Aretha's strong reverence for her family background and her religious grounding. "How do you sing?" Frost asked. "Religiously" came Aretha's reply. "What sort of gospel?" was Frost's next question. Aretha didn't hesitate: "My father's gospel." Frost persisted, Guralnick recalls. " 'Which father?' he asked, perhaps with irony. 'Both fathers,' said Aretha, without any [irony]. When she sang, it was fairly cut and dried until, toward the end of the show, she sat down alone at the piano and embarked on Thomas A. Dorsey's 'Precious Lord, Take My Hand,' one of the oldest and deepest inspirational numbers in the contemporary gospel repertoire." From there, Aretha's performance on that Frost broadcast harkened to her roots in the church, and she began to "get happy," Guralnick observed. She astounded viewers with an expressive, emotive style of singing that traces back to churchgoers who "get the spirit" during especially moving services.

Indeed, Aretha is an artist who combines her family heritage of community involvement and spiritual dedication with her art. "I have to really feel a song before I'll deal with it," Aretha said in 1983. "Just about every song I do is based on either an experience I've had or an experience someone I knew had gone through."

Born in Memphis, Tennessee, on March 25, 1942, Aretha grew up in a prominent and loving household in Detroit. Her parents—C. L. and Barbara Franklin—were pillars of their predominantly black Detroit community. Her father was a noted evangelist and singer, and Aretha adored listening to her mother sing in church and around the house. In later years many of her longtime friends would note a remarkable similarity between Aretha's voice and Barbara's. By the time Aretha was in her mid-teens, she had decided that she wanted to make her mark in life through singing. At the age of fourteen, she had cut her first gospel record, accompanied by the formidable talents of musicians from her father's church, New Bethel Baptist.

Thanks to her exposure to church music, Aretha's early mastery of a unique soulful singing style earned praise from such musical notables as MAHALIA JACKSON, B. B. King, and Dinah Washington. While she was still in grade school, Aretha's talents became known to many other black artists who befriended the shy young girl whenever they visited her father's church. Because of segregation, many black performers had to stay in the Franklin home rather than the "whites only" hotels, while in Detroit. After graduating from high school, Aretha set out to become a pop music singer. She spent the next several years performing in night-clubs and revues along the legendary "chitlin' circuit"—the network of black clubs that existed throughout the Deep South and in some north-ern states.

She signed a contract in 1960 with Columbia Records and spent the next several years recording pop albums that didn't earn much notice. But by the mid-sixties Aretha had moved to Atlantic Records, where the producers knew how best to utilize her strong voice and creative phras-ing techniques. In the next decade Aretha produced a string of hit records that became instant classics, including "I Never Loved a Man (the Way I Love You)," "Chain of Fools," "Respect," "I Say a Little Prayer," and Stevie Wonder's "Until You Come Back to Me (That's What I'm Gonna Do)."

One of her proudest moments was receiving an award from the Southern Christian Leadership Council in February 1968. The award was presented to Aretha by Dr. Martin Luther King Jr., the civil rights leader who had been a longtime friend of Aretha's father. Sadly, Aretha would sing the gospel classic "Precious Lord, Take My Hand" at King's funeral service after he was assassinated in April 1968.

Aretha experienced a personal and professional slump beginning in 1979, when a devastating tragedy struck the Franklin family: Aretha's beloved father was shot by a burglar who broke into his Detroit home. The brutal incident left C. L. Franklin comatose. Aretha, then married to actor Glynn Turman and living in Los Angeles, rushed to her father's side. She remained in Detroit for five years, helping her family care for her father. After C. L. Franklin died in 1984, Aretha mourned his loss but slowly began putting her career back on track.

In the mid-eighties she again changed companies, signing up with Arista Records. Aretha reentered the pop music market and claimed center stage with several million-selling recordings, including "Freeway of Love," "Jump to It," and international hits recorded with British pop stars George Michael and Annie Lennox.

After so long at the top of the soul and gospel worlds, Aretha announced that she was beginning a new phase of her extraordinary life. In 1997 she told television talk show host Rosie O'Donnell that she had enrolled in the classical music program at the Juilliard College of Music in New York. Music fans were delighted to hear Aretha confessing that she'd always loved the art of operatic singing. After a long string of appearances at the televised Grammy Awards, she stunned her fans by singing an operatic aria at the 1997 ceremony. It was a breathtakingly risky performance by a woman who had won more than eight Grammy Awards during her thirty-year-long career of soul and gospel singing.

As she entered her fifth decade in the fluid world of pop music, Aretha had received numerous awards. In addition to the trove of Grammy Awards, Aretha had received NAACP Awards, Essence Awards, and commendations from various national, congressional, and presidential arts commissions.

For a shy little girl who always strived to express herself through singing, Aretha made a powerfully long-lasting contribution to the nation's culture. As she saw it, she was merely living up to the legacy of all those singers and artists who set an example for her:

"They call me 'Lady Soul,' so let me tell you something about soul," Aretha said as she accepted a Grammy Award. "Soul is something creative, something active. Soul is honesty. I sing to people about what matters. I sing to the realists; people who accept it like it is. I express problems, there are tears when it's sad, and smiles when it's happy. It seems simple to me, but to some, feelings take courage."

44

Nikki Giovanni

1943–

Poetry and Memory

THE HIP-HOP ARTISTS of the nineteen nineties owed a debt of gratitude to black American literary pioneers like Nikki Giovanni. Although she came of age after slavery ended in America, Nikki Giovanni felt the tragedy that her forebears endured. As a prominent member of the black arts movement of the late sixties, Nikki incorporated her ancestors' stories—and the struggles of her contemporaries—into vivid essays and poems. "I write out of my own experiences, which also happen to be the experiences of my people," Nikki said in an interview several years ago. "Human beings fascinate me. I just keep trying to dissect them poetically, to see what's there." The result, some forty years after she emerged as one of the brightest lights in the literary firmament, was a body of work that made Nikki one of the world's most respected poets of the late twentieth century.

"Hers is a committed and social rage," *Time* magazine noted in 1972. "She is capable of scalding rhetoric and one senses a dynamic intelligence." Indeed, Nikki exemplified the finest tenets of classical poetry, while also updating the honored tradition for modern times. From humble beginnings in Ohio to the halls of America's leading universities to the vanguard of black literary expression, Nikki followed a proud tradition of African-American women who improved the national understanding of race and gender issues.

As author of more than two dozen essay and poetry collections, recipient of numerous literary awards both in the United States and abroad, Nikki is a living example of black women's vital role in shaping our nation's cultural history. Sometimes angry, often graphic and detailed, Nikki's poems have chronicled the struggle for identity and national democracy among blacks, women, and other minority groups. And throughout all the professional accolades, Nikki still maintains a strong love for the simple practicalities of life—a cool spring day, a good book, a beautiful sunrise. "I used to watch the clouds roll by whenever I visited my grandmother in Knoxville, Tennessee," Nikki recalled in an interview. "I still am fascinated by the smaller things, like why corn pops, and how mother robin knows when to sit on the eggs, and when it's safe to leave. I like sunsets, and I love to be up early in the morning to see the sunrise."

Born in Knoxville, Tennessee, on June 7, 1943, Nikki was the second child of Jones and Yolande Giovanni. Later that summer, Nikki's family moved north to Cincinnati, Ohio. Like thousands of other Southern blacks, the onset of World War II provided the Giovannis an opportunity to find work in the larger industrial cities, work that was scarce in the Deep South and not easily available to black Americans. Nikki lived with her maternal grandparents, Emma and John Watson and attended Austin High School. A precocious student who kept mostly to herself, Nikki graduated early from high school.

In 1960, at the age of seventeen, Nikki enrolled at Fisk University in

Nashville. A historically black university, Fisk was one of the preeminent colleges in the nation, a school steeped in the proud history of the former slaves who had helped establish the school. Nikki enjoyed the college life, but was soon dismayed to learn some bitter news from home: Her beloved grandfather, John Watson, had died. She lost interest in school and was dropped from the school's rolls after leaving the university without permission. For the next couple of years, Nikki worked behind a counter at a local drugstore and took some courses at the University of Cincinnati. All the while, the young woman wrote poems and kept journals, her innermost thoughts recorded carefully and silently.

In 1964 Nikki felt confident enough to return to Fisk University. By this time, the civil rights movement was gaining momentum in the Deep South, and Nikki was caught up in the activism of the time. She helped establish a Fisk chapter of the Student Nonviolent Coordinating Committee and took part in several protests and demonstrations around Tennessee. As Nikki saw it, the struggle to end racial discrimination required all sorts of skilled activists—lawyers, businessmen, *and* writers and artists.

After graduating from Fisk in 1967, Nikki began working with writers' workshops in Tennessee and in some northern cities, including Detroit and Philadelphia. By 1968, as the nation reeled from assassinations, race riots, and social unrest, Nikki had helped found the Cincinnati Black Arts Festival. She had edited a literary journal called *Conversation* and received a Ford Foundation Fellowship to attend the University of Pennsylvania. Later that year, after attending the funeral of slain civil rights leader Dr. Martin Luther King Jr., Nikki moved east once again. This time she settled in New York. She had been awarded a coveted National Foundation of the Arts grant and began studying at Columbia University's School of Fine Arts.

At the age of twenty-seven, Nikki even founded her own publishing enterprise. Her first collection of poems, *Black Feeling, Black Talk,* created a stir in the literary world. As a novice poet, Nikki showed remarkable maturity and a keen eye for the issues of the day. That same year, she published a second collection, *Black Judgement.* By 1969 Nikki was well known in the growing community of black poets, playwrights, and artists living in New York. Local cultural organizations like the Harlem Council of the Arts soon recognized Nikki's drive and talent and helped her find funding to continue her writing and publishing. Meanwhile, Nikki took teaching jobs, including lecturing positions at Queens College and Rutgers University. During the last year of the decade, she gave birth to a son, whom she named Thomas Watson Giovanni in honor of her grandfather. Around the literary cafes and coffeehouses of Greenwich Village, Nikki mingled with the top poets and artists of the era. It was an exhilarating time, when political and social upheaval gave artists plenty of meaningful issues to build their work around.

In 1970 Nikki turned her considerable skills to editing the works of others, publishing *Night Comes Softly,* a collection of poetry by black women writers. During the next few years, Nikki's universe of teaching, writing, and lecturing expanded. She became intrigued by the "spoken word" movement, and in the early seventies began making recodings of some of her poems. She also became a regular contributor and editorial consultant to several serious arts journals. In 1971 a recording of her reading her own poems, *Truth Is on Its Way,* became one of the most popular albums of the year, bringing Nikki to the attention of artists in Europe and Africa.

She traveled abroad for the first time in 1971 and was warmly welcomed by poets and writers who admired her poetry and recordings of her readings. In 1972 the National Association of Radio and Television Announcers gave Nikki their annual award for Best Spoken Word Album, a stunning achievement for an artist still in her formative years. But Nikki, always a prodigy, fit easily into the rarified circles in which she now traveled. By the mid-seventies she traveled and lectured constantly, wrote several book reviews and essays, gave poetry recitals at Lincoln Center in New York City, and published a lengthy conversation between herself and novelist James Baldwin.

As college campuses throughout the nation continued to roil with students protesting the Vietnam war and ongoing racial discrimination in America, Nikki found devoted fans in university communities around the nation.

At the same time, the highbrow literary world was recognizing her work. In 1973 Nikki was named one of eight Women of the Year by *Ladies' Home Journal.* She also toured Africa lecturing, and was awarded a commendation from the American Library Association. The year was a banner one for Nikki as she also received a Life Membership and Scroll from the National Council of Negro Women and saw into print another poetry collection, *Ego-Tripping and Other Poems for Young Readers.*

For the next several years, Nikki's life was a whirlwind of teaching, writing, touring, and lecturing. She received several honorary degrees from leading universities, including the University of Maryland and Smith College. Her spoken-word albums, including the popular *Like a Ripple on a Pond* and *The Way I Feel,* became classics of the black arts movement genre. But, in 1978, a personal setback temporarily curbed Nikki's rise. Her father became ill. As always, family was very important to Nikki, and she returned to her hometown with her son in tow to help her ailing father. Nikki soon realized that she would have to help her parents as they entered their twilight years. Her income—like that of other poets—was not substantial, but Nikki threw herself into helping her parents. For the next several years, she continued writing poetry, focusing on books and recordings for children.

In 1979 her special attention to children's literature led President Jimmy Carter to name Nikki an honorary member of the President's Commission on the International Year of the Child. That same year, Nikki published another poetry collection especially for children—*Vacation Time.* After the death of her father in 1982, Nikki returned to teaching full-time, accepting a visiting professorship at Ohio State University. Although she had traveled the globe, Nikki found a safe and productive home at the well-regarded university. Two years later, she accepted a professorship in creative writing at the College of Mount Saint Joseph, a small, liberal arts college located on the banks of the Ohio River. She remained there for two years, relishing the peace and quiet and stability of the small community and raising her son. In 1987 Nikki moved on again, this time to Virginia, where she became a visiting professor of English at Virginia Polytechnic Institute and State University.

The Public Broadcasting Corporation brought Nikki's work into millions of American homes later that year when it broadcast a special program on her, *Spirit to Spirit: The Poetry of Nikki Giovanni.* For the first time, thousands of Americans encountered Nikki's extraordinary work and witnessed the vital, gripping way she gave her readings. She was appointed to the Ohio Humanities Council in 1987 and served as a judge on the prestigious Robert F. Kennedy Memorial Book Awards panel. In 1988 another poetry collection, *Sacred Cows . . . and Other Edibles,* earned Nikki new fans. For the next decade Nikki taught and wrote, her works striking chords among a vast array of readers worldwide. In 1989 she accepted a tenured professorship at Virginia Polytechnic Institute and continued writing and lecturing abroad.

In some instances critics viewed her work as "feminist" political rhetoric, while others saw Nikki's writings as purely personal espousals of life, love, and identity. Yet after receiving dozens of honorary awards, teaching at important universities, and publishing a body of work that included important cultural touchstones, Nikki Giovanni remained America's premier representative of the little-understood literary figure: the poet.

As she told a group of Illinois elementary school pupils during an interview in the late eighties, her life has been defined by sheer love of poetry and the art of self-expression: "Writing poetry isn't baking a cake or cleaning the shower," Nikki told them. "It is not a job we can quantify. It is a journey without end that we experience until we feel a point of completion."

45

Angela Davis

1944–

Fighting for Equality,
From Courthouse to Classroom

THE LIFE OF ANGELA DAVIS is a dramatic manifestation of the deep divisions in modern America. Born to a middle-class family in the Deep South, Angela was an unlikely candidate for political controversy. Yet, after being fired from her teaching job for her political beliefs, she sparked a nationwide debate over democracy in America.

During the late sixties Angela was among the thousands of young idealists who began questioning the structure of political power in the United States. As the war in Vietnam intensified and the domestic struggle for racial equality deepened, many college-educated young adults sought to use radically new modes of political expression. From California to Ohio, in university towns large and small, public demonstrations against military buildup, racial discrimination, and the assassinations of leading figures like John and Robert Kennedy, Dr. Martin Luther King Jr., Medgar Evers, and Malcolm X, brought a sense of urgency to the national consciousness.

Further, the ongoing cold war between the United States and the Soviet Union compounded social tensions in the United States during the late sixties. In many educational and business institutions, a hint of sympathy for Communism among workers or students was cause for concern. Angela's abrupt dismissal from a major university led her to question many aspects of our national political system. And, in a shocking episode, she ultimately was arrested and tried on charges that many believe resulted from her controversial political outlook. The trial created a sensation, but Angela was acquitted, in 1972.

In the decades after that headline-making trial, Angela became a committed and tireless fighter for the basic tenets of democracy, including especially freedom of political and religious expression. In 1980, as a Communist party candidate, she became the first black woman to run for the vice presidency of the United States. As a dedicated scholar, she has shared her powerful personal experiences and her sharply honed academic training with thousands of eager college students. Since the mid-nineties she has held a teaching position at the University of California at Santa Cruz, one of the nation's leading public universities. In 1995 she joined a group of African-American women writers and scholars in protesting the Million Man March, a large, "men only" demonstration organized by Nation of Islam leader Louis Farrakhan. Along the way, Angela authored numerous books and essays, including a 1998 exploration of feminist themes in the works of twentieth-century female blues singers.

For many black women activists, politicians, and scholars, Angela was a role model of towering strength, a woman who faced down incredible obstacles in order to stand up for her beliefs. "Some people call me brilliant [but] I just work hard," Angela wrote in her diary. During an adventure-filled life of disappointment and triumph, Angela proved time and again that the hard work of black American women helped this nation to grow and prosper. Indeed, as a child growing up in a segregated town in the Deep South, Angela always believed that blacks played an important—if overlooked—part in national success.

Born on January 26, 1944, Angela was the bright and inquisitive daughter of Frank and Sallye Davis. The Davis family lived in Birmingham, Alabama, where many of the key events of the civil rights movement would later occur. During her early years Angela was surrounded by a large extended family with deep roots in the South. Because blacks in Birmingham had to endure "separate-but-equal" social conditions, there was a strong sense of community and support among African Americans.

Angela took seriously her parents' admonition that she study hard and do well in school. Both parents were teachers, and they kept a close watch on her educational progress. Their vigilance paid off, for Angela was one of the top students in her high school. In 1961 the shy, studious girl learned that she'd been accepted at a top college—Brandeis University. Leaving the familiar, friendly environment of Birmingham seemed somewhat intimidating to young Angela, but she knew she had to seize this opportunity.

Angela excelled at Brandeis. She wrote in her diary during her sophomore year: "My first year and a half here at Brandeis was very successful. But, it's not enough. I want . . . to travel abroad, go places, see new things, explore. I have the chance to study at the Sorbonne in Paris, France, for my entire junior year of college. All because I study and do well in my classes. . . . Not many nineteen-year-olds have this chance, so I'm going," Angela concluded. "Look out France, here I come!" Indeed, she was accepted into the prized international program. At the Sorbonne, she learned about classic literature, art, and philosophy. It was an enriching experience, and the thoughtful young girl began exploring many of the intricacies of life.

In the fall of 1963 Angela was shocked to learn of some horrible news from home: someone had lobbed a bomb into a Baptist church in the heart of Birmingham's black community. Four little girls were killed in the blast, and millions of Americans nationwide were horrified at the brutal act. For Angela, news of the terrorist attack sent chills of fear and anger coursing through her. She had attended that church in her youth and actually knew the four girls who had died in the explosion. The shock and pain of the terrible event left an indelible scar on young Angela's burgeoning political psyche.

It was an important moment in Angela's political awakening, and she never forgot the sadness and outrage she felt over that bombing. Subsequently, Angela began to set her sights on answering some the questions of leadership and power that had started within her. "Something has to be done," she wrote in her diary after the bombing. "I can no longer keep my mouth shut and not say anything about all of this. I guess this shy girl is gonna have to break her shell."

Angela returned to the United States and graduated from Brandeis at the top of her class. Seeking to expand her growing political awareness, she decided to go to graduate school. At the University of California (UC) in San Diego, Angela found herself caught up in a cultural movement. (And like many political activists in the vanguard, she allowed her reddish-brown hair to grow into a large, round Afro, symbolizing a rejection of the widely held belief that "straightened" hair represented the standard for beauty.)

All across California, college students were beginning to ask some of the same questions that Angela was pondering—questions about equality, power, and leadership in America. One of her favorite professors at Brandeis had been a Marxist expert named Herbert Marcuse. Now under his tutelage in California, Angela embarked on an impassioned exploration of different political and social philosophies; she applied for a doctorate, and studied for a time at the prestigious Goethe University in Frankfurt, Germany. Moreover, she joined the Communist Party, USA. Throughout, Angela became a reliable and provocative scholar, and soon she was hired as an assistant professor at UC Los Angeles.

By the end of the sixties, however, an air of unease had begun to settle over some public universities. With volatile demonstrations occurring frequently on college campuses, some university presidents sought ways of expelling lecturers and professors who were suspected of encouraging student radicalism. In California, Republican governor Ronald Reagan was an avowed anticommunist and member of the board of trustees of the University of California. By the time Angela's name appeared on a list of professors, she had earned some notoriety.

In addition to joining the Communist party, while studying and teaching full-time, Angela was also becoming active in social movements outside of the campus. Her advocacy work on behalf of George Jackson, one African-American man awaiting trial in Soledad Prison, had raised the eyebrows of some administrators in the UC system.

On June 19, 1970, Angela made headlines across the nation when Governor Reagan issued a statement in which he defended an earlier decision to fire Angela from the university: "This memorandum is to inform everyone that . . . Angela Davis, Professor of Philosophy, will no longer be a part of the UCLA staff. As head of the Board of Regents, I, nor the board, will not tolerate any Communist activities at any state institution. Communists are an endangerment to this wonderful system of government that we all share and are proud of."

Time magazine dubbed her "Angela the Red," and her dismissal was seen as a key development in an ideological battle that was brewing in the nation. For her part, Angela maintained her resolve to help fight oppression in all its forms. In 1970 her association with the Jackson brothers would bring about a crucial event in Angela's young life.

One day in the late summer of 1970, the brothers made a daring attempt to escape from custody. Their trial was to take place at the Marin County Courthouse in Northern California, and the media turned out in droves to cover it. But as the trial was about to begin, the brothers drew guns and began firing at sheriff's deputies. When it was over, one of the brothers lay dead in the Hall of Justice, the other was wounded, and three law enforcement officials, including the judge, were killed. In the days following the harrowing encounter, authorities learned that at least one of the pistols used by Jonathan Jackson was registered to Angela Davis.

Angela went underground, fearing for her life. As the Federal Bureau of Investigation placed her on their ten-most-wanted list, Angela moved furtively around the nation, from California to Florida and dozens of tiny towns in between. The state authorities in California wanted to charge her with conspiring with the brothers, and Angela despaired of receiving fair treatment if she surrendered.

In September 1970, while still on the lam, she wrote in her diary: "What am I gonna do? . . . I returned to the States after the 16th Street Church bombing with a desire to do something. A desire to help the

movement." Instead, she found herself at the eye of a growing social
storm in America, and a fugitive from justice. It was a heartbreaking,
confusing time, and Angela began questioning her own actions.

During this period, dozens of members of the Black Panther party
and other revolutionary groups around the nation were engaging in
gun battles and dangerous encounters with law enforcement officials.
The atmosphere was tense, and Angela knew that her life was in
danger because the FBI had identified her as being "armed and dangerous" while she was on the run. She did not condone the shooting of
the law enforcement officers, but she knew that few Americans would
believe her. She spent more than two months hiding out from the
authorities, relying on a dependable network of activists and supporters to help her.

Yet the chase could not go on forever, and eventually Angela was
caught. On a crisp autumn day in 1970, she was surrounded by police
officers in a New York City motel. She had been hiding there with
David, a compatriot. Later Angela described her capture in a letter to
her beloved mother:

> They done caught your baby girl. Oh well, I couldn't run forever. I
> would have gone crazy living my life on the run that way. Oh Ma,
> you should have seen it. It was like "Angela the invincible," or some-
> thing. There were at least ten cars that picked David and I [sic] up at
> the motel in Manhattan.

Her arrest and imprisonment made headlines around the world, and
some supporters mounted a "Free Angela" campaign that echoed similar efforts on behalf of the famous Black Panther Huey P. Newton
when he was imprisoned a few years earlier. Her case was complex and
tinged with the political turmoil of the era. For months, Angela was
confined to a jail cell while she awaited trial. It was a solitary, cold
environment, but she was determined to survive the ordeal. While incar-
cerated, Angela read, exercised, and meditated and was closely involved
in her lawyers' defense plan. She sat tall in the courtroom during each
appearance.

Two years later, the jury determined that there was insufficient evidence to prove that Angela had given the guns to the Jackson brothers.
On June 4, 1972, her diary entry read:

The trial was a complete victory. After 13 weeks. The prosecution attempted to prove their case based on circumstantial evidence and on the [belief] that I was obsessed with one of the defendants on trial at the time of the murders. . . . Of course, like every other brother or sister in Marin County, I wanted the Soledad Three to get off, but not bad enough to kill innocent people. I had nothing to do with those murders.

Indeed, Angela's acquittal ushered in a new spirit of determination among some former "radicals." As the seventies progressed, many African Americans who had been on the front lines of "revolutionary" activism began seeking ways to work within the system in order to effect changes. For Angela, the next decade was filled with personal and spiritual exploration. She lectured nationwide and around the world about the need to end racial and gender oppression. She published a book of essays and wrote her autobiography. Published in 1974, *Angela Davis: An Autobiography* rendered her life story in sharp detail and with admirable honesty. She continued to support the principles of communism, and twice ran for vice president as a member of the Communist Party.

In the nineteen eighties, she began teaching philosophy and women's studies at San Francisco State University and became active in many local and national issues. When officials at San Francisco State declined to grant her tenure, Angela refused to give up on her wish to continue educating students. She wrote a critically acclaimed book, *Women, Culture, and Politics,* examining gender and power issues around the globe and taught at the San Francisco Art Institute.

Angela became a sought-after lecturer at colleges and community groups around the nation, and she cofounded an organization called the National Alliance Against Racist and Political Oppression. In 1988 she published an impressive collection of her lectures, *Women, Culture and Politics.* As with her autobiography and other essay collections, the book became an instant favorite among college students around the nation. In the early nineties she began teaching at the University of California at Santa Cruz.

More than twenty years after her dismissal from the institution, she returned to find a new atmosphere of tolerance and acceptance. She was granted tenure, and currently holds the prestigious Presidential Chair in African-American and Feminist Studies at UC Santa Cruz.

Active in numerous social causes, Angela was also serving on the board of the Black Women's Health Project, a grassroots organization devoted to increasing funding and education for the health and welfare of African-American women. Angela continued to be a vocal supporter of social causes and equality around the globe.

As she told an enraptured audience at Spelman College in Atlanta in 1987, she was simply trying to uphold her belief in the value of our shared humanity: "As we organize, lobby, march, and demonstrate against racist violence, we who are women of color must be willing to appeal for multi-racial unity in the spirit of our sister-ancestors. Like them, we must proclaim: We do not draw the color line."

46

Alice Walker

1944–

Folklore, Feminism, and the Color of Woman

WITHOUT A DOUBT, Alice Walker's immense and superb body of work has made a significant mark on modern American literature. Like the academic and literary organizations who showered her with awards and praise for more than twenty years, millions of American readers believe that Alice Walker has played a big role in improving this nation.

Indeed, Alice traveled the world championing the causes of the poor and exploited, from Africa to Cuba to the American Deep South. Hers was as much a journey of the mind and soul as it was one of fact-finding and political action. For all her international fame, Alice remained a deeply spiritual person who valued honesty and kindness far more than financial worth or critical acclaim. "If I didn't have the love of the people and of the earth and of the life force itself, I couldn't bear it," Alice told an interviewer. "I couldn't know that children are being subjected to all the things that they are being subjected to. I would just turn away, I think, as many people do. People go into drugs, they go into television, and they go into many things," Alice said. "But you can also go in through love."

Born in Eatonton, Georgia, on February 9, 1944, Alice Malsenior Walker was the eighth child of William Lee Walker and Minnie Tallu-lah Grant Walker. As the last child in a large family, Alice grew up in a poor but close-knit home. Her parents were sharecroppers who barely earned enough money to keep their eight children fed and clothed. They lived in a rickety shack not far from the childhood home of the famous twentieth-century novelist Flannery O'Connor. Years later, Alice con-fessed that she had felt some resentment that the O'Connor home—called Andalusia—had been preserved by historical and literary societies in homage to the writer after her death, while the homes of some black Southern writers were allowed to languish.

After becoming a financially successful novelist, Alice returned to the creaky old property where she spent her earliest years and reflected on the way her childhood had shaped her life. Back in the late forties, Alice could not have dreamed of the direction her life would ultimately take.

Minnie and William Walker were poor, but they also instilled a strong sense of pride and love in their children. Alice's great-great-grandmother had been Cherokee Indian, a fact which fascinated Alice and planted within her an interest in other ethnicities and cultures. As a child, Alice listened carefully whenever her mother or father told stories that they had heard from their parents. She learned that her father's forebears included a strong matriarch named Mary Poole, who had been a slave. Listening to stories of how Mary Poole had managed to survive the terrible life of slavery—including a forced walk from Virginia to Georgia while carrying two infants—left a deep impression on young Alice.

Though she loved her mother, Alice realized that her mother's world was serious and filled with hard work—and not a lot of time for her youngest daughter. "I was the last child, and my mother didn't want, really want eight children," Alice told an interviewer in 1992. "And she didn't really bite her tongue about saying that, either." All the same, Minnie Walker protested when the white landowner on the farm where they sharecropped questioned her decision to send her children to school. At that time, the children of sharecroppers were expected to leave their classrooms in the small, colored-only schools they attended for months at a time to work in the fields. But, thanks to her mother's persistence, Alice stayed in school for full terms, even after a tragic accident that could have ended any hope of her continuing her education.

One day, Alice was playing outdoors with some of her older brothers. Theirs was an erratic relationship, with Alice spending much time and energy trying to escape her brothers' taunts and pranks. Her brothers began teasing her with a BB gun, which wasn't unusual. But this time one of them shot it off directly at Alice's face. The small metal pellet bored into Alice's eye. After several hours of uncertainty, Minnie and William were relieved to learn that their daughter had not suffered brain damage from the injury. But the shooting left Alice blind in one eye, a tragic event that caused the young girl to retreat even further into herself.

Because her face was scarred, she felt inferior to the other children in her village. (An uncle later paid for Alice to have surgery to remove much of the dead scar tissue from around the injured eye.) Always a bright student, Alice turned away from her playmates and into the world of books and writing. Looking back, she realized that she was deeply depressed in the first few years after the shooting. "I no longer felt like the little girl I was," Alice remarked years later. "I felt old, and because I felt I was unpleasant to look at, [I felt] filled with shame. I retreated into solitude, and read stories and began to write poems."

Alice graduated as valedictorian from her small Georgia high school and was awarded a scholarship to Spelman College in Atlanta, a women's school founded in the days when blacks in the Deep South could not attend universities with white students. Spelman's students included the daughters of some of the most prominent black politicians and businesspeople in America.

When Alice said goodbye to her family to head off to college, her mother startled her by giving her three gifts—a suitcase, a sewing machine, and a typewriter—symbolizing freedom to leave, financial independence, and her choice of career.

By the time Alice reached the end of her freshman year, the civil rights movement was in full steam. Alice threw herself into organizing, participating in sit-ins and other demonstrations with student activists who protested segregation in the South.

In 1962 she was invited to attend a meeting with Dr. Martin Luther King Jr. in Atlanta. Moreover, Alice had been selected to take part in the Youth World Peace Festival in Europe, and her dedication to ending racism brought her into contact with a whole new world of political and social activists. Her new status as a politically active student didn't go over well with the solid middle-class administrators at Spelman, and Alice came close to expulsion.

Nevertheless, Alice's commitment to fighting for causes she believed in was undiminished. She traveled to Europe with the Youth World Peace organization and spent an entire summer traveling around the continent. Alice, observant and open-minded, began to develop a love of other cultures that would characterize her writing in later years. She eventually returned to the United States and attended the historic March on Washington in August 1963. Alice, like millions of people around the world who heard Dr. Martin Luther King Jr.'s "I Have a Dream" speech, was forever changed by the minister's words on that day.

She returned to Spelman for her junior year and applied and was accepted into a writing program at Sarah Lawrence College in New York. Alice packed her bags and headed North. That was a difficult decision, because Alice didn't want to leave the South during the height of the civil rights movement. She knew she would be one of just a few black women attending Sarah Lawrence.

By her junior year at Sarah Lawrence, Alice had become a favorite student of two well-known literary figures of the era—the poet Muriel Rukeyser and writer Jane Cooper. Noticing the beginnings of a great writer in Alice, the two women encouraged her to continue working on stories and poems. Alice had been writing more frequently and by the age of twenty-one had earned praise from legendary black writer Langston Hughes after Rukeyser, her mentor, sent Hughes one of Alice's stories. In 1965 Alice took part in a special program to send American students to Africa. She traveled to Senegal and other African nations and returned to the United States worldly and convinced that her mission in life would somehow return her to Africa.

Over the next few years, Alice endured several challenging experiences, including an unwanted pregnancy that caused her to consider ending her life. With the help of a close friend, Alice underwent a "safe" abortion (at a time when abortion was illegal in most states) and wrote deeply personal poems that helped her survive the difficult decision.

After graduating from Sarah Lawrence, Alice decided to return to the South. In Georgia, she helped register poor rural blacks to vote. She continued to find time to write and eventually returned to New York, where she took a job with the city welfare department.

In her early twenties, Alice began to gain some attention for her writing. Some of her poems and short stories had been published in literary journals, and Alice was thrilled to learn that she had won a scholarship from the Bread Loaf Writer's Conference. During the mid-sixties, however, the sit-ins and demonstrations in the South continued riveting the nation's attention.

In 1966 Alice returned to the South, and once again threw herself into helping the fight to end segregation. During a voter registration drive in Mississippi, Alice met a white law student named Melvyn Leventhal. He, too, was passionate about ending racial discrimination, and the two idealists fell in love. When Melvyn decided to return to New York to finish law school, Alice went with him. When the couple married, Alice was relieved to realize that her new husband encouraged her love of writing. In the early seventies she wrote an essay titled "The Civil Rights Movement—What Good Was It?" which won first place in *American Scholar* magazine's annual essay contest. Thereafter, Alice became determined to concentrate full-time on writing.

She was accepted at the MacDowell Colony, an established retreat for writers working on projects and in need of solitude and creative support. Alice spent a few months at the quiet colony in New Hampshire, pondering issues and situations that would eventually find their way into short stories, essays, and novels. When her husband took a job with the National Association for the Advancement of Colored People working on civil rights cases, the young couple returned to Mississippi. For the time being, Alice put her burgeoning writing career aside, working as a teacher for a local school while Melvyn represented several racial discrimination cases for the NAACP.

It was an exciting time, and Alice had mixed feelings about living in the South again. Her family did not understand why she had married a white man, and she found herself somewhat estranged from them. When Alice became pregnant, she rejoiced. But it was not to be. When, in 1968, Alice learned of Dr. Martin Luther King Jr.'s assassination, she became despondent. After attending his funeral, she returned to Mississippi. Stressed out, and despairing that all the work of the civil rights movement had been in vain, she suffered a miscarriage. It was a heartbreaking experience, and Alice continued to concentrate on teaching.

During the next couple of years, Alice and Melvyn remained in Mississippi, and she accepted a teaching job at Jackson State College. Her first volume of poetry, *Once,* was published, and Alice began gaining confidence in her writing abilities. She was starting to find her "voice," a critical juncture for anyone serious about the art of writing.

To her great joy, Alice became pregnant again. Inspired and confident, she also resumed writing fiction. Her first novel, *The Third Life of Grange Copeland,* was completed the week she gave birth to her daughter, Rebecca. Over the years, even as her marriage disintegrated, Alice took to motherhood well. Her teaching and writing careers also blossomed, and Alice took a job at Tougaloo College in the South, followed by a prestigious fellowship at Harvard's Radcliffe College.

In 1972 she received an offer to teach writing at Wellesley College in Massachusetts. While at the women's liberal arts college, Alice distinguished herself as an innovative, supremely well trained teacher. She focused on women writers, and ultimately became one of the first college professors in the nation to emphasize the work of black women writers.

In the course of her research, Alice made a discovery that would haunt her for years to come. She came across the neglected works of ZORA NEALE HURSTON, a Southern writer who had been successful during the Harlem Renaissance. Alice became preoccupied with Hurston's work and played an important role in reviving interest in the Florida woman's writings. Through much of the seventies Alice published essays and stories about Hurston's life, including an article for *Ms.* magazine that revived attention in Hurston's work. Alice even traveled to the tiny Florida town where Hurston had died many years earlier. She was buried in a pauper's grave, a sad, ignoble resting place for one of the greatest writers of the twentieth century. Alice bought a proper gravestone, and had it placed at Hurston's grave.

Thereafter, Alice seemed to plunge even further into her own writing. In 1973 her first collection of short stories was published. *In Love and Trouble: Stories of Black Women* won critical acclaim and earned Alice the ire of some black women. They found her description of some of her male characters as unfairly brutal. But Alice said she knew of men who mistreated women and was simply describing what she had witnessed. Her second book of poetry, *Revolutionary Petunias and Other Poems,* was also published during this period.

It was a creative, prolific time for Alice, and she edited a book about her hero and former pen pal, Langston Hughes, and began winning literary awards for her stories. By the mid-seventies she had accepted an editing position at *Ms.* magazine. In 1976 she published her novel *Meridian,* which concerned the struggles of a young black woman in the Deep South during the civil rights movement; it was widely hailed for its intelligent, emotional exploration of personal commitment. By the end of the decade, Alice had been awarded a prestigious Guggenheim Fellowship, which made it possible for her to concentrate on writing full-time.

Her marriage had ended amicably in divorce in 1977, and she moved to San Francisco. There she entered a romance with a black intellectual, Robert Allen. Allen was editor of the journal *Black Scholar* and shared Alice's love of literature and activism. Over the next few years

Alice saw some of her most creative periods of work. She published another book of short stories, *You Can't Keep a Good Woman Down*, and continued winning literary accolades. By now she had a small, loyal group of readers, including feminists, college students, and thousands of African-American women who were moved at seeing some of their own experiences reflected in Alice's work.

Along with Allen, she moved to a woodsy, secluded town in northern California. For Alice, who grew up in an isolated rural setting, the calm surroundings of Mendocino helped her concentrate on her writing. And in 1982 she finally completed a novel that she had been working on piecemeal for many years. Published in 1983, *The Color Purple* was a breakthrough work for Alice. Centering on the tragic and inspirational lives of fictional black characters in a small Southern town, the book startled American readers with its frank discussions of sex, domestic abuse, the legacy of slavery, and black Americans' longing for their African roots. The book won the American Book Award and the Pulitzer Prize and elevated Alice to the upper ranks of the literary world.

Still, some black American women criticized Alice's portrayal of the lead male character in the book. Cruel, uncouth, and unforgiving, the character—referred to throughout the book as "Mister"—sparked a controversy that followed Alice for years.

The Color Purple was a critical and commercial smash. When record producer Quincy Jones and film director Steven Spielberg told Alice they wanted to film the book, she agreed to serve as a consultant. The film, starring WHOOPI GOLDBERG and Danny Glover, came out in 1985. Years later, Alice would write about her disappointments with the film. In 1996 she published her version of the script (which Spielberg had not used) in *The Same River Twice: Honoring the Difficult*. This book also included journal entries and notes that Alice made during the heady days when *The Color Purple* was at the top of the bestseller lists and on its way to the silver screen.

Alice learned to extract valuable lessons from even the most difficult situations. Her writing through most of the nineties concerned spiritual pursuits, and reflections on the subjects of meditation, global environmental issues, and the plight of oppressed women around the world.

Intensely private, Alice said that it wasn't easy to publish some of her inner thoughts about her life. But she continued to write about a wide range of subjects, living in the stillness of Mendocino, where her daughter, Rebecca, was a regular visitor. For discussing politically and socially controversial issues, Alice gained a whole new kind of literary respect with *The Temple of My Familiar,* published in 1988, and *Possessing the Secret of Joy,* in 1991, which caused a minor furor because it concerned the rite of female circumcision practiced in some African and Middle Eastern nations. Ever imbued with a commitment to speaking out about the cruel injustices done to women around the world, Alice did not apologize for writing about the controversial subject.

During this period Alice also founded a publishing company, Wild Trees Press, and spoke increasingly about the spiritual side of her life. In 1997 she published another book of essays, *Anything We Love Can Be Saved,* which focused on her commitment to social activism and spiritual growth. And in a scary episode, she contracted Lyme's disease. Fortunately, doctors were able to treat the disease, and Alice turned to meditation and Buddhism.

By the late nineties Alice also returned as a contributing editor to *Ms.* magazine, and continued working on important projects dealing with spiritual and social issues, including the plight of women in America and worldwide. Many fans of her novels said they were willing to wait while Alice pondered her next fiction story, knowing that, whatever the subject, it would most certainly be a book from Alice's heart.

47

Susan Taylor

1946–

Publishing the Black Woman's Experience

IN TWENTY YEARS Susan Taylor rose from an entry-level job as part-time beauty editor of a new and unknown magazine to one of the best-known and most influential black women in America. Under her skilled eye *Essence* magazine grew into a powerhouse publication with a loyal readership of more than five million black women. It was a long climb, but Susan accomplished it with vigor, dignity, and integrity.

Moreover, like BETTY SHABAZZ and other prominent black women who have maintained careers while struggling to raise their families alone, Susan is a staunch advocate of women's key role in shaping the future of America. "Women work overtime, do double, triple duty, juggle ten balls at once," Susan wrote in *Essence* in 1988. "Children, careers, husbands, schoolwork, housework, church work, and more work—and when one of the balls drops, we think something is wrong with us."

Born in New York on January 23, 1946, Susan was a smart, inquisitive child. Her parents, Lawrence and Violet Weekes Taylor, were Caribbean immigrants who owned a clothing store in Harlem. She excelled at the Catholic schools she attended, and was also popular among her fellow students and teachers. When she fell in love, it never occurred to her that she should not marry her boyfriend William Bowles, owner of a profitable hairdressing salon.

Her husband had started having affairs with other women while Susan was still pregnant with their daughter, and she struggled with the difficult question of whether she should sever the relationship. Ultimately, her strong sense of self-esteem won out, and Susan divorced her husband. She worked hard for many months, but despaired that she might lose her apartment or become unable to care for her child. She earned about $500 per month working as a beautician, but rent for her modest New York apartment was nearly $400 per month.

After her divorce, Susan realized that she would have to take control of her life. At age twenty-four, she discovered that becoming an adult would involve challenges and sacrifices above and beyond anything she had ever experienced. She was afraid of what the future held for her, but Susan was also determined to overcome that fear.

"Fear keeps us immobilized," she said during a lecture in Detroit in 1995. "Fear keeps us from seeing opportunities. It's only when we realize that we're connected to something other than ourselves that we lose our fear and know we live in a universe of abundance."

Indeed, Susan mustered her resources and set out to find more meaningful work. It was a stressful time, and soon Susan began experiencing physical signs that she was on the verge of a breakdown: a squeezing pain in her chest convinced her that she was about to suffer a heart attack. Her doctor told her that she must immediately reduce the stress in her life. Susan was stunned. Walking home from that medical appointment—"I had no money to ride the bus, let alone take a cab," Susan recalled many years later—she came upon an unexpected source of inspiration. A local church was having an afternoon service, and she decided to attend. There she heard some words that have continued to define her life. "I went into that church and went to the service, and a Rev. Al Miller . . . said, 'With your mind, you control your world. God is alive in you,' " Susan recounted years later.

At that instant, Susan realized that she could in fact seize control over her life. After all, she was in good health, and the combined wisdom of the doctor and the minister helped convince her that she was smart enough and strong enough to get out of her bleak predicament. Sure enough, in a matter of weeks following that eventful day, Susan had landed a second job.

After seeing a copy of a little-known magazine, *Essence,* in a local store, Susan went to the publication's offices and applied for a job as a part-time beauty editor. The small publication was just beginning when Susan was hired, and she began to help turn it into a successful addition to the world of women's magazines.

A lack of a college degree didn't hinder Susan, as her warm and outgoing personality and stylish flair quickly endeared her to her coworkers and the magazine's budding readership. Between the mid-seventies and eighties *Essence* would cement its position as the veritable bible of health and beauty for millions of underserved black American women. Prior to the seventies popular magazines like *Glamour, Vogue, Seventeen,* and the *Ladies' Home Journal* offered lifestyle tips and health and beauty guidance to millions of mostly white, mostly middle-class readers around the nation. With the exception of a handful of magazines like *Ebony, Jet,* and the teen publication *Right On!,* no mainstream magazines existed for the modern black American woman.

But Susan was blessed with a particularly modern outlook. Having suffered the pangs of a failed marriage early in her life, Susan was devoted to the idea that black American women needed to feel that they could accomplish their dreams on their own terms.

Speaking from her own experience, she urged the magazine's readers to "use missteps as stepping stones to deeper understanding and greater achievement." By 1985 Susan was the top editor at *Essence,* and she decided to go to college. She enrolled in Fordham University, where she earned an undergraduate degree, in 1990.

Named publisher of *Essence* shortly thereafter, she is one of the few African-American women in United States history to head a successful monthly publication. As she sees it, she is merely living up to the long legacy of strong black women who came before her. "We are the first generation of black people in four hundred years who can live our dreams," Susan wrote in 1988.

During the mid-nineties Susan announced that she would cut back on her duties at the magazine. She also enrolled in a religious studies program at a top seminary in New York and told her readers that she was embarking on a deeply felt spiritual path. All the same, she remained a guiding force at *Essence* and continued to write a monthly column filled with words of encouragement, advice, and personal insights covering a range of issues facing black women, from health care to crime and violence to motherhood and marriage to religion and faith.

Her column was a popular part of *Essence*'s success, and Susan became synonymous with the image of a proud, self-sufficient, modern African-American woman. She was also a popular inspirational speaker. She wrote two books chronicling her thoughts and opinions gathered over her long career in publishing, and one of her books, *Lessons in Living,* published in 1993, sold more than 300,000 copies. Susan received numerous NAACP and Urban League Awards, as well as other media and business commendations. In the late nineties she remained happily married to Kephera Burns, a documentary filmmaker.

As she once wrote in her popular column, "In the Spirit," Susan believed in the value of the individual and in the high level of commitment, intelligence, and compassion that black women have contributed to the United States. "Each of us should be articulate and passionate about one issue," Susan once wrote. "The responsibility for positive change begins with you and me."

48

Whoopi Goldberg

1950–

Combining Acting With Activism

FROM A SCRAPPY STREET KID hanging around New York stage doors to celebrity, Whoopi Goldberg has cut a wide swath through America's entertainment world. As only the second black woman to win a coveted Academy Award, she is a living monument to the often-overlooked contributions of black American women to the film industry. Like HATTIE MCDANIEL and Dorothy Dandridge before her, Whoopi Goldberg is one of the best known and most beloved actresses of this century. And as evidenced by her trenchant quips and sharp political commentary, Whoopi is a staunch believer in the importance of black American women in this nation's historic development.

Born Caryn Johnson on November 13, 1950, Whoopi grew up in a loving household in Manhattan's Chelsea District. Her mother, Emma, ran a Head Start child-care program, and young Whoopi was a devoted fan of live theatre. At a time when many black American teens were feeling the first winds of social and political revolution, Whoopi decided to concentrate on learning theatrical crafts. (Her nickname was bestowed upon her by friends who noted that one of her personal quirks produced a sound similar to that of a "whoopee cushion." After a first marriage that later ended in divorce, she officially adopted the name Whoopi Goldberg.)

Aside from her mother's strong example, Whoopi's earliest impressions of black women in America were formed in front of the television set. As an adolescent, Whoopi first began to recognize the contribution of black American women by watching the landmark NBC situation comedy *Julia*. "I was about thirteen when that show came on the air, and to see this beautiful woman [Diahann Carroll] playing a nurse, a single mother whose husband had died in the war, was a real triumph," Whoopi wrote in her 1997 autobiography, *Book*. "A black woman who wasn't working as a maid! . . . Who walked with her head high and her eyes dead ahead! To be represented in a way that was intelligent . . . was a serious thing," Whoopi recalled. "It said, Yeah, we're out here, same as you, trying to raise our kids and do our jobs. Same as you."

In her teens years, Whoopi became a fan of New York's thriving community theatre scene. For a time she took part in a program for young actors, and there she first discovered her talents. But before she could really begin to explore the acting world, her life took a temporary detour in the form of a child. Whoopi dropped out of the Catholic high school she had been attending and began working to support her daughter.

The next several years took Whoopi to the Southwest and to California, where she worked at menial jobs like bricklaying and hairdressing. But when she found herself on public assistance, she suffered no qualms about taking the government's help to keep her family afloat. "I lived on welfare, as a young mother out in California, and there was no shame in it for me," Whoopi wrote in *Book*. "I'm actually proud of what I was able to do for me and my kid, and I'm not fool enough to think I could have done it on my own."

In San Diego she spent several years working as a hairdresser before a friend steered her toward the San Diego Repertory Company. At last Whoopi got a good sense of the actor's life. By the mid-seventies she had begun making a name for herself in the small network of community and experimental theatre groups in California. In 1974 she joined the Blake Street Hawkeyes, an avant-garde troupe based in San Francisco. After a young life spent watching musicals and legitimate theatre performances on Broadway, Whoopi won a role in the chorus of the groundbreaking musical *Hair*. By the end of the seventies she was a well-known young actress with a loyal following among other actors and fans of contemporary theatre. And in 1984 Whoopi succeeded in putting together a one-woman show, *Whoopi Goldberg on Broadway,* that thrilled critics and theatergoers alike. Its funny and poignant characterizations—a drug addict named "Fontaine," a little black girl who longs for flowing blond hair, and others—made Whoopi's show the sensation of the season.

By the mid-eighties she was storming the gates of Hollywood. First there was a breakthrough role as the lead character, Celie, in the film version of Alice Walker's Pulitzer Prize–winning novel *The Color Purple,* directed by Steven Spielberg. Whoopi's performance earned her an Academy Award nomination for Best Actress. She later starred in more than a dozen feature films, including *Sister Act* and *Boys on the Side.* Her crowning achievement in film, though, was reached in 1991, when she received an Academy Award for Best Supporting Actress, for her role in the hit film *Ghost.* As Whoopi mentioned in her acceptance speech on that historic night, she was only the second black woman (Hattie McDaniel was the first) ever to receive the coveted film acting award.

She returned to the theatre periodically, including another successful one-woman show, *Whoopi Goldberg: Direct from Broadway,* which was broadcast on HBO. Throughout her increasing success, Whoopi remained dedicated to working for social causes. In 1987 she cofounded, with comedians Robin Williams and Billy Crystal, Comic Relief, a charitable organization to help the homeless. Audiences worldwide got a good dose of Whoopi's quick wit and keen political eye when she hosted the 68th Annual Academy Awards in 1996, and the 34th Annual Grammy Awards in 1992.

Yet Whoopi refuses to rest on her laurels. In 1997 she again opened on Broadway, this time in a revival of the Stephen Sondheim musical *A Funny Thing Happened on the Way to the Forum.* The show was a smash, and Whoopi earned rave reviews for her portrayal of a Greek slave who turns the community upside down by falling in love with a member of royalty. In a profile of Whoopi following the show's opening, the *New York Times* reviewer remarked: "Welcome to the Goldberg variations on this 1963 musical classic, itself a vaudevillian spin on the classic Roman comedies of Plautus. . . . She emerges as a thorough, winningly game professional who understands that someone has to be in charge here. And as she ably demonstrated as the . . . emcee of the Academy Awards, Ms. Goldberg knows how to take charge, even in a part that is not exactly tailor-made for her."

With the publication of her autobiography in 1997, Whoopi conquered another aspect of popular entertainment. And, as she said in the pages of *Book,* she expects to have many more exciting journeys to share with her fans in the years to come.

"I am the epitome of what the American Dream basically says," Whoopi told an interviewer during the late eighties. "It says you could come from anywhere and be anything you want in this country. That's exactly what I've done."

49

Oprah Winfrey

1954–

Embodying the Dream, Honoring the Legacy

MORE THAN PERHAPS any other woman in contemporary America, Oprah Winfrey is an example of the ways black women have helped improve this nation. In fact, from America to Britain, from Israel to South Africa, from Japan to Norway, people see Oprah as embodying the American Dream. With her Emmy Award–winning television program, *The Oprah Winfrey Show*, broadcast in more than 130 markets

281

internationally, Oprah is one of the most popular figures of the late twentieth century. Her entertainment empire is enormous. It is a multi-million-dollar company, but at its core is a philosophy of love, redemption, and forgiveness. Oprah's is a universal message that connects with people of every stripe.

If there were any doubts about Oprah's influence and popularity, they were washed away in the aftermath of a Texas judge's March 1998 ruling in her favor in a lawsuit brought against her by a group of Amarillo cattlemen after she televised a show focusing on a deadly cattle virus. The trial was an important test of the First Amendment to the U.S. Constitution, and legal scholars and journalists watched the six-week-long trial anxiously to see whether Oprah would be found guilty of "wrongfully disparaging" the beef industry. She had denied the charges and stood trial in Amarillo to defend herself.

During the trial, Oprah rented a local theater to tape her daily talk show. The cattlemen soon learned that their opponent had a much larger support base than they had ever dreamed. For a month, hundreds of Texans flooded into Amarillo to attend the tapings of the show. Oprah was gracious, organized, and incredibly composed during the stressful situation. And when the trial ended, and the judge ruled that the cattlemen had little basis for their lawsuit, Oprah appeared before an adoring crowd in front of the courthouse. Looking relieved, somber, and happy all at once, Oprah spoke about her love of our American democracy, and the U.S. Constitution. "Free speech not only rules," Oprah said, triumphantly. "It rocks!" The next day, her expressive image was visible at the top of newspapers and television programs around the globe.

It was a remarkable moment, for many reasons. Oprah had come a long way before reaching that joyous scene on the Amarillo courthouse steps. Few Americans—man or woman, black or white—have enjoyed the high level of public admiration and fascination that Oprah experiences. Yet after an eventful life of uncertainty and disappointments, of self-doubt and self-improvement, of financial success, public criticism, and, ultimately, critical acclaim, Oprah's courtroom victory was a stunning affirmation of her belief in the power of black American women. With regularity, Oprah had reminded her viewers and fans that she was a fortunate individual who had benefited from the strong spirits who had come before her, those famous and unknown black American women who had served as a bridge between the nation's past and its future.

"I am where I am today because of the bridges that I crossed," Oprah told *Essence* magazine in 1987. "Sojourner Truth was a bridge. Harriet Tubman was a bridge. Ida B. Wells was a bridge. Fannie Lou Hamer was a bridge."

Indeed, Oprah's example of human kindness, sharp business skills, personal bravery, and dedication to democratic ideals will stand as a significant bridge for millions of Americans in the years to come. But as Oprah has indicated on more than one occasion, her early life was tough preparation for the commercial success and personal awareness that lay ahead.

Born in a tiny Mississippi town called Kosciusko on January 29, 1954, Oprah was a smart, observant girl. Her mother and father, Vernita Lee and Vernon Winfrey, did not marry. In her earliest years, Oprah lived with relatives on a small, rural plot of land in the Deep South. Oprah's mother had taken a job in far-off Milwaukee, Wisconsin, and left Oprah in the care of her grandmother. Oprah's grandmother was a stern but loving guardian and taught her grandchild to read at an early age. "My grandmother gave me the foundation for success that I was allowed to continue building upon," Oprah said in 1991.

Attending church each week was also an important part of Oprah's early foundation. Her birth name was supposed to have been Orpah, a biblical name, but when her mother filled out the hospital documents, somehow the letters got transposed.

During those early years, church and the Bible played a big part in Oprah's life. Because of her grandmother's careful tutelage, Oprah was a regular guest in the pulpit at Sunday church services. She startled parishioners by reciting long poems and Bible passages on many occasions. Dressed in crisp, clean dresses, with her hair carefully combed and braided, the precocious little girl displayed a strong speaking voice, perfect diction, and the beginning signs of that elusive quality known as "stage presence." Looking back, Oprah realized that even as a child, she had envisioned her life taking some form of a public role.

Watching her grandmother at work around the farm where they lived—cleaning, washing clothes outdoors, doing yardwork—helped convince Oprah that she must try to make her life different somehow.

"I remember standing on the back porch . . . and my grandmother was boiling the clothes because, you know, at that time, we didn't have washing machines, so people would boil clothes in a great big pot," Oprah recalled. "And I was watching her from the back porch, I was four years old, and I remember thinking, 'My life won't be like this. My life won't be like this, it will be better,' " Oprah said.

Young Oprah was not arrogant or pretentious, she simply had a keen sense that her life would hold different challenges than those faced by her mother and grandmother. At age six, Oprah moved to Milwaukee to live with her mother. It was a culture shock for the young girl. Her life there was very different from the safe, protected environment of her grandmother's rural Mississippi farm. Not long after going to live with her mother, Oprah became the victim of emotional and sexual abuse at the hands of some males in her new neighborhood.

"I was living with my mother and living under circumstances that a lot of young children have to deal with even today," Oprah said in 1991. Indeed, her strong dedication to improving the plight of American children is now a cornerstone of her popular talk show. And to hear her tell it, it was something of a miracle that she survived those harsh years in Milwaukee when she was a troubled adolescent: "I was raped when I was nine by a cousin and I never told anybody until I was in my late twenties. Not only was I raped by a cousin, I was raped by a cousin, and then later sexually molested by a friend of the family, and then by an uncle," Oprah remembered with sadness. "It was just an ongoing, continuous thing. So much so that I started to think, you know, 'This is the way life is.' "

In 1990, during a live interview with a woman who had multiple personalities, Oprah realized that her childhood trauma of abuse had had a profound effect on her subconscious. When the revelation hit Oprah, she became emotional and had to struggle through the remainder of the interview. It was her first step toward learning not to blame herself for the abuse she had endured. But long before that point, Oprah had few alternatives for dealing with the abusive men in her family.

Desperate, Oprah began running away from home to escape the abuse. She was placed in a juvenile home at the age of thirteen, and felt very much alone. At age fourteen, she learned that she was pregnant. The baby was born prematurely, however, and died shortly afterward. Oprah was beside herself, and wondered what she would do with her life.

Her mother, Vernita, was also worried about her daughter. She sent Oprah to live with her father, in Nashville, where she soon regained her balance. Vernon Winfrey was a strict disciplinarian who gave Oprah a firm set of rules that he expected her to follow. There would be no more late nights for the teenager, and no more cutting school. Vernon also required Oprah to read a book a week and then write a report to be given to him at the end of each week. It was a new and challenging world for the troubled girl, and she blossomed under the discipline.

Oprah realized that she loved her father, and now thanks him for encouraging within her a love of reading. "As strict as he was, he had some concerns about me making the best of my life, and he would not accept anything less than what he thought was my best," Oprah recalled years later.

The next few years were a period of meaningful growth for Oprah. In 1971 all her early training in public speaking paid off. Where her childhood church exposure to public speaking had been exhilarating, Oprah's bleak years in Milwaukee had temporarily dimmed her ardor for the spotlight. Nonetheless, she ran for the coveted title of Miss Black Nashville in 1971 and won. Her next stop on the beauty pageant circuit was the state competition, and Oprah was chosen Miss Black Tennessee in 1971. In 1972 she enrolled at Tennessee State University and applied for a job at a local television station. (She had already worked for a local radio station for a brief period.) During her audition for the television news job, she mimicked one of her idols—network newscaster Barbara Walters. The composed, intelligent young woman greatly impressed the station bosses, and she was hired. It was the first of many crucial steps on her climb to television stardom.

She was, at nineteen, the first black woman to anchor a local news broadcast in Nashville. And within months of starting her job at WTVF, Oprah was a local celebrity. At the same time, her own personal experience with hardship and abuse made her a rather unlikely television journalist.

"My openness is the reason why I did not do so well as a news reporter," Oprah said during a 1991 interview. "Because I used to go on assignment and be so open that I would say to people at fires, people who had lost their children, I'd say to them, 'That's okay, you don't have to talk to me.' Well, then you go back to the newsroom and the news director says, 'What do you mean they didn't have to talk to you?' And I'd say, 'But she just lost her child, and you know, I just felt so bad,'" Oprah recalled. "So, I didn't do very well. I was too involved. I'd go to funerals of people and not go in. . . . I wouldn't want to talk to them, disturb them, or cry on the air."

Her empathy with those in pain would later make Oprah one of the most powerful personalities in the world. But in those early years at local television stations Oprah had to find another way to maximize her incredible screen presence and ability to encourage people to speak comfortably about their situations. In 1976 she moved to a Baltimore, Maryland, television station, where she served as coanchor for the next two years. Her calm, friendly demeanor appealed to Maryland viewers, and soon Oprah was offered a shot at hosting her own show. On the local talk show, *People Are Talking,* Oprah interviewed local officials, visiting celebrities, and just plain folk who had done interesting things. At age twenty-two she became a staple for many Baltimore television viewers, and her audience grew and grew during eight years at WJZ-TV.

Yet, during this period, Oprah's personal demons began to resurface. Now, instead of staying out late, Oprah began a romance with food that would last for years. In her bestselling 1996 book *Make the Connection,* Oprah tells how she began to overeat out of anxiety and deep-seated feelings of inadequacy. She didn't know it then, but her inner torment over having been abused as an adolescent was playing havoc with her life. "I didn't realize at the time that by overeating, I was trying to fill something deeper, something unconscious. If you had asked me then or even ten years later, I would have answered: 'I love chocolate chip cookies.' The fact that I was lonely, somewhat depressed, and having a hard time adjusting to the new job never entered my mind."

And so, for the next several years, Oprah embarked on a battle of the bulge. As with many television personalities, the subject of weight and personal appearance is important. In Oprah's case, she would try diet after diet, losing and regaining pounds over and over again without really managing to confront the reason why she tended to overeat.

All the while, her professional star continued to rise. In 1984 she was offered a job as host of a morning talk show in one of the nation's top markets—Chicago. She moved back to the Midwest and became a fixture on local television as host of *A.M. Chicago.* Oprah's show became so popular that it regularly trounced all other morning news shows in Chicago. During this period, Oprah also had an opportunity to explore another childhood dream: acting.

She had read ALICE WALKER's Pulitzer Prize–winning novel *The Color Purple* and loved it. When filmmaker Steven Spielberg decided to make a movie of the book, Oprah auditioned for a key part, that of a strong black woman named Sophia who refuses to bow to the racist whites in the story's small Southern town. Spielberg chose Oprah to play the part, and she played it magnificently. Critics nationwide hailed her performance, and Oprah received an Academy Award nomination. It was a joyous development for a woman who had dreamed of acting stardom while still a young girl in a poor Mississippi household.

Along the way, Oprah signed a contract to host her own talk show. In 1986 *The Oprah Winfrey Show* aired its first nationally syndicated broadcast. At the time the popular talk show *Donahue,* hosted by Phil Donahue, offered afternoon viewers a steady diet of serious subjects and news-related topics. Oprah's show was revolutionary—and somewhat controversial. Guests would speak to Oprah and audience members about a host of formerly taboo subjects—rape, incest, drug abuse, and crimes they'd committed. Many of the show's themes made Oprah uncomfortable, but she couldn't deny that her ratings were among the highest in daytime television history. Soon her afternoon talk show replaced *Donahue* as the top daytime talk show in the nation. And critics began to complain that her show, and later those of several copycats, such as *Jerry Springer, Maury Povich,* and *Montel Williams,* were offering little more than sorry freak shows to titillated viewers. Oprah agreed.

During the first few years of her show, Oprah had seen enormous financial success and won several daytime Emmy Awards for best talk-show host. Yet Oprah knew she had to offer her viewers something more positive. In 1988 she seized control of her professional fate. She was already one of the highest-paid television personalities in the nation. But when her contract came up for renewal, she formed her own production company and bought her show from its original owners, Capitol Cities/ABC.

Oprah called her new production company Harpo Productions (*Harpo* is *Oprah* spelled backward) and bought an entire studio facility in Chicago. As she envisioned it, her company would produce not only her highly rated and financially successful talk show but important films as well. Oprah directed her staff to steer clear of the lurid subject matter that was popping up on other talk shows. She made a responsible decision to offer her viewers positive and useful explorations of life, and her ratings continued to climb.

Meanwhile, she continued her struggle with a weight problem. In *Make the Connection,* Oprah described how all the success failed to help her answer the question of why she continued to overeat: "Now, looking back, I see no difference between myself and a junkie, scrambling for a needle and whatever dope might be around. Food was my dope," Oprah recollected. "In that first year of working in Chicago, I had gained twenty-eight pounds."

When *Newsweek* magazine wrote about Oprah's success in Chicago, the story referred to her as "nearly 200 pounds of Mississippi-bred black womanhood." Oprah was mortified, yet still denied to herself that she had a problem. "At that time, I was 202 pounds, but telling myself I didn't look a pound over 180," she wrote. For the next several years, Oprah continued on a roller coaster of losing and regaining weight.

When, in the early nineties, she reached 237 pounds, Oprah decided she had better begin to make some serious changes. The turning point was the Daytime Emmy Awards ceremony, in which Oprah was the winner of yet another trophy for best talk-show host. Walking up to the podium to receive the award, all she could think of was how awful she looked in the short-skirted ensemble she had chosen to wear. Calling it one of the most humiliating moments of her life, Oprah set out to end her battle with herself once and for all. With the help of a trainer and nutritionist, Oprah finally began to "make the connection."

Thanks to a faithful regimen that included gymwork, jogging, and a liberal but healthful diet of grains, vegetables, and "regular food," Oprah found peace with herself. She began trying to keep her weight in the low to mid-150s, but not beating up on herself if she gained extra pounds from time to time. "And that's okay, I've accepted that," Oprah wrote in 1996. "The most important part is to understand that it's not as much about the weight as it is about making the connection. That means looking after yourself every day and putting forth your best effort to love yourself and do what's best for you."

Indeed, Oprah's newfound inner happiness benefited millions of television viewers around the world. Her Book Club—in which Oprah asked viewers to read certain titles and then take part in discussions about the books—ignited a frenzy of interest when it premiered in 1996. Since then, millions of viewers who might not otherwise have bothered are reading books like TONI MORRISON's *Song of Solomon* and Ernest Gaines's *Lesson Before Dying*. And Harpo Productions had aired some of the most highly rated television movies of all time, including a 1998 broadcast of DOROTHY WEST's popular novel *The Wedding*.

Oprah announced in late 1997 that she would continue her talk show for at least two more years. She produced a film of Toni Morrison's 1987 Pulitzer Prize–winning novel, *Beloved,* and starred in the picture. And after Oprah's amazing victory over the Texas cattlemen in March 1998, she gained new fans who came to see her as a living monument to the commitment to democracy. At the young age of forty-four, Oprah, the once-troubled girl from a small Mississippi town, had already secured her place in history as a woman who changed America.

50

Florence Griffith Joyner

1959–1998

Racing Into Olympic History

AN OUTSTANDING SPRINTER even while in high school, Florence Griffith Joyner didn't slow down much in the twenty years that followed. With a dedication to rigorous physical training, a healthful diet, and a deep reservoir of personal confidence, the woman affectionately known as Flo-Jo was the only American woman to ever win four medals in a single Olympic track and field competition. With a legendary capacity for concentration, Florence contributed mightily to America's standing as a powerhouse in international track competition.

As a devoted mother and wife, she was also a vocal spokeswoman for improving the mental and physical health of millions of African-American children. In the early nineties she was appointed cochairperson of the President's Council on Physical Fitness and Sports; Florence was also director of her own nonprofit youth foundation, Flo-Jo International, an organization designed to encourage healthy development of inner-city children. Always the picture of charm and excellent physical fitness, Florence was an innovative designer of women's athletic wear. Hers was a full, productive life of helping others by offering her own story of determination, hard work, and keen intelligence as a living role model.

The trajectory of her life—from humble beginnings in a low-income household to the top of her chosen field—was similar to that of many successful African-American women. Florence was born on December 21, 1959, in Los Angeles, the seventh of eleven children. Her parents, Florence and Robert Griffith, lived in the Watts section of the city and struggled to support their large family. During the sixties Watts was alive with the sights and sounds of social change. Florence and her siblings watched as social upheaval and political activism brought civil unrest to their neighborhood. In 1965, when she was still in elementary school, thousands of residents in the predominantly black neighborhood faced off with the Los Angeles Police Department in several nights of street fighting and looting. The Watts community was devastated.

While growing up in a crowded housing project, Florence resolved to survive the precarious world of poverty and unhappiness that sometimes characterized portions of her community. In high school, she began concentrating on her physical education classes and displayed a remarkable speed and strength on the track oval. Her ability earned her acceptance at California State University, Northridge.

Florence's parents were thrilled and proud to learn of her admission. The public university system in California was among the best in the nation at this time. For many students like Florence, attending one of the dozen Cal-State universities provided an affordable way to obtain a solid education. Indeed, after her worldwide success in track and field, Florence would become a staunch supporter of numerous educational charities. While at Northridge, Florence first developed the work habits and training regimen that would ultimately make her the fastest woman in the world.

And when she later transferred to the University of California in Los Angeles, her local reputation as a forceful runner received another boost. UCLA was a jewel among college sports programs. Few other universities nationwide could match its reputation as a top-notch producer of athletic champions.

For Florence the next few years were a blur of track meets and training schedules. She helped make the UCLA women's track team one of the strongest competitors in U.S. amateur athletic history. She also set her sights on the biggest track event of all—the Olympics. By the early eighties, Florence was a familiar presence on the world amateur track competitive circuit. In 1981 she became the American record holder in the relay event at the World Cup; she won important NCAA track competitions in 1982 and 1983 and became a crowd-pleasing heroine to millions of track enthusiasts around the globe.

In 1984 Florence made her first significant mark on the Olympic stage. On her home turf, when the Olympic Games took place in Los Angeles, Florence electrified the cheering crowd by winning a silver medal in the 200-meter race. It was a triumphant moment, and one that Florence would manage to top only a few years later. In October 1987, she married Al Joyner, a track star and influential trainer of track athletes.

By the time of the Olympic Games in Seoul, Korea, Florence was a bona fide star of the athletic universe. Along with her new sister-in-law, heptathlete Jackie Joyner-Kersee, Florence would become the queen of a tight-knit group of African-American competitive runners.

At the Seoul Games, Florence enthralled the crowd with her powerful, competitive spirit. Adorned in stylish trackwear that she designed herself, Florence raced into the history books, winning three gold medals and one silver. It was a startling achievement, even more so considering the hurly-burly nature of that year's Olympiad in Seoul. "Only the races started on time," Florence recalled of that week of competition.

After her triumphs at the Olympics Florence became a devoted contributor to the cause of improving the physical health and well-being of Americans. She retired from Olympic competition and gave birth to a daughter, Mary Ruth, in 1991.

Along with holding several world-record track titles, Florence was a shining example of health, beauty, and personal accomplishment. With glamour and panache—and a svelte, five-foot seven-inch frame, luxuriant long hair, sculpted fingernails, and high cheekbones—she was the embodiment of black women's strength, beauty, and perseverance. And with the wisdom of one who made her dreams a reality, she continued to offer helpful encouragement and a vivid example of all that Americans can accomplish with hard work and self-determination:

"I love working with kids," Florence said in a 1993 *New York Times* interview. "Talking with them and listening to them. I always encourage kids to reach beyond their dreams. Don't try to be like me. Be better than me."

On September 21, 1998, Florence Griffith Joyner died in her sleep. It was later determined through an autopsy that she had a seizure and suffocated—a sad and unexpected end to a life of professional excellence and personal achievement.

SELECT BIBLIOGRAPHY

In addition to the books and articles cited in the text, the following works have been selected to complement *Fifty Black Women Who Changed America.*

Angelou, Maya. *I Know Why the Caged Bird Sings.* New York: Random House, 1969.

_____. *Gather Together in My Name.* New York: Random House, 1974.

_____. *Singing and Swinging Like Christmas.* New York: Random House, 1976.

_____. *The Heart of a Woman.* New York: Bantam Books, 1981.

_____. *All God's Children Need Traveling Shoes.* New York: Random House, 1986.

Bernard, Jacqueline. *Journey Toward Freedom: The Story of Sojourner Truth.* New York: Harcourt, Brace, 1967.

Bontemps, Arna. *The Poetry of the Negro.* New York: Doubleday, 1949.

Bradford, Sarah E. *Harriet Tubman: The Moses of Her People.* New York: Corinth Books, 1961.

Brooks, Gwendolyn. *A Street in Bronzeville.* New York: Harper Brothers, 1945.

_____. *Annie Allen.* New York: Harper Brothers, 1949.

_____. *In the Mecca.* New York: Harper & Row, 1968.

Caesar, Adolph. *Ma Rainey's Black Bottom.* New York: New American Library, 1985.

Chisholm, Shirley. *Unbought and Unbossed.* Boston: Houghton Mifflin, 1970.

Cloyd, Iris, ed. *Who's Who Among Black America.* Detroit: Gale Research, Inc., 1988.

Dee, Ruby. *My One Good Nerve: Rhythms, Rhymes and Reasons.* Chicago: Third World Press, 1987.

Dunham, Katherine. *A Touch of Innocence*. New York: Harcourt Brace, 1959.

Duster, Alfreda M. Barnett, ed. *Crusade for Justice: The Autobiography of Ida B. Wells*. Chicago: University of Chicago Press, 1970.

Evans, Mari, ed. *Black Women Writers, 1950–1980*. New York: Anchor Press, 1984.

Evers, Myrlie, with William Peters. *For Us, the Living*. New York: Doubleday, 1967.

Giovanni, Nikki. *Black Feeling, Black Talk, Black Judgement*. New York: Morrow, 1970.

_____. *Cotton Candy on a Rainy Day*. New York: Morrow, 1978.

Guralnick, Peter. *Sweet Soul Music*. New York: Harper & Row, 1986.

Hansberry, Lorraine. *A Raisin in the Sun*. New York: Random House, 1959.

_____. *To Be Young, Gifted, and Black*. 1959.

_____. *Les Blancs: The Collected Last Plays of Lorraine Hansberry*. New York: Vintage Books, 1972.

Harrison, Daphne Duval. *Black Pearls: Blues Queens of the 1920s*. New Brunswick, N.J.: Rutgers University Press, 1988.

Hemenway, Robert E. *Zora Neale Hurston: A Literary Biography*. Chicago: University of Illinois Press, 1977.

Horne, Lena. *Lena*. New York: Doubleday, 1965.

Hurston, Zora Neale. *Their Eyes Were Watching God*. Bloomington, Ind.: Indiana University Press, 1937.

_____. *Moses, Man of the Mountain*. Philadelphia: Lippincott, 1939.

_____. *Dust Tracks on a Road*. Bloomington, Ind.: Indiana University Press, 1942.

Jordan, Barbara, with James Haskins. *Barbara Jordan*. New York: Dial Press, 1977.

Jordan, June. *Some Changes,* New York: E. P. Dutton, 1970.

Lorde, Audre. *From a Land Where Other People Live*. Detroit: Broadside Press, 1973.

_____. *The Cancer Journals*. San Francisco: Spinster Press, 1980.

Morrison, Toni. *Sula*. New York: Bantam, 1975.

_____. *Song of Solomon*. New York: Knopf, 1977.

_____. *Beloved*. New York: Knopf, 1987.

Rose, Phyllis. *Jazz Cleopatra: Josephine Baker in Her Time*. New York: Doubleday, 1988.

Terrell, Mary Church. *Confessions of a Colored Woman in a White World*. Washington, D.C.: Ransdell, 1940.

Walker, Alice. *Revolutionary Petunias*. New York: Harcourt-Brace, 1971.

_____. *Meridian*. New York: Harcourt Brace Jovanovich, 1976.

_____. *In Search of Our Mothers' Gardens*. New York: Harcourt Brace Jovanovich, 1983.

PICTURE ACKNOWLEDGMENTS

1. Phillis Wheatley, *Corbis*
2. Sojourner Truth, *Corbis*
3. Harriet Tubman, *Corbis-Bettmann*
4. Ida B. Wells Barnett, *UPI/Corbis-Bettmann*
5. Mary Church Terrell, *Photographer Collection Moorland-Spingarn Research Center, Howard University*
6. C. J. Walker, *Photographs and Prints Division, Schomburg Center for Research in Black Culture, The New York Public Library, Astor, Lenox and Tilden Foundations.*
7. Mary McLeod Bethune, *Corbis-Bettmann*
8. Zora Neale Hurston, *Boston Public Library (Author's Collection)*
9. Alberta Hunter, *Frank Driggs/Corbis-Bettmann*
10. Bessie Smith, *Frank Driggs/Corbis-Bettmann*
11. Hattie McDaniel, *UPI/Corbis-Bettmann*
12. Marian Anderson, *Copyright Bob Dean/Boston Globe Photo*
13. Ella Baker, *Copyright Bettye Lane*
14. Josephine Baker, *UPI/Corbis-Bettmann*
15. Dorothy West, *Michael Robinson/Chavez/Boston Globe Photo*
16. Katherine Dunham, *UPI/Corbis-Bettmann*
17. Mahalia Jackson, *UPI/Corbis-Bettmann*
18. Dorothy Height, *Jack O'Connell/Boston Globe Photo*
19. Rosa Parks, *Copyright Ted Dully/Boston Globe Photo*
20. Billie Holiday, *Frank Driggs/Corbis-Bettmann*
21. Gwendolyn Brooks, *UPI/Corbis-Bettmann*
22. Fannie Lou Hamer, *UPI/Corbis-Bettmann*
23. Lena Horne, *Copyright John Blanding/Boston Globe Photo*
24. Ella Fitzgerald, *UPI/Corbis-Bettmann*
25. Ruby Dee, *UPI/Corbis-Bettmann*
26. Shirley Chisholm, *UPI/Corbis-Bettmann*
27. Eartha Kitt, *UPI/Corbis-Bettmann*

28. Leontyne Price, *Corbis-Bettmann*
29. Maya Angelou, *Copyright David L. Ryan/Boston Globe Photo*
30. Lorraine Hansberry, *UPI/Corbis-Bettmann*
31. Odetta, *UPI/Corbis-Bettmann*
32. Toni Morrison, *UPI/Corbis-Bettmann*
33. Audre Lorde, *Photo by Thea James/Inman Square Photos*
34. Sonia Sanchez, *Marion Ettlinger*
35. Barbara Jordan, *Copyright Jack Shehan/Boston Globe*
36. June Jordan, *Photo by Linda Sue Scott*
37. Betty Shabazz, *UPI/Corbis-Bettmann*
38. Johnnetta Cole, *University Photography Copyright Emory University*
39. Mary Frances Berry, *John Blanding/Boston Globe Photo*
40. Marian Wright Edelman, *Janet Knoh/Boston Globe Photo*
41. Tina Turner, *UPI/Corbis-Bettmann*
42. Charlayne Hunter Gault, *Copyright Wendy Maeda/Boston Globe Photo*
43. Aretha Franklin, *Copyright Pat Greenhouse/Boston Globe Photo*
44. Nikki Giovanni, *UPI/Corbis-Bettmann*
45. Angela Davis, *Reuters/Corbis-Bettmann*
46. Alice Walker, *Copyright Janet Knott/Boston Globe Photo*
47. Susan Taylor, *Copyright Bill Brett/Boston Globe Photo*
48. Whoopi Goldberg, *Reuters/Corbis-Bettmann*
49. Oprah Winfrey, *Copyright 1996 Harpo Productions, Inc. All Rights Reserved. Photo credit: Skrebneski*
50. Florence Griffith Joyner, *Reuters/Corbis-Bettmann*

INDEX